JELLINEK'
PROGRESSION

Institute for Recovery
(847) 735-1827

DISEASE
& RECOVERY

These progression and recovery symptoms are based on the common experience of those suffering from Jellinek's disease. Every symptom does not occur in every sufferer or in the same sequence. The entire process may take years or it may occur in a very short time.

JELLINEK'S DISEASE

The New Face of Alcoholism

JELLINEK'S DISEASE

The New Face of Alcoholism

KATHLEEN WHALEN FITZGERALD, PH.D.

Whales' Tale Press
P.O. Box 27
Lake Forest, Illinois 60045

Published by Whales' Tale Press
P. O. Box 27, Lake Forest, Illinois 60045
1-800-914-1887
www.whalestalepress.com

Originally published under the title "Alcoholism: The Genetic Inheritance".

Library of Congress Cataloging-in Publication Data

FitzGerald, Kathleen Whalen; Jellinek's Disease: The New Face of Alcoholism

Bibliography: Page 252
Includes Index.
1. Alcoholism. I. Title
RC565.F563 1993 616.86'1 87-9114

ISBN: 1-882195-04-3

Printed in the United States of America
New Revised Edition Under New Title.

Cover Illustration by Deborah Koff-Chapin, The Center For Touch Drawing
Original artwork © 2001 Deborah Koff-Chapin. Find out more about her work at www.touchdrawing.com. The image was inspired by the songs of Jonathan Klate in memory of his son Ozzy, as featured on the album "The Muse at the Edge of Forever." www.Realisy.com

Text Design by Chris Harnesk & Pam McGinty

This work is dedicated to the loving memory of Geraldine O. Delaney, Founder, Little Hill Alina Lodge, Blairstown, New Jersey.

Mrs. Delaney pioneered the use of the term *Jellinek's Disease,* a merciful breakthrough for those individuals and families suffering from active alcohol addiction, for those 'reluctant to recover' and for those who are committed to their recovery today.

May her vision continue to be our strength and may generations that follow flourish in sobriety.

Acknowledgments

Many people were sent into my life at the right time and they have become instrumental in the conception, writing and publication of this book. For them I am profoundly grateful. Specifically:

Lionel J. Schewitz, M.D., who pointed me in the right direction.

Rita Gross, M.S.W., who saw that I got there. May she rest in peace.

Geraldine O. Delaney, who first said, "If we would use the term 'Jellinek's disease' rather than 'alcoholism' people would be breaking down the doors to get treatment." Mrs. Delaney provided the inspiration for this book.

We are especially indebted to Monica M. Oblinger, Ph.D., Professor, Department of Cell Biology and Anatomy, Finch University of Health Sciences, The Chicago Medical School. Dr. Oblinger has most generously revised the information regarding the biology and neurochemistry of addictive illness and introduced some of the latest research, concepts and medical insights in the field into this latest edition of the book. Thank you, Monica!

Contents

Prologue

"You have but to know an object by its proper name for it to lose its dangerous magic."
ELIAS CANETTI

"Kathleen, please come in here and give me some help," called my mother. I put my book down, went to the kitchen, and with clenched fists and shaking voice, asked her, "Why did you give me that name? I just hate it!!"

She turned from the sink, dried her soapy hands, looked me square in the eyes and said softly, "Your father and I loved that name and we wanted you to have it."

That was my first lesson in ***reframing***.

The reframing of a picture is a common practice, wherein the old and cracked wooden frame can be replaced by a thin metal frame or a wide Lucite frame or a lush, brassy, ornate frame. As the frames change, the picture takes on visual, emotional, and artistic differences, but it remains the same picture.

One of the basic goals of psychotherapy is the reframing of our childhood by holding the trauma or pain up to the light of day, naming what happened, owning it, and pushing through the pain to resolution so that we are not tormented by the hidden, haunting memories of long ago. The historical facts remain the same, but at the hands of a skillful psychotherapist, the ancient pains and traumas become neutralized and lose their sting. Bad times and hurtful people get reframed and lose their power to hurt us further.

As we change the name of a person, place, illness, food, car, position, street or business, we reframe them socially, politically and perhaps even financially. All of the inarticulated assumptions, constricted expectations and emotional charges are changed in an instant.

In the 70's, classrooms became "pods" as social experimentation was carried out in the schools. Kids were the little beans who could be added and subtracted by bean counters. Social engineering was carried out by reframing the purpose of education.

Colored People became Negroes who became Black who are now African-Americans. The folks are the same, but the change in nomenclature reflects the change in the self-definition of a people.

The former harassed "secretary" walks taller as an "administrative assistant". Calumet Parkway becomes Martin Luther King Drive. Accenture, the consulting arm of Arthur Anderson, distances itself from the legal troubles of the accounting side by a swift name change.

Borneo is now Brunei, an independent sultanate distinguishing itself from being a former British protectorate. If you look for the Gilbert Islands you will find Kiribati, now an independent member of the Commonwealth. Geographical renaming is essential to self-determination.

The "reframing by renaming" is demonstrated nowhere better than Hollywood. Samuel Goldfish became Samuel Goldwyn and built an empire. Can you imagine Dino Crocetti and Jerome Levitch rather than Dean Martin and Jerry Lewis? Norma Jean Mortensen, holding her white dress blowing over the street vent, or singing "Happy Birthday, Mr. President" to a bemused JFK?

Nathan Birnbaum, Gracie Allen's widower, smoking cigars, playing God and living to be 100? Marion Morrison swaggering into a bar, dragging Maureen O'Hara over the fields of Ireland, commanding a submarine with Japanese destroyers listening overhead? Charlie Carter receiving the Ten Commandments, racing a wild chariot in Ben Hur, raising a rifle to a cheering mob of the NRA?

Who would not go to Estee Lauder's, rather than Josephine Metzer's? To Elizabeth Arden's rather than Florence Lewis'? Could your breath be taken away by Frances Gunn singing "Somewhere over the Rainbow"? What would have become of Caryn Johnson if she hadn't morphed into Whoopi Goldberg?

In "the Meaning of Culture", John Cowper Powys writes, "Deep in the oldest traditions of the human race dwells the secret of the magical power of names." Names are indeed magical, as they can trick us into seeing what is not there, hearing what is not spoken, convincing us to skip the logic and take things as they appear, not as they really are.

As we as a people grow in compassion, sensitivity, authenticity, we have categorically rejected shaming labels that hurt and wound others. (Unfortunately, this movement has been trivialized as "Political Correctness", implying good manners rather than a deep and abiding respect for others who may be different.)

By the use of more sensitive language, we have gone far in building a more inclusive society where none are outside the definition of "American". We no longer speak of Spics, Krauts, Micks. Bums are now "the homeless" and jailbirds are "the imprisoned". Persons may be physically or mentally "challenged, rather than defective.

Perhaps no area reflects this grèater wisdom that the medical field, where more sensitive language dominates terminology that was formerly shaming and guilt-producing. Many shameful illnesses have been renamed to honor the scientist or physician who first discovered or diagnosed them, thus reframing the essence of the illness itself.

Down's Syndrome children were Mongoloids; conjoined twins were Siamese; Tourette's Syndrome were shouters and screamers; the Alzheimer's Diseased were simply senile; those with bipolar or obsessive-compulsive disorders were called nuts or crazies; the Hansen's Diseased wore leper bell's; those with Korsakoff's Psychosis had wet brains; those with Parkinson's Disease were shakers, twisters and pill-rollers. Yet drunks are still alcoholics.

In veterinary medicine, even animal illnesses carry the name of the scientists who first designated a cluster of symptoms as an illness. Rabbits get a bacterial infection called Tyzzer's Disease; dogs contract Cushing's Syndrome and Addison's Disease; the cornea of the eyes of German Shephards can become ill with Uberreiter's Disease; opossums and armadillos get Chaga's Disease; Aujeszky Disease creates a mad itch in pigs; Chediak-Higashi Syndrome is an immunodeficiency that kills mink, mice and killer whales.

Derzsy's Disease creates hepatitis in geese and Bang's Disease describes contagious abortions in cattle; Merek's Disease is a herpes virus in chicken and quails; Marie's Disease is a hypertrophic osteopathy of sheep, horses and cattle; and Pacheco's Disease infects parrots, macaws and cockroaches.

In 1956, the American Medical Association classified alcoholism as a bona fide disease. In 1960, Dr. E. M. Jellinek of Yale University wrote ***The Disease Concept of Alcoholism***, defining the chronic, progressive and fatal nature of this illness. He watched a family member drink and deteriorate. He took notes, saw a pattern of illness developing and charted the steady, predictable progression of the early, middle and late stages which lead to death.

A wise woman once said, "If we used the term 'Jellinek's Disease', people would be breaking down the doors to get into treatment." Jellinek's Disease is the most easily treatable, most neglected health problem in the United States today. This tragic neglect springs from denial: I'm not an alcoholic and don't need help. Consequently, only 3-5% of alcoholics recover.

The major reason for this denial is the name by which it is known: alcoholism. It is replete with negative social and moral implications: skid row, boozers, bag ladies, winos, lushes, the days of wine and roses, suicides, road rage, a father murdering his children, priests abusing kids. No wonder we are in denial - which of us would want that label slapped on our foreheads?

In steadfastly calling "alcoholic" those of us who are biochemically and neurologically unable to metabolize alcohol as the other 90% of the population are, we focus on the chemical substance that causes the pathology. We discuss the symptoms, miss the essence, and give it free reign to hide in mythology, misconception and misunderstanding.

Furthermore, alcoholism is an ism like doctrines or theories or styles: fascism, cubism, imperialism, realism, Thomism, heroism. What other fatal illness is an ism? Cancerism? Fluism? Diabetesism? AIDSism? Alcoholism is not a theory or doctrine or style.

Jellinek's disease is a chronic, fatal illness that affects 18 million Americans. One out of every four kids in our classrooms has a parent with Jellinek's Disease. It kills thousands, destroys families and reduces our roads and highways to streets of slaughter. This nefarious ism costs us $276 billion annually. And insurance companies don't have to pay for treatment of an ism.

Jellinek's disease is responsible for:

30% of all suicides

55% of all auto fatalities

60% of all child abuse

65% of all drownings

85% of all home violence

It is estimated that when a woman suffers from Jellinek's disease, her husband leaves her in 9 out of 10 cases; when a man contracts it, his wife leaves in 1 out of 10 cases.

To the degree that we call an illness by the name of a sin or social problem and to the degree that myth, misconception and misunderstanding surround an illness, recovery is blocked. The myth of Jellinek's Disease is that its victims are weak-willed, sinful, selfish. As if they sought and reveled in their illness. As if they felt no pain. As if they ought just to control themselves. It is easier to control diarrhea that to assert one's will over alcohol.

With all due haste, it is imperative that we embrace the term "Jellinek's Disease", the proper name for what is presently misnamed "alcoholism." Not only for the 18 million of us whose lives are cut short by 33.5 years, suffering needlessly from this simple metabolic disorder. Not only for the thousands who are waiting to be killed beneath the speeding, careening wheels of a drunk driver.

Not only for the one in four of our kids who throw up on the way to school. Not only for the hundreds of thousands of abused wives and children. Not only for the victims and perpetrators of crimes. Not only for those dying of cancers, heart diseases, diabetes, mental illnesses that are alcohol-related. For all of us, for we are all intimately effected.

If there were any other disorder that was so wide-spread, cost so dearly and had such minimal recovery rates, governmental, medical, legal, educational and religious organizations would be standing on their collective heads, screaming to find out what we were missing and what was wrong. It's simple: change the name; reframe the illness; get well.

Chapter One

Jellinek's Disease: A Chronic, Fatal, Progressive Illness

When you are old and grey and full of sleep,
And nodding by the fire, take down this book,
And slowly read, and dream of the soft look
Your eyes had once, and of their shadow deep.
WILLIAM BUTLER YEATS

Helen opened the Chippendale secretary and drew out a new bottle of Harvey's Bristol Cream. Slowly, she poured it into a Baccarat brandy glass. They had received Baccarat for their wedding thirty-six years ago. She knew that if Paul were home he would tell her to put it into a sherry glass, but Helen loved the feel of the snifter and the way it rested so safely in her hand.

Placing the bottle on the floor, she sat in the wing-back chair by the fire. The white birchbark curled and crackled. Mahler's Ninth Symphony filled the darkened room. Helen smiled into the fire as the warmth of sherry stole over her.

Ah, Helen, do not go gentle into that good night. Now, who was that? Yeats? No, no, Dylan Thomas. And what was that he wrote about not remembering if it snowed six days when he was twelve or twelve days when he was six? It is a better thing to forget than to remember, Helen smiled to herself, for she was so good at not remembering.

The grandfather clock struck nine. The logs were now only soft, glowing powder in the fireplace. The room was chilled. Empty, the bottle of sherry lay on its side. Helen slept deeply as the snow drifted before the great Gothic door.

A thousand miles to the east, Allison sat in her small, private cubbyhole room off the kitchen, fingering the snapshot in the thin silver frame. The year was 1948. Allison was three and her mother, Helen, was twenty-eight. Allison, her hair in little pigtails, faced the camera; Helen, her thick brown hair in a soft pageboy, smiled at her daughter. Their faces touched.

Four . . . five . . . six . . . Allison counted the telephone rings. Seven . . . eight . . . She slammed the phone down. She felt like vomiting. Where is she? What in the name of God has happened?

She placed the picture facedown. Tears rolled down her cheeks. It's all over. I wish she were dead. God, I wish she were dead. You can't go home again, Allison . . . There is no more home.

Christmas was only two weeks away and Allison knew they would not go back home to Chicago. Her husband simply would not put up with another of her mother's scenes: Cold turkey, spilled gravy, Helen tripping and falling and drinking.

So many times Allison had fantasized being back home, shopping with her mother at Saks, getting their hair and nails done, a leisurely lunch at the Drake. Allison dreamed of the time when her own daughter, Sara, would be with them.

That's all over now. The children, Sara, now 15, and John, now 13, wanted to stay in Connecticut for Christmas to be with their friends. They did not want to see their grandmother. They did not know her any longer.

Allison bent the edge of the silver frame in her clenched hand. She went into the kitchen and poured herself some scotch.

Paul's stomach knotted as he turned up the snowy drive. He pushed the button under the dash and the garage door slowly opened. He parked the car, reached for his briefcase, and made his way to the back door. The snow clung to his shoulders and hair.

Paul found himself working every night, later and later. There were the briefs to go over, the junior partners to confer with, the clients to call, the old friends to meet for a drink or two. He wasn't getting the work done during the day–he was too distracted. And to be honest, he really didn't want to come home. He didn't have to look at her at the office.

He put the key in the lock, paused, and slowly turned it. He smelled their dinner drying in the oven. No sounds came from the library but he knew Helen was in there. The clock struck ten. Paul opened the oven. Nothing had been touched. Without taking off his coat, he sat at the table and buried his face in his hands. *Christ Almighty!*

Is this all there is? Sixty-four years old–more money than I can ever spend–good health–the firm–our future. How long we planned for this time. What has happened? It's all a nightmare. The kids are gone now–Allison in Connecticut and David doesn't call.

The thought of his son brought a fresh hurt. Paul had envisioned David taking over the firm when he was ready to retire. Now David was gone and wanted to have nothing to do with them. Paul was tired and ready to enjoy what he had worked for so long, yet he was terrified of having nothing to do, of being alone with her.

How could this have happened? When he had first met Helen that warm April evening, he had fallen in love with her and had known that someday he would marry her. He had loved her unpredictability; she had treasured his steadiness.

Back then, Helen never drank, on principle–her father was an alcoholic. She simply did not drink. After much coaxing, Paul had persuaded her to have a little white wine with dinner. Now that was all a blur. Helen had become a shell of the woman he had loved. She had become so predictable.

Paul took off his coat and threw open the library door. The stale smell hit him. He looked down at her bruised legs, her bloated belly, her mottled face with puffy eyes. *My God, she looks like a beached whale.* He grabbed the glass out of her hand, scooped her out of the chair, and like every other night, carried her up to bed. The hardwood stairs creaked under him. They mocked him. At the top of the stairs, he paused, turned and looked down. *It would be so easy . . .*

THE LABYRINTH OF ADDICTION

Helen, Paul, Allison, and David are caught in the labyrinth, blindly running from the mad monster alcohol who holds them hostage. If they pause, it hears their breathing; if they move, it hears their footsteps; if they look to the east, it comes from the west. Faster and faster, they must keep running down the convoluted corridors of rage, shame, and insanity.

The snorting monster at the very center of the labyrinth of alcohol demands human sacrifice and greedily takes its toll from young and old, from male and female, from rich and poor. And the world laughs and points in judgment at those trapped inside, as if those inside freely chose to be there.

Helen and her family did not choose life in the labyrinth. They were all bound and chained by the unalterable nature of alcohol's addiction, over which she has no control. Her *Switch* was tripped. They are all locked into a disease; a chronic, progressive, fatal disease caused by the workings of the body chemistry Helen has inherited.

A NEW DEFINITION OF ALCOHOLISM

A new definition of alcoholism, which highlights behavioral signs including impaired control and denial was developed in 1992 by a joint committee of the National Council of Alcoholism and Drug Dependence (NCADD) and the American Society of Addiction Medicine (ASAM). The new definition states: "Alcoholism is a primary, chronic disease with genetic, psychosocial, and environmental factors influencing its development and manifestations. The disease is often progressive and fatal. It is characterized by impaired control over drinking, preoccupation with the drug alcohol, use of alcohol despite adverse consequences, and distortions in thinking, most notable denial. Each of these symptoms may be continuous or periodic."

Over the years, there has been a collective push to define alcoholism. When the book, *Alcoholics Anonymous*, was first written in 1939, Dr. William D. Silkworth, in his introduction, writes that the action of alcohol on chronic alcoholics "is a manifestation of an *allergy*; that the phenomenon of craving is limited to this class and never occurs in the average temperate drinker . . . It has never been permanently eradicated. The only relief we have to suggest is entire abstinence".

An allergy is a pathological response to substances that are without comparable effect on the average individual. Sixty years ago, with what was known at the time, Dr. Silkworth was completely accurate. His use of the term "allergy" helped many to move out of the shame of being out of control into a more scientific place to understand alcoholism.

In 1960, Dr. Jellinek published *The Disease Concept of Alcoholism.* The word "concept" has a tentative feel about it, like it is an idea, rather than fact. (We have always felt that some children jump around in school and have trouble concentrating; we now have diagnostic categories of ADD and ADAH that we know are true from brain studies.)

In 1994, D.C. Lewis wrote of a disease "model" of addiction, suggesting that the criteria be used which includes the degree to which:

1. the condition has a clear biological base
2. is marked by identifiable signs and symptoms
3. shows a predictable course and outcome
4. the condition or manifestation are not cause by volitional acts

Finally, in 1997 Dr. Alan I. Lesher wrote in *Science* that "Addiction is a Brain Disease and It Matters". He states that the brain has a mechanism that changes from use/abuse to addiction at some point when the *Switch* gets tripped. That is when the disease begins and, as such, meets all the identifiable criteria for a physical condition being truly an illness.

In short, over the past 60 years, professionals dealing with alcoholism have gone from describing it as an *allergy* to a *concept* to a *model* and finally to the simple, metaphorical *Switch*.

Over and over, Helen is locked into a pattern of behavior that consumes her mind with the thought of alcohol, possesses her body with the demand for alcohol, and subjects her will to its overpowering charm. Her mind and body and will, once free, are programmed in a repetitive, predictable chain of events over which neither she nor her family may exercise any control.

While various psychosocial factors may contribute to heavy drinking, they do not make one physically dependent upon alcohol. *Without physical dependence, Jellinek's disease can not exist.*

A disease is simply anything that interferes with the health of the body and with its ability to function normally. Jellinek's disease destroys the body and its ability to function within a normal range. This diseased state has not been sought out by its victim, and as such, is an involuntary illness.

Helen's disease is caused by her unusual body chemistry. She is an alcoholic and the body chemistry of alcoholics is different from others. From earliest infancy, probably even from the moment of conception, alcoholics would react differently to alcohol if they were so exposed.

As one ravaged by cancer or leprosy did not try to get the disease, so one destroyed by Jellinek's disease did not seek his illness.

The majority who drink are genetically immune: They have no inherited weakness toward developing alcoholism. However, there is a large minority of people who are genetically programmed for alcoholism. They have simply inherited an alcoholic body chemistry.

Those with Jellinek's disease have inherited a body chemistry that, in the presence of alcohol, produces the addiction, the disease.

Unlike the flu or the measles, Jellinek's disease is chronic and will only cease to exist when the afflicted draws his last breath. No one outgrows it, nor does it simply run its course. Therefore, once Jellinek's disease has been contracted, the individual will always have it, either in an active state if he continues to drink, or in a latent state if he ceases to drink. For this reason the alcoholic who no longer drinks calls himself "a recovering alcoholic," rather than "a recovered alcoholic." Jellinek's disease is never over.

Unlike a chronic slipped disc or a chronic allergy to ragweed, whose symptoms remain more or less the same without treatment, Jellinek's disease progresses from a less destructive state to a point of insanity or death. Again the analogy of cancer is particularly apt: Beginning with the deviation of a single cell into a cluster of deviant cells, a microscopic tumor appears, grows, spreads, metastasizes, and finally kills its host. However, with Jellinek's disease, there is never a remission, never a cure.

Like cancer, the early stage of Jellinek's disease is hidden. Its earliest manifestation–a greater physical tolerance than most for alcohol–is an ironic, almost infallible sign of the onset of an irreversible process that will end in the total loss of tolerance that signals the latter stage of Jellinek's disease.

THE METABOLISM OF ALCOHOLISM

While medical science cannot at this time assert that a particular gene, a particular enzyme, or a particular neurotransmitter actually ***causes*** alcoholism, there is much known about the biochemistry of alcohol addiction.

We know that the alcoholic does not metabolize alcohol in the same manner that the rest of us who drink alcohol do. We know that his liver functions differently from the time of that very first drink. We know that certain unique developments occur in the alcoholic's brain–changes to the cells, between the cells, within the cells–that do not occur in the rest of us.

We know that the chemistry and biology within the body of an alcoholic responds abnormally to alcohol. His body reacts by first adjusting to alcohol's impact, then accommodating its presence, and finally becoming addicted. What is not normal for others becomes normal for him.

Scientists have long been searching for the biological signs, those genes or enzymes or brain waves that may designate future alcoholics. The entire area of alcoholism research holds great promise of unwrapping the secrets of the liver, of the brain, of the mechanism that may one day reveal to us why and how 18 million Americans have contracted Jellinek's disease and which of their children are marked for alcohol impairment.

The majority of ethanol (alcohol) that enters the body turns into acetate by a process known as oxidation. The remainder is not metabolized but is excreted through sweat, urine or breath (and the latter is the basis for the breathalyzer test used by police).

ADH

The major route of the metabolism of ethanol is its oxidation in the liver. An enzyme called ADH (alcohol dehydrogenase) speeds up the conversion of ethanol to a molecule called acetaldehyde. There are several ADH genes, two of which show variations in people.

These variant forms are called ADH2 and ADH3. The variants are prevalent in Asian populations and are thought to protect individuals from developing alcoholism. These variant genes make an enzyme that converts alcohol to acetaldehyde more quickly than normal

Acetaldehyde is toxic and when its level in the blood increases, this causes people to feel uncomfortably ill, to experience facial flushing and other symptoms such as rapid heartbeat and headaches. When alcohol is converted rapidly to acetaldehyde and the levels of acetaldehyde in the blood build up quickly (as occurs in people with the ADH2 and ADH3 variant genes), this produces negative ill feeling sensations very quickly.

It has long been thought that the negative rapid physical effects of drinking in people with the variant ADH genes are a deterrent that discourages people from alcohol abuse.

A similar situation occurs with another important enzyme involved in metabolizing alcohol. The second phase of alcohol metabolism in the body is accomplished by an enzyme called acetaldehyde dehydrogenase (ALDH). ALDH converts acetaldehyde which is toxic to acetate. Acetate is non-toxic and is rapidly converted to carbon dioxide and water. So the ALDH can be thought of as the enzyme that "detoxifies" acetaldehyde.

Some individuals have a defective aldehyde dehyrogenase gene (ALDH2) which doesn't "detoxify" acetaldehyde as quickly as normal and this allows acetaldehyde levels to become elevated in the blood stream. Such higher acetaldehyde levels cause ill feelings, sweating, flushing, nausea and shaking.

It is noted that the past use of the drug Antabuse to deter drinking was based on the drug's ability to inhibit aldehyde dehydrogenase and make people feel very ill after consuming alcohol. Certain individuals, mainly of Asian ancestry, have a variant ALDH2 gene that doesn't metabolize acetaldehyde efficiently. This gene is considered protective against alcoholism because it makes them sick.

Thus, the presence of a gene that enables either too rapid a metabolism of alcohol to acetaldehyde (ADH variant) or too slow a metabolism of acetaldehyde into non-toxic metabolites (ALDH2 variant) are linked to a lower rate of alcoholism in such individuals.

ADH & ALCOHOLISM

Is the converse of this situation true? Are there "variants" of ADH or ALDH that are associated with alcoholism? One could speculate that this is not unreasonable. That is, individuals who "clear" alcohol rapidly and also metabolize acetaldehyde rapidly would be expected to have a higher tolerance to alcohol because they clear alcohol blood levels rapidly and do not accumulate high levels of toxic acetaldehyde.

Such individuals may be more susceptible to increased drinking because they do not "feel" the negative effects of elevated acetaldehyde levels as intensely or as quickly as people who processes alcohol differently. In fact, a considerable amount of research has shown that individuals with a "low response" to alcohol are more likely to become dependent on alcohol compared to those with an initial "high response".

Thus in an ironic twist of biochemical fate, the person who can "drink like a fish" from the very beginning is more vulnerable to developing alcoholism than is the person who is "knocked on their butt" by a single beer. Folk wisdom has traditionally attributed this higher capacity to the "hollow leg" phenomenon. Alcoholics can literally "hold" more booze in their hollow legs; normal people do not have "hollow legs".

However, variants of genes in the alcohol metabolic pathway that predispose people to alcoholism have not been identified. It is also likely that a higher alcohol clearance rate in some people precipitates heavier alcohol intake to get the same effect and this higher intake is cumulative in effecting many other systems that are impacted by alcohol and its metabolites.

WOMEN

In this regard, recent studies have begun to unravel the reason that women and female animals are more susceptible to the toxic effects of alcohol. It has been known that females show more liver, heart, skeletal muscle, pancreatic and brain damaging effects from toxic amounts of alcohol than do males. While this had been previously attributed to smaller body size and higher fat percentage, recent work has shown that women have a less active form of the gastric (stomach) type of alcohol dehydrogenase enzyme than do men.

The stomach is the first stop for an alcohol-containing drink. While the liver is the primary site for metabolizing alcohol, the process begins in the stomach with "first pass" metabolism. While the metabolism of alcohol in the stomach compared to the liver is quite modest, it is clear that the initial "first pass" metabolism in the stomach is important. In women, there is a much lower ADH activity in the stomach and thus there is less metabolism of alcohol in the stomach and this produces a higher blood alcohol level for a given dose of alcohol than occurs in men.

GABA

Recent studies on the genetic linkage of alcoholism have involved studies of southwest American Indian as well as Asian populations. When "linkage" in the same gene regions appears in different human populations, interest in what genes are in those areas of the chromosome map is sparked. Researchers identified a chromosome 4 region near the alcohol dehydrogenase (ADH) gene cluster as being possibly linked to alcoholism resistance. Another gene, among hundreds present at the locus of interest, is for a GABA receptor. The receptors for the neurotransmitter GABA have long been suspected of having some involvement in alcoholism vulnerability. They have also found evidence that one region of chromosome 11 appears to be linked to an increased alcoholism risk. Further studies to narrow down which of the many genes in those areas may be relevant to a higher risk for alcoholism are needed and will be of great interest.

After ingestion, alcohol begins its journey to the stomach, enters the blood system, is detoxified in the liver and is excreted through breath, urine and sweat. While this process is common to all, it is only in the organ of the brain that alcohol and other drugs establish the fateful grip of addiction: the *Switch* gets turned on in the brain. Abuse or over-use becomes addiction.

In a 1997 *Science* article, "Addiction is a Brain Disease and It Matters", Dr. Alan I. Leshner graphically depicts the irreversibility of chemical addiction and thereby the contracting of an illness. (People in AA have traditionally referred to this as "crossing the red line", the no going back biochemically).

Once the *Switch* has been tripped, the addict has to leave the room. There is no turning off the *Switch*. Recovery means staying out of the room, one day at a time. Relapse means returning to the room where the lights grow even brighter.

GENERAL NEUROBIOLOGY

Neurons release various chemicals called neurotransmitters to send messages to other neurons. Scientists have known for years that many drugs of abuse block the *reuptake* of one or more of the neurotransmitters that are used by neurons to communicate with each other. To understand this process, it must first be noted that neurotransmitter molecules are used by neurons to communicate with each other.

The first cell in the circuit (the presynaptic cell) releases the neurotransmitter molecules into the tiny space where two neurons come into close contact. This space is called a synapse. Neurotransmitter molecules diffuse through the synaptic space and then bind to specific molecular targets called receptors that are located on the second cell (the postsynaptic cell). This lock and key type binding stimulates a series of biochemical and membrane changes in the post-synaptic cell. Once this biochemical "communication" has taken place, the neurotransmitter molecule undocks, is released back into the synapse and the presynaptic neuron pumps it back into the terminal and recycles it for subsequent reuse. This is called the "receptacle".

Proteins called transporters and which are located on the presynaptic neuron accomplish this recycling. These molecules grab onto neurotransmitters located in the synapse between two cells and pump them back into the cell that initially released them, thus ending the signal. Addictive drugs (cocaine in particular) block the transporter for dopamine as well as for other neurotransmitters. This blockade raises the level of dopamine located extracellularly in the synapses. Thus, the "signal" is prolonged as molecules are left in the cleft for longer periods and can continue to interact with receptors. When this excess dopamine signalling occurs in the "pleasure centers" of the brain, reinforcing sensations are produced.

BRAIN REWARD CENTERS/CIRCUITS

Alcohol is an addictive drug that shares common sites of action in the brain with other addictive drugs. Namely, the brain's "reward" circuitry is effected by alcohol and other drugs of addiction. The brain systems involved in motivational behavior are commonly called the *pleasure centers.*

In the scientific literature the terms "reward centers or circuits" are used to describe the brain wiring that underlies motivation, learning and emotion. This core circuitry of the brain is usurped by alcohol and other addictive drugs. The drugs do so by using the brain's own neurotransmitters and wiring.

Among the most important neurochemicals in addiction is the neurotransmitter dopamine. Dopamine is the intrinsic brain chemical that let us feel pleasure. It has often been referred to as the chief "feel good" transmitter of the brain.

Dopamine levels in particular brain regions are increased by activities that naturally feel good - sex, food, drink, warmth, safety. Addictive drugs also increase dopamine signalling in these same brain regions.

Alcohol intake appears to increase dopamine concentrations in the brain regions involved in reward and pleasure. It also increases the levels of other neurotransmitters such as serotonin that the brain uses for positive emotional states. Thus, alcohol and other drugs provide a seductive, deceptive, and evolutionarily powerful signal within the brain. This signal says "Yes, I want this. I need this in order to survive."

At low doses, alcohol stimulates the pleasure/reward centers by increasing dopamine. It hits the bull's-eye. As the pleasure/reward centers are stimulated, the primal needs that normally drive us calm down and are satiated, albeit artificially and temporarily. Thus, addictive drugs can be thought of as agents that tap into the oldest survival circuits of the brain - the centers that signal reward when food, sexual or other needs of the species have been met.

NUCLEUS ACCUMBENS

What and where are these reward centers in the brain that people strive to stimulate using alcohol and drugs? One of these is the nucleus accumbens. This is a cluster of neurons located deep in the brain. It is a primitive center that is activated when dopamine is released from axon endings in the nucleus accumbens (Nac).

Its activation causes the individual to feel pleasure. Thus stimulation of the nucleus accumbens is at the heart of reinforcement and reward. People and animals tend to repeat actions that provide reinforcement and pleasure. Since alcohol and other addictive drugs provide a deceptive but massively powerful signal in this primal circuit, they are easily adopted as "surrogates" to nature's own rewards. They trick the deepest part of the brain to register that all is well.

REWARD DEFICIENCY THEORY

One current theory about addiction is called the "reward deficiency syndrome" and was put forth by Dr. Kenneth Blum and his colleagues in 1996. At its core, this theory suggests that the brain of a person predisposed/vulnerable to developing alcoholism or other drug addictions is unable to generate sufficient reward stimulation from natural means. For example, the person may produce or release inadequate amounts of dopamine (and perhaps other neurotransmitters) or have abnormal receptors or wiring in the reward system. An inborn chemical imbalance in the reward circuitry could manifest itself as anxiety, anger, craving for something to relieve the negative emotional state.

The syndrome has been postulated to be a form of sensory deprivation of the brain's pleasure systems. When a drug comes along that stimulates these centers which have languished without adequate input, the individual clearly knows that a very special and dramatic event has occurred. Frequently an alcoholic feels not "high", but normal with the first drink. They feel very very good, because they have felt "off" or "less than" they should have been feeling.

In fact, the pleasure/reward system of the brain was discovered in the early 1950's by Dr. James Olds who implanted electrodes into a rat brain to study behavior. He found that placement of such electrodes into the limbic reward pathways would motivate the rats to press a bar to get electrical stimulation into the reward centers.

It was found that they would press the bar endlessly, thousands and thousands of times. They would stimulate themselves to the point that food, sex and even sleep was abandoned. During the past few decades it has been learned that these same regions are present in people and that the dependence on alcohol, opiates, cocaine and other chemicals uses this same neuronal reward circuitry of the brain.

In normal individuals, brain chemistry and external stimulation work together efficiently to provide the person with an overall feeling of well being as normal needs are met. In others, genetic anomalies, stress, or neurochemical anomalies keep the person in a negative emotional state that begs for alleviation, begs for reward or pleasure. Alcohol acts on various neuronal circuits and can provide such relief to the screaming, reward-deficient brain.

The nucleus accumbens (Nac) does not exist in isolation. Its major input is the ventral tegmental area (VTA) of the midbrain. The circuit uses dopamine as its neurotransmitter and the VTA neurons are responsible for delivering and releasing adequate amounts of dopamine into the nucleus accumbens.

There are also other inputs to the nucleus accumbens. For example, opiate receptors are present on accumbens neurons and thus the brain's endogenous (its own natural) opiates as well as opiate drugs can stimulate these neurons. It has become apparent from research over the past decade that all four classes of addictive drugs relate to and effect this basic reward circuit of Ventral tegmental area --> Nucleus accumbens. Of special interest is the 2001 *Neuroscience* article, "Addiction and the Brain: The Neurobiology of Compulsion and its Persistence."

Alcohol and other sedatives, nicotine, stimulants like cocaine and amphetamine and opiates (like heroin or morphine) all effect this reward circuit of the brain, albeit in different ways. In addition to having this common site of action in the brain the various types of addictive drugs also have unshared, unique actions on the brain which determine the specific behavioral effects of a given drug (for example, motor stimulation vs. sedation).

While many drugs mimic or alter the action of one or more of the brain's own transmitter molecules, addictive drugs do this in the reward circuits of the brain that are involved in motivational behavior. Cocaine enhances the action of dopamine and other neurotransmitters by blocking the transporters that remove the neurotransmitters from the synapse. Amphetamine causes neurons to release more dopamine, increasing stimulation of the responsive neurons. Nicotine mimics acetylcholine at the nicotinic receptor. Opioids mimic the brain's endogenous endorphins and stimulate dopamine release.

Alcohol, among other effects, alters the activity of a particular receptor for GABA, a very prevalent neurotransmitter in the brain that can effect dopamine release and also effects several other neurotransmitters. How do these seemingly different events alter the function of the reward circuit?

Cocaine and stimulants are perhaps the simplest to understand since they elevate dopamine levels directly in the nucleus accumbens, the brain's deep pleasure center. Cocaine blocks the molecules in the membrane of the cells in this region that pump dopamine out of the synapse and thus inactivates it. When reuptake of the transmitter is blocked, more dopamine stays in the synapse and continues to stimulate the neurons in the reward center.

Similarly, stimulants that cause the neurons of the ventral tegmental region to release more dopamine into their target zone, the nucleus accumbens, increase stimulation of the reward circuitry. Opioids are more complex in their action but receptors for the body's own opioids exist on neurons in the nucleus accumbens. Thus these cells can be directly stimulated artificially by the drug which uses the brain's natural or endogenous opioid receptors in the reward centers.

In addition, opioids also act on neurons of the VTA and stimulate them to release more dopamine at their terminals in the nucleus accumbens. Normally, the firing rate of the VTA neurons is held constant and "in check" by input from inhibitory neurons located in other brain regions. Opiates turn off the activity of these inhibitory neurons that normally hold the VTA neurons in check. The Night Watchman is put to sleep. Thus, the VTA cells fire more and release more dopamine.

Alcohol is also complicated in its mechanism of action. However, both alcohol and nicotine appear to be able to "disinhibit" neurons in the VTA. The sites at which alcohol acts may be multiple and include other brain areas besides the nucleus accumbens. In addition, alcohol also effects other neurotransmitters of the brain.

However, one of its central effects appears to be the disinhibition or freeing up of the VTA neurons. This increases the firing of these neurons which leads to increases in doparnine levels in the nucleus accumbens. Thus, all roads lead to Rome: dopamine levels or signalling in the nucleus accumbens are increased. The pleasure/reward center is "turned on". Once the *Switch* has been flipped, it cannot be turned off, or as recovering alcoholics state, "I crossed that thin red line."

ADDICTION & THE MEMORY

Recent brain imaging studies have revealed that the nucleus accumbens with its pleasure/reward focus may not be the only player in addiction. Alcohol and other drugs initially commandeer the brain's reward circuits. However, with time and continued use, the brain's circuitry begins to rewire. The exact nature of the rewiring is not yet understood but it is clear that once it occurs, the ability to feel pleasure normally erodes and is replaced by drug craving.

One key to this is the formation of new, strongly positively charged memories. Alcohol and drug use stimulates the formation of deep emotionally charged memories. The wiring of the brain enables this since the nucleus accumbens lies at the crossroads between the limbic system (control of emotion) and higher centers that control the initiation of movement and that store memories. The emotional circuits give salience to events, people, and things. This is illustrated in the 2000 *Neuron* article, "Addiction, Dopamine and the Molecular Mechanism of Memory."

Thus, these circuits enable us to form memories with strong or weak emotional components. At its core, this circuitry is how we learn. Drugs of abuse, because they effect the pleasure/reward centers much more intensely than any normal behavior (like eating, sex or winning the lottery) generate vivid memories with positive, rewarding emotional overtones. Such deeply positive emotional memories help to sustain cravings and relapse.

In addition, other areas of the frontal cortex that mediate judgement are impacted by alcohol and drug use and become weak and damaged. The wiring that signals the connections between behavior and its consequences "short circuits" and misfires. Thus, driving while drunk with children in the car is no longer seen as a behavior that is dangerous and that should be avoided.

One of the brain neurotransmitters, dopamine, is involved in circuits that mediate movement, motivation and pleasure. A body of research has shown that nearly all drugs that are abused by people elevate dopamine levels in some brain areas in an extreme way that is far beyond what is achieved by normal pleasurable activities like eating, watching a sunset, or sex. A type of brain imaging that can monitor and display brain signaling patterns in living subjects is called Positron Emission Tomography (PET) imaging.

DOPAMINE RECEPTOR

When PET was used at the Brookhaven National Labs as described in a 2001 *Journal of Neurochemistry* report, to examine dopamine receptors in the brain, it was found that dopamine receptor levels were much lower in alcoholics and cocaine addicts than in normal subjects. Because of the lower levels of the receptors, more dopamine is needed in the addicted subjects to stimulate the brain's pleasure centers to the same level as could be achieved in normal subjects. It is as the hearing-impaired need the volume turned up. Drugs may provide a means to such an elevation in dopamine signaling by artificially elevating dopamine transmission in the face of lower receptor levels. Whether the lower receptor levels are causative or a result of drug abuse remains to be determined.

A very highly cited study in 1990 suggested that a genetic anomaly that effects the dopamine D2 receptor (called the Al allele) was linked to alcoholism. The study did not suggest that this was "The Gene" for alcoholism but rather that the Al-D2 variant was correlated with this disease. In subsequent work, this same genetic anomaly was found in people with other addictive compulsive disorders and diseases such as drug addiction, smoking, compulsive overeating, pathological gambling, attention-deficit disorder.

This led Dr. Kenneth Blum to propose that a common biological basis existed for these. He called this "reward deficiency syndrome". In its simplest form, the syndrome is a failure of the brain's pleasure mechanisms and an inability of the individual to derive adequate reward/reinforcement/pleasure from "normal" activities. The inadequacy comes from a failure of the brain's reward system. One way in which this could occur is through a dopamine receptor which is defective and does not signal properly. This is not the persons fault; they are born that way.

Scientists at Brookhaven National Laboratory have recently shown that increasing the level of the D2 receptor for dopamine in the brain can turn rats that prefer alcohol into light drinkers, and those with no preference into teetotalers. This is the turning up the volume for the hearing impaired — they can hear normal tones.

The D2 receptor in the brain is important for generating signals that are experienced as pleasure and reward. While a considerable amount of research had shown that alcohol and other addictive drugs increase brain dopamine levels, they also deplete the very receptors that dopamine needs to have its effect. A depletion of the D2 receptors and thus a reduction in "brain reward signals" may stimulate alcoholics to increase their alcohol intake in an effort to regain the stimulation and reward that is so seductive. A vicious cycle just to feel "normal" is in full throttle in the brain of alcoholics.

D_2 GENE THERAPY

In a very exciting 2001 study using gene therapy, researchers tested the hypothesis that increasing the level of D2 receptors might decrease alcohol intake. They injected a "disabled" virus that was altered to carry the D2 receptor gene directly into the nucleus accumbens, the brain's main pleasure center.

Once they determined that the gene delivery was effective (the animals were making more D2 receptor protein), they examined how the injected gene effected the drinking behavior of rats that had been previously trained to self-administer alcohol. Among animals that preferred alcohol, gene therapy to deliver more D2 gene produced a very significant drop in their preference and consumption of alcohol. The suggestion from this work is that overproduction or overexpression of D2 receptors may be protective against alcohol abuse. This of course remains to be confirmed.

THE CYCLE OF ADDICTION

In the alcoholic, the delicate, harmonious way in which our brain cells were designed to sustain life, to think, to remember, to react to danger, to pray, to enjoy a spring morning is profoundly disrupted. Everything is out of whack.

The person is caught in a ever-tightening spiral: The nerve cells cry out for more alcohol to feel normal; the person drinks to avoid withdrawal; the liver metabolizes what it can but is becoming cirrhotic from over-work; the nerve cells cry out for more; the person drinks more; the liver tries to keep up with the intake; the nerve cells need more.

On some level, perhaps without realizing or knowing just why, Helen found herself losing control of her drinking. As the biological *Switch* was tripped, the alcohol became the chemical surrogate for reward.

Taste grew into desire, desire into craving, craving into obsession, obsession into compulsion, compulsion into an addiction that consumed her. Choice had ceased to exist.

Helen was left with nothing but frustration, rage and guilt as she daily struggled for control over her drinking. Who could comprehend the utter shame she felt as, again and again, she promised herself and vowed to her family that she would not take another, only to find herself throwing a drink down her throat to quiet the screaming cells that were demanding more and more.

The illusion of peace that came so softly, so sweetly with that first drink overcame her best intentions. She was hooked. That sweet, first rush that quieted her nerves was dashed as she was forced to reach for another drink. Then another. Then another.

This is the meaning of alcoholic impairment, of Jellinek's disease.

A HEREDITARY DISEASE

It always has been commonly accepted that alcoholism runs in families. But unlike red hair, or a talent for art, which are recognized as hereditary, the explanation offered has been that children raised in alcoholic homes somehow learn it; and in some perverted, guilty way, want it, court it and deserve it. At best, when inheritance is admitted, it is an inherited weakness of moral fiber that is adjudged to be the cause.

Indeed, alcoholism does run in families. It has been scientifically proven so. We know that it is transmitted ***genetically***; not through the mind or the environment but through the body chemistry. And like all inherited traits, it manifests itself where it will, among rich and poor, without respect of person, without the volition of parents or children.

Helen most probably inherited Jellinek's disease from her father, despite the fact she abhorred his drinking and vowed never to be like him. He in turn inherited his disease from one or both of his parents, who may not have had the disease themselves, who may have never drunk alcohol, who unwittingly transmitted the gene for that unique body chemistry.

The origins of Jellinek's disease are laid at the time of conception and come through that same mystery of creation that brings a shape of the nose, a unique smile, an ear for music and the myriad other dynamics handed down from one generation to another in the hidden secrets of the cell.

In a 1973, Donald W. Goodwin, a psychiatrist and researcher in the field of alcoholism, conducted a landmark study using Danish case records of 30-year-old Danish males who had been adopted at 6 weeks of age by non-alcoholic families. He found that:

1. Those who had been born of alcoholic fathers were 3 times more likely to develop alcoholism than those from non-alcoholic fathers; and
2. The sons of alcoholic fathers developed alcoholism at an earlier age.

In a second study in 1974, Goodwin compared sons of alcoholics who had been raised by the alcoholic parent and their brothers who had been adopted by non-alcoholic families. He found that the sons who were raised in the non-alcoholic environment were just as likely to become alcoholic as those who remained with their natural family.

Goodwin also found in a comparison of children born of alcoholic parents with those born of non-alcoholic parents that both groups were virtually indistinguishable with regard to psychiatric problems such as depression, anxiety neurosis, personality disturbance, psychopathology, criminality, and drug abuse. Mental problems do not cause alcoholism.

These studies by Goodwin have been replicated with the same results, putting to rest any remaining nature versus nurture debate. Nature won.

In other words, one does not become an alcoholic because one is under stress, lonely, depressed, nervous, or over-worked. One does not become an alcoholic because one makes money or does not make money, because one prays or does not pray, because one has a violent temper or is blessed with a tranquil disposition.

One becomes an alcoholic because one is biologically vulnerable and tests this vulnerability by drinking.

DR. JELLINEK AND THE DISEASE CONCEPT

When Dr. Jellinek wrote ***The Disease Concept of Alcoholism*** in 1960, research in the area of alcoholism and other addictions was in an infant stage. Knowledge of the cell and of brain chemistry was primitive compared to today: The opiate receptors, where heroin and morphine land and begin to effect the brain, were not discovered until the 1970's; the entire understanding of endorphins, the brain's natural pain-relieving and pleasure-causing neurotransmitters, was also not arrived at until this time.

Dr. Jellinek's writing's came before the many discoveries of the last 40 years when developments in the area of brain physiology and pharmacology were primitive. Yet there were pioneers in the field of alcoholism research who anticipated the exciting findings that were just around the corner.

H.E. Himwich wrote in a 1956 article: "There is a physiological mechanism; for the cells of the body–and especially those of the brain–require the presence of alcohol for their function, as indicated by the grave disturbances that develop on the withdrawal of alcohol. This viewpoint places alcohol in a class with morphine and the barbiturates as a substance for which a physiological need can be created."

Also in the same article, P. H. Hoch wrote: "Alcohol acts like a narcotic which is incorporated into the metabolism of the nervous system"

L. D. MacLeod stated in 1952: "There may be an interaction between alcohol and certain systems involving acetylcholine resulting in an exaggeration of the intoxicating effect of alcohol."

S. C. Little and M. McAvoy, researchers in brain pathology, stated in a 1952 article, "On the basis of electroencephalographic studies it must be concluded that there is a cerebral condition predisposing to alcoholism."

These and many other researchers were groping for the truth about a phenomenon that has plagued mankind for centuries. As sophisticated as they were, they simply did not have the tools to enter into the mysteries of the cell and its chemistry to understand how and why an individual could be doomed to pursue the consumption of alcohol to the point of death.

MYTH OF THE ALCOHOLIC PERSONALITY

Jellinek's disease is, by definition, a physical, biochemical, degenerative, addictive illness. It is a primary disease that causes other diseases. It begins in that three pound organ called the brain.

It does not have its origins in the mind, therefore it is not a mental illness, although it results in mental problems. Likewise, it does not have its origins in the soul, although it leads to spiritual bankruptcy. And more importantly, it does not have its origins in a strange or perverted personality, although it twists the personality and creates a stranger.

In an attempt to explain alcoholism, we chose the broad term, "alcoholic personality". It means that alcoholics, even before they began drinking, were somehow different from the rest–perhaps too loud or too quiet, a little off-beat, unable to fit in.

By the time people who are advanced even to the middle stage of their disease (much less those who are in the chronic stage) get into treatment, they manifest similar personality symptoms that are not acceptable in society. They harm people–their own families and friends, themselves. They cause pain and break the laws of both God and man. They begin to act alike and look alike; the rest of society watches in horror and disgust and tries to figure it out.

The problem with the term "alcoholic personality" is that it uses the ***effects*** that the disease produces to describe its ***cause***. There is simply no such thing as the alcoholic personality.

After her husband lost the 1988 presidential election, Kitty Dukakis drank rubbing alcohol. *Newsweek* put her picture on its cover, entitled, "The Alcoholic Personality". Nowhere in the body of the text was there any reference to her alcoholic biochemistry, only to her alcoholic personality. No wonder the public is confused. Quite simply, Kitty's *Switch* had been irretrievably flipped on.

Helen and the 18 million other Americans who suffer from Jellinek's disease did not begin life with any more character disorders or personality problems that the rest of the population. Helen did not begin to drink because she was lonely, depressed, enraged. She did not begin to drink because she could not cope with life. She did not begin to drink because she came from a broken family or was abused as a child. She did not begin to drink because of stress or school competition or because of a threat of nuclear holocaust.

The myth of the alcoholic personality has been destroyed by a 1983 study published by George Vaillant, M.D., of the Harvard University Medical School. The study followed 660 young men from 1940 until 1980, from adolescence into late middle age. These men were drawn from two distinct social/economic groups: 204 were sophomores at Harvard University; 456 were junior high school boys from the inner-city of Boston.

A significant element of this study and one that makes it so valuable in terms of understanding the natural history of Jellinek's disease is that the research did not begin at the end when the disease was full-blown and work its way backward to when the men were boys and had not yet begun to drink. It began at the beginning when the subjects were young and no one knew or suspected who, if any, would develop Jellinek's disease.

After forty years of extensive research, it was clearly shown that there were ***no significant personality characteristics to predict those who would contract Jellinek's disease from those who would not***.

Dr. Vaillant stated that in their youth, future alcoholics were as psychologically stable as those who would not develop problems with drinking. He likewise stated that it was difficult to comprehend that the personality did not develop the alcoholism; the alcoholism developed the alcoholic personality.

The one consistent predictor of alcoholism, Vaillant found, was the factor of an alcoholic parent. Those boys with an alcoholic parent were ***5 times*** as likely to develop alcoholism than were those boys with no alcoholic parents, despite the stability (or lack of it) in the family. Jellinek's disease, because it springs from a skewed body chemistry, is clearly inherited.

It may be passed from mother to son, from father to daughter (as in Helen's case), from grandparent to grandchild , even skipping a generation or two. This heredity component may be obscured by the fact that a parent or grandparent never touched the stuff. Whatever reason (religious, medical, social) stopped the former generation from drinking also precluded it from testing its vulnerability to alcohol.

In other words, because there was no apparent alcoholism in one's ancestral line does not rule out the fact that, as in other genetically transmitted diseases, the abstinent ancestors may well have passed on to their children and to their children's children their vulnerability to alcohol. As these vulnerable children, who may have no knowledge that they are sitting ducks for alcoholism, test out their vulnerability, they kick off the disease.

Occasionally, a family's drinking history can be concealed because of shame or because of not speaking ill of the dead. This does a disservice to young people who have a right to know and need an accurate picture of their family history in regards to alcoholism. This may well determine their choice whether to drink or not.

An alcoholic woman, recently out of treatment, had learned of the hereditary nature of her disease but was perplexed because she believed that she was the first alcoholic in her family; she felt guilty that perhaps she had spawned a new alcoholic gene to plague those who came after her.

Her father had a beer once in a while, but his family's drinking history had never been discussed. Upon investigation, the woman found that an entire generation of uncles who had died young—reportedly of heart disease, cancers, accidents, fires. Upon closer scrutiny, all had been heavy drinkers. Thus, it is clear that she inherited the gene from her father.

If Helen had been born into a family of Jewish or Italian origins, where wine and spirits were used for religious or family celebrations and the culture frowned upon easy social drinking and punished drunkenness, Helen might not have tested her vulnerability to alcohol and would never have become physically dependent upon it.

A culture includes the unwritten rules, beliefs, and values by which its people live. As long as a culture remains relatively isolated and its young do not marry outsiders, the culture remains intact. When a group of people seek to become assimilated into the larger society and its young people marry into other groups, the distinct culture breaks down and with it, the rules, beliefs, and values by which its people have lived.

More and more Jewish people are presently experiencing Jellinek's disease. It is not that suddenly the genetic strain is becoming weaker or that the stress of assimilation is too great and they are resorting to drink. Rather, there are those Jewish people who have always been vulnerable to the effects of alcohol but have not had the freedom to test their vulnerability, as have the Irish or German. The cultural constraints have loosened and it has become acceptable, even desirable, to drink. And if one drinks and is biochemically predisposed, one will contract Jellinek's disease, regardless of race or religion.

Helen, as millions of other young American women and men, began to drink because she lived in a society that basically condoned the use of alcohol and provided ready access to it. She joined the ranks of the Jellinek's disease victims because the chemistry and metabolism of her body was so calibrated that her illness was inevitable; the only way she could have avoided it was to abstain completely from any and all liquor.

But Helen did have access to liquor. If this were not the case, despite the other factors, she would not have contracted Jellinek's disease. The accessibility of liquor is another critical factor.

Before the radical changes within the Catholic Church in the middle 1960's, nuns, for the most part, did not drink except for special occasions when they would have a single glass of wine with Christmas or Thanksgiving dinner. Although most of them belonged to cultural groups, e.g., Germans, Irish, Poles, French, that approved of drinking, individual nuns could not (or did not have the opportunity to) test their vulnerabilities because liquor simply was not available.

As they experienced more freedom in dress and had money to spend, many nuns began drinking like the rest of society, and, like the rest of society, developed Jellinek's disease at the same rate because of their own genetic susceptibility.

Again, these nuns were not distinguished by any premorbid psychological problems; they did not demonstrate the alcoholic personality before they had access to liquor. This came ***after*** their chemistry and metabolism were out of control and their personalities were distorted by their addiction; after their *Switch* had been tripped.

Over 40 years ago, Dr. Jellinek addressed the issue of whether alcoholism was a self-inflicted condition. In refuting that theory, he wrote, ". . . in our culture, drinking is a custom to which society attaches an astonishingly great importance" and added that it comes close to being an institution our society.

Secondly, he comments, alcohol addiction is insidious because "the changes toward a pathological process are imperceptible . . . since it develops within the context of an activity that belongs to the 'normal' and even valued behaviors of a society." In a random survey of California residents, 91% of the people agree with the statement that alcoholism was a real illness, but 41% also believed that alcoholics drank by choice. Do people with brain cancer secretly have control over the metastasis of their tumors? This ambivalence in the public's mind is most certainly felt by the untreated alcoholic who truly feels so sick and spends so much time trying to control her drinking. The result is shame heaped upon shame. No wonder denial flourishes. What is an alcoholic to do but continue in the madness? There is no way out.

One of the basic cultural norms of American society is the use of alcohol. It is a value to learn how to drink, because our family gatherings, our business transactions, our recreational and sporting events demand that one knows how to drink.

In a memorable scene from ***The Catcher in the Rye***, Holden Caulfield and his friends, in New York on holiday from prep school, laugh at a group of single women from the Midwest who order gin and tonic in a restaurant. Everyone knows you don't drink gin and tonic in the winter.

The cultural values of our society are quite specific as to what, when, and how we drink. It is unfortunate that these same cultural values do not accommodate those whose body chemistry punishes them for accepting these values.

Chapter Two

Progression of the Disease: From Tolerance to Death

When a man dies, he does not just die of the disease he has: he dies of his whole life.

CHARLES PEGUY

Steve bolted out of bed, ran into the bathroom, and threw up. As he hung over the toilet, cold sweat ran down his back, under his arms, behind his knees.

He rested his head on the edge of the bathtub. The white ceramic was cool and steady and he could hold his head still. He rinsed his mouth, threw cold water on his face, and avoided looking in the mirror. Hanging onto the wall, he made his way back to his bedroom, left the door open, and lowered himself back into bed.

If he kept his eyes open, the room spun, the pictures and windows twirling before him. If he closed his eyes, his brain spun madly in his head and he'd get sick again.

If he sat up, he'd fall over; if he lay completely in bed, he'd be twirling like a top. Steve kept one foot on the floor, on the hard stuff of reality, and the other under the sheet. He covered his head with the pillow, tunneling a small passage for air.

His mouth was dry. He hadn't the energy or the steadiness to navigate the stairs down to the kitchen for orange juice, or even an ice cube.

Steve lifted his hand before his face. His high school class ring with its red stone caught the beam of light from the closed window. Santa Carla High School, Class of 1999. What had happened?

Steve Carburry. I am Steve Carburry. I am the same person I was. Honor student. Co-captain of the baseball team. Scholarship to USC. Steve Carburry, dizzy, drunk, on my ass, getting kicked out of the lousy community college. They're on me, all the time. If they'd only get off my goddamn back and leave me alone. How did it happen? Only three years ago I was sitting at the top of the heap. Now I'm a loser.

Life had started to change for Steve the summer between his junior and senior year. The previous fall had been the best season of his life. He had gotten his driver's license and his father had bought him a Honda Civic. Steve was backup left fielder for the Santa Carla team and the coach planned to start him in his senior year. He had done well on his college boards. College was on his mind constantly.

Steve and his friends went to the beach and drank beer. He didn't drink much around the house. He drank only when he was out with the guys. He could hold his beer better than the others. Beer didn't seem to bother him; it just magnified his personality. He seemed brighter, funnier, friendlier. Steve felt uncomfortable at a party without beer. He could chug a can in sixty seconds. He found he would be on his second or third while the others were still on their first.

The guys liked to brag about their drinking. Steve didn't. He seemed to take it seriously, like he took baseball and school. When they boasted about drinking, Steve would change the subject.

His father noticed empty beer cans in the car. Steve said they had a party and had forgotten to throw them away. One morning his mother said she could smell beer on his clothes; he told her he could smell onions on hers. He simply did not like to talk about it. He changed the subject. Mrs. Carburry did not pursue the subject any further; her father drank. She had run away from home in Nebraska when she was seventeen and had never returned. She hated drinking and every time she saw Steve with a can of beer in his hands or with glassy eyes from drinking, her stomach cramped as it did when she was a girl in Nebraska.

On Labor Day of his senior year, the boys went to the beach for the day. They brought beer. The following morning, Steve woke up with a black eye and his shirt was torn. He could not remember what had happened; the entire night seemed sliced from his mind. He looked out the window. The Honda stood in the driveway. He didn't remember driving home.

School started in September. In his senior year, Steve became a different person. He would begin to study and find himself unable to concentrate. He could not focus his thoughts and he felt jumpy, like he had to keep moving. A beer before he started his homework would calm him down, steady his nerves, focus his thoughts. By the end of the evening, he had consumed several beers. He worked quicker and more accurately than if he had nothing to drink. Before a game, he would have a few beers and his performance was better.

Beer helped him concentrate, helped him perform, but people in his life were becoming a problem. His mother, previously so proud and so accepting of everything Steve did or wanted, told him he was drinking too much. He would characteristically leave the room, change the subject, or if that wouldn't work, he'd blow up and say he was old enough to live his own life and didn't need interference from her.

He started to hide beer in a cooler in his closet, behind his duffel bag. He'd crush the empties, stick them at the bottom of his wastebasket, and every morning, he'd get rid of them.

His girlfriend, Amy, started to complain that he was preoccupied with something and didn't pay enough attention to her. He told her to quit nagging and to stay out of his head. She gave him his ring back. He told her to go to hell.

Steve and his father had always been close, but changes between them were beginning to occur. They didn't seem to have as much to say and when they were together, the air was strained. Steve felt his father's disapproval in subtle ways. If Steve came into the room when his father was watching TV, his father remembered something he had to do in the yard. He stopped attending Steve's games.

Steve would find his father scowling as he read the paper or ate, and he would answer in one word. One night he found his father in the kitchen. It was dark except for the light from inside the refrigerator. His father looked at Steve as he came into the kitchen. "There were eight cans of beer in here this morning. Now there are only two. I haven't had any. Your mother doesn't drink beer. Your brother, Skip, doesn't drink." His father slammed the refrigerator door and left the kitchen. After that, Steve was careful to replace any that he took, and he kept his own supply hidden from the family.

Steve's senior counselor also noticed the changes that had come over him. His studies were still going well, but teachers reported that he was irritable and verbally volatile if challenged. His friends seemed to be drifting away as good old steady Steve was becoming unpredictable, testy.

The guidance counselor requested a meeting with Steve's father. The counselor noted the changes in Steve's behavior. Mr. Carburry became upset and challenged the counselor's credentials, pointing to Steve's high scholastic standing and his athletic accomplishments, his scholarship to USC. The counselor could not argue with the facts. He concluded the interview quickly. He could see that he was getting nowhere with someone who had so much to defend.

As Steve and his father got into the car, Steve turned to his father. "Thanks, Dad. Sorry about that." Mr. Carburry did not look at his son, but said in a low, controlled voice, "That guy knows what he's talking about. You know that and I know that." Neither of them spoke for the rest of the way home.

Steve was relieved that his father did not confront him about his life or whatever was causing the problem. He did realize that he was starting to drink too much, and he knew that he had to get his life together–college was coming next year.

Steve decided to cut out the beer. Enough was enough. That's the way a guy could really lose control. Steve stopped drinking on Valentine's Day, made up with Amy, and felt that his life would get back to normal. He had not really lost much, but things were getting out of hand.

Four months without a drink. Steve felt great, and if he ever thought he had a problem with booze, his long period of abstinence showed him that he had nothing to fear. He could take it or leave it. No problem at all. It was just a question of mind over matter, and he would be more careful in the future. And, if the truth be known, he actually felt better without it. He knocked off twelve pounds and the tension around the house seemed to ease up. Nothing was really ever discussed, but they all knew what was going on. This was just the way the Carburrys handled things: The less said, the better.

The end of May brought more parties, graduation, the senior prom. Amy's parents had a sunrise breakfast after the prom. She and Steve and their friends sat around the pool as the sun was coming up. The home was on a cliff overlooking the Pacific and everyone was in a quiet mood after all the parties of the night before. The Mexican housemaid brought out frosted glasses of champagne on a silver tray. The graduates toasted their four years together.

Steve took a glass. You don't graduate every day of your life. You're not eighteen forever. The cool champagne was a perfect way to begin your first day as a free man, and as the maid made her way around with the champagne bucket, Steve enjoyed a refill.

After the breakfast, the graduates headed for home. Steve stopped and bought a six-pack. As he came in the door, his father was leaving for work. He smiled broadly at his son, the graduate, who had gotten his life back in order so easily. He spotted the six-pack in Steve's hand. His face froze. He got into his car. He said nothing.

Steve was back on beer that day. He found himself drinking differently. He needed more. Two or three beers used to get him through; now he needed a whole six-pack, and he was losing track again of how much he was drinking. Steve no longer bothered to count; he couldn't. Once he began to drink, he'd continue until he couldn't remember anything.

A week later, he ran a red light and collided with an elderly man who was driving slowly. Mr. Carburry was at the police station within minutes and made a few phone calls. The elderly man was cited for driving without a license. Mr. Carburry did not confront his son, but didn't talk to him for two weeks.

Toward the end of the summer, Steve was brought home for "lewd and disorderly conduct," but again, a few calls were made and the family name was kept out of the papers. Steve continued to drink. His parents began to fight, his father growing sullen and his mother given to tears. His twelve year old brother stayed away as much as he could. Steve was going downhill fast; his whole family was going downhill fast.

That September brought relief to everyone. Steve left early for USC. Getting away from home, from the same place and the same people, might help. They all thought that what Steve needed was a change of scene. He had pulled himself together before, he would do it again. Everyone has his weakness. Steve had his inner resources, and once he was on his own, he would draw from his strength and overcome his drinking.

By the middle of November, the Carburrys received a letter from the registrar's office saying that Steve's scholarship was in jeopardy. They drove to L.A. to meet with Steve and his adviser. All agreed that Steve should seek counseling for his problems.

Steve had an appointment at the Student Health Service. The social worker focused on Steve's adjustment problem from a small high school to a large university, talking of separation anxiety, attachment to family, etc. The subject of Steve's drinking did not come up. Steve did not keep his next appointment.

By the beginning of the second semester, Steve had lost his scholarship and by June, he was told not to come back. His drinking had escalated. His driver's license was suspended. He came home and enrolled in the local community college. His old friends stayed away from him, but he found new ones. His new friends were heavily into drugs and spent their days on the beach or in bars. They did not go to school or work. Steve ran with a bad crowd.

In what seemed like a flash, Steve lost his tolerance. After two beers, he knew that he had it, but he had no choice. He couldn't stand to be without it, yet it was destroying him. Two beers now had the same effect that ten beers had only a year before.

He felt he was losing his mind. He stayed in his room most of the time, and when he did go out, he was dazed and unfocused. It had all happened so fast.

Steve heard a car pull up the driveway. He heard voices beneath his window. The doorbell rang. His mother answered it. Steve heard the heavy voices from the foyer . . . a hit and run . . . young mother killed . . . whose car was the Honda . . . where had the car been last night? Steve buried his face in the pillow. He remembered nothing.

EARLY, HIDDEN STAGE

Picture 5 adolescents, age 16, experimenting with their first beer. They are all from the same high school, sharing a similar social and economic background. None of these boys has any psychopathology, personality disturbance, criminality, or drug abuse. They are normal, well-adjusted 16 year old boys. Consider their unique responses to their first experience with alcohol:

BOY 1: Giggles, drinks quickly, feels slightly dizzy.

BOY 2: Doesn't like taste, begins to feel slightly aggressive, continues drinking.

BOY 3: Flushes, feels nauseated, sips slowly so as not to call attention to himself.

BOY 4: Feels nothing emotionally or physically, the alcohol has an effect on him similar to water.

BOY 5: Likes the taste, feels slightly mellow.

If one could predict future Jellinek's disease sufferer from among the five boys, who would it be? Which one most probably resembles Steve in the hidden stage of his disease?

Boy 4, the young man with no apparent physical or emotional response, is in the early, hidden stage of Jellinek's disease. As his body begins the slow, steady process of adaptation to alcohol, his tolerance will increase and his physical and mental functioning will be enhanced by alcohol.

Jellinek's disease is elusive. And paradoxical. There is no other illness whose early, hidden manifestations are the opposite of its later development. One does not develop an expanded lung capacity prior to the onset of emphysema nor a strengthening of the muscles prior to multiple sclerosis. Yet an increased tolerance and heightened physical and mental functioning at the beginning of Jellinek's disease herald the eventual loss of tolerance and inability to function that marks the end.

And it is because of these and many other contradictory symptoms that Jellinek's disease goes unrecognized. It is the disease that tells you it's not a disease. If the five boys above were to be stopped and questioned about each other's response to their first beer, they would all agree that Boy 4 "would never be an alcoholic . . . see how he holds it." He was not even approximating being drunk, yet he was the one most in jeopardy.

In this early, hidden stage, there is nothing that would distinguish the boy, like Steve, who is reacting pathologically from the boy who is reacting normally. He does not sound, think, or behave like an alcoholic. There is seemingly no problem and he has no reason to even think that there will be one.

No one is worried. And because of his initial high tolerance, which is becoming even higher, he himself rests secure in the knowledge that he has nothing to fear from alcohol. And he even takes pride in his ability to handle the effects of drinking better than others can.

Dr. James Milam states in ***Under the Influence*** that this early stage is characterized by the liver and central nervous system adjusting to alcohol, increased tolerance, and improved functioning.

At some point, a switch from heavy drinking to addiction occurs. Alan Leshner proposed that a metaphorical *Switch* is thrown in the brain as a result of prolonged drug use. Once the "*Switch*" is thrown, the individual no longer uses drugs in a voluntary manner but rather in a compulsive, addictive manner where drug seeking and use continues even in the face of seriously negative health and social consequences.

THE SWITCH IS THROWN

Many believe that there may be a biological basis to this *Switch* and strive to determine the root case of the brain disease that is addiction. It is postulated that the addicted brain is different from a non-addicted brain. It is different biochemically, physically and functionally. Many changes accompany the switch from voluntary to compulsive alcohol and drug use. However, three categories of long term changes appear to be involved.

I. *Adaptations and changes occur in brain regions that control "somatic" or body functions*. This type of change is best seen in alcohol and opioid addiction. The adaptations are such that when the chronic drug is removed, physical signs of withdrawal emerge. Some of these can be life-threatening. For example, with alcoholism, withdrawal symptoms can include hypertension, rapid heartbeat, tremor, and even major grand mal seizures.

II. *Adaptations in the reward circuitry of the brain*. These adaptations are complex and not yet entirely understood. However, the plasticity of the brain is evident. That is, the brain has an ability to change its wiring, its stimulation properties, its response to various drugs and endogenous molecules; these processes are activated by drug use. Basically, the reward system of the brain is altered. Early in the process, the drugs have major reinforcing/reward effects. However as tolerance ensues, the person experiences less of a "high" and needs more drug to get the same reward stimulation as before. With dependence, the high may not be achieved at all but the low that exists without the drug is avoided. The pleasure/reward center and its receptors, transporters and response have been altered.

III. *Adaptations in memory circuits*. Places, people, functions associated with drug/alcohol use become connected in such a way that cues may stimulate intense drug cravings. This link between addiction and the molecular mechanisms of learning and memory is one of the hottest areas of research in addiction today. The brain pathways of learning and memory and those of addiction converge and the details of this convergence are beginning to be dissected and understood.

The "rewiring" of the brain's memory circuits by the powerful reward inputs help to consolidate strong positively charged memories of drug use that persist even in the face of reduced drug effects. The brain has "learned" and consolidated responses to drug cues and these trigger habitual behaviors. Evidence from this has come directly from brain imaging studies of addicts vs. normal people. Presented with visual drug use cues, such as a martini glass with olives, the alcoholic subject's brain shows activity in discrete regions where memory is stored that are not seen in normal subjects. This is called "euphoric recall".

How long do these brain changes last? When a drug is withdrawn, the somatic withdrawal stage lasts 3-14 days. The motivational/reward system withdrawal stage may take weeks to months to recover. The emotional memories that drive craving and foster relapse can last a lifetime. It has been suggested that the biological switch from casual or heavy drug use to addiction occurs when the third category of brain changes occurs. Where in the brain these changes occur is actively being researched and areas of the hippocampus, amygdala, dorsal striatum and frontal cortex are being studied.

ADJUSTMENT/ADAPTATION TO ALCOHOL

The body accommodates stress by adapting to it, not fighting it: when eyesight is lost, the hearing sharpens; when a program of exercise is begun, unused muscles ache and then harden; when light is directed to the eye, the pupil contracts.

Alcohol is a source of stress to the body. In the early, hidden stage, alcohol assaults the cells of the body, throwing their delicate chemical balance of fats, proteins, and hormones out of whack. To accommodate this onslaught, the cells make subtle changes in the structure and chemistry of their membranes to continue functioning smoothly.

In time, however, the continued onslaught of alcohol completely destroys the fragile balance of the cell's membrane and consumes the cell's very life.

As a person with Jellinek's disease experiences rising acetaldehyde levels, he must consume more alcohol to override its devastating effects. It is imperative to continue drinking once he starts. In everyday language, "the hair of the dog that bit you."

This is not a psychological compulsion, something one does because one's ***mind*** is hooked. The ***body*** is hooked. It is a screaming out by every cell in the body for alcohol, the only substance that will provide a moment's relief. Only those who are in the later stage of Jellinek's disease can truly understand the sweetness and comfort of the initial drink as the alcohol rushes to the cells to bathe them, to console them, and to give them what they so desperately need.

INCREASED TOLERANCE

The high tolerance level at this early stage of addiction is the result of adaptation by the brain and the entire central nervous system to the presence of increasingly and necessarily larger amounts of alcohol. The alcoholic's body, even at this early, hidden stage, uses alcohol more efficiently and more quickly since less and less of it is metabolized in a normal manner and at a normal rate. Because of this speeded-up system, it must tolerate greater amounts of alcohol and function better with increased amounts.

This tolerance is not a ***learned response***. When it is said that alcoholism runs in families, it does not mean that this tolerance has been taught, like good manners. It is in the very nature of the body's response to alcohol that is beyond the purview of the intellect or the will.

People cannot adjust their central nervous system so that it may accommodate a larger volume of alcohol. It simply happens because an alcoholic's body is so designed and his chemistry is so regulated. He did not have to learn it.

This tolerance is not because he drinks too much to cover up his emotional or psychological problems. ***Increased and regular drinking does not develop tolerance; tolerance develops the drinking. Someone who develops migraine headaches from chocolate cannot develop a tolerance for chocolate by eating huge amounts of it; one will simply develop huge headaches***.

Rather than developing tolerance because one drinks too much, one drinks too much because of the high physical tolerance. An increase in the amount and frequency of drinking is a sign of an increasing tolerance, a primary mark of an early Jellinek's disease sufferer.

When the alcoholically impaired becomes tolerant to alcohol's effects, he is responding to changes which are occurring inside himself. He is not responsible for initiating these changes. He is not even conscious that these changes are taking place.

IMPROVED PHYSICAL AND MENTAL PERFORMANCE

Improved functioning is another characteristic of the hidden stage of Jellinek's disease. A non-alcoholic may feel euphoric, relaxed, with one drink. He may have a heightened sense of his own well-being.

However, since alcohol is a central nervous system depressant, the non-alcoholic will begin to slur his words, fall, and become disoriented if he drinks too much. However, when he stops drinking, the blood alcohol level (the percentage of alcohol to blood volume, .08 signifying legal intoxication) will drop and he will return to normal.

However, the alcoholic, in the early, hidden stage of Jellinek's disease shows improvement of performance as his blood alcohol level rises. With increased drinking, his performance remains steady, high, on target. He does not slur words, pass out, crack up a car. He is feeling better, more normal than when not drinking. And in reality, his body is more normal, for it is responding to the adaptations and adjustments his cells are making to accommodate the abnormal impact of alcohol.

With a few drinks, he feels better, thinks more clearly, speaks with greater articulation, is more alert, and functions on a higher level. If one drink is good, two must be better. If he is able to drink within his tolerance, this maximizing effect of alcohol will last and he will not get drunk; he will maintain this higher level of performance and will keep on a buzz until he stops drinking.

When he stops drinking, his blood alcohol level will plummet and his physical and psychological performance will drop rapidly. Some are able to maintain their drinking levels within their unique tolerance zones for long periods of time; they are neither drunk nor sober; they perform well, if not better, than most; this is a way of life.

However, regardless of the time that one remains in the hidden, adaptive stage, the day comes when the metabolic adaptations and chemical accommodations are over and the individual afflicted with Jellinek's disease is out of control, responding only to the demands of his cells.

This is what happened to Steve.

MIDDLE, CRUCIAL STAGE

The early stage in the progression of Jellinek's disease is called "hidden." This is well named because the radical, irreversible changes that the alcoholic is experiencing are hidden within the body, effecting the stability of his enzymes, fats, proteins, and hormones.

Slowly, his cells are being distorted by alcohol; ever so slowly, his organs and his brain are changing to keep themselves comfortable in the presence of increasing amounts of alcohol.

The person with Jellinek's disease sees only good results from his drinking: He feels good, has more fun, thinks better, performs more efficiently. Everything's cool.

Yet, everything is not really cool. It has been written that "everything that is hidden shall be revealed." Jellinek's disease is progressing like a pregnancy and it is only a matter of time before it shows.

The apparently benign effects of this early stage of drinking are over. Drinking is becoming unpleasant, even harmful. He is beginning to need that first drink and can't stop when he begins. He is never sure what will happen when he does drink; sometimes he can handle it, but more frequently, he simply can't predict when he will drink, how much he will drink, where he will drink. He feels guilty and remorseful, making promises that he can't keep and can't even remember.

He avoids people and is losing interest in everything but drinking. He is having trouble at work, but he is still able to hang on, relying on past successes and on others who are loyal or who owe him. He doesn't want to discuss anything about his drinking and knows that if he could just get away and change his job or his wife or his kids, everything would get back to normal.

While there is no one moment in time when the person with Jellinek's disease leaves the early stage and enters the middle stage, there are definite, predictable changes that occur. The early stage may last for years or months or only weeks; the certain fact is that, like the man in the song who was doomed to ride the subway in Boston forever, he will never again return to the seemingly innocuous early stage.

LIKING VS WANTING

These are two different things for the addicted person but similar things to the normal person. We tend to want the things that we like. However, when drinking or taking addictive drugs moves from casual use into compulsive use, the individual begins to dissociate liking from wanting. They may despise their active addiction and the drug itself, but they want it desperately nonetheless.

What can explain the dissociation of like and want? What biological change enables drugs to become the chemical surrogates of natural reinforcers and to dictate what the organism "wants"? What are these long term adaptations in the brain which have been referred to as "drug-induced neural plasticity"?

Excessive bombardment or stimulation of receptors and neurons by drugs causes long-lived changes in the signaling properties of neurons. These changes appear to occur in three systems of brain neurons: 1) *neurons in the motivational control/reward areas* that regulate motivated behavior (e.g. the dopaminergic system from the midbrain ventral tegmental area (VTA) to the nucleus accumbens (Nac), 2) *neurons in associative memory systems* that produce the strong learned associations of cue-dependent/context dependent drug and alcohol craving, and 3) *neurons in the physical control areas* that mediate physical withdrawal symptoms if the drug is withdrawn. Not all addictive drugs produce physical dependence (as defined by the presence of physical withdrawal symptoms). Alcohol and opiates produce physical dependence while cocaine or amphetamine do not.

LOSS OF CONTROL

The hallmark of this stage is loss of control. Dr. Jellinek defines loss of control as meaning "that any drinking of alcohol starts a chain reaction which is felt by the drinker as a ***physical*** demand for alcohol."

The Jellinek's disease victim has moved into the twilight zone; the sun is setting, night is not yet here. His drinking can no longer be seen or felt with any clarity. He cannot predict how much he will drink and soon he is drinking more than he wants. Even when he has promised his wife, his kids, his dead mother, God, anyone, that he won't drink. He simply has to drink.

LOSS OF TOLERANCE

The cells of someone with Jellinek's disease have changed and rearranged themselves to accommodate alcohol. They have become so different that they have functioned well, even flourished in the presence of increasingly large amounts of alcohol. This has been described as ***tolerance***.

This occurs over a relatively long period of time and the change in the tolerance level is so subtle that it often goes unnoticed. A person with Jellinek's disease finds that he needs seven or eight beers to do what six beers did; slowly, he needs 10, then 12, a case or more. His tolerance is building.

And because he is sensitive about his drinking, and even prides himself on it, he feels that he will never have a problem with drink. He started out being able to hold more than his friends and now he can hold even more than he used to. Nothing to worry about.

And yet, on some level, he does notice that he is drinking more. He may observe this with curiosity or pride, rarely with fear or concern. Others around him may be getting concerned.

If his car took a tank of gas to get from one point to another and if, over a period of time, it took a tank and a half or two tanks, he would worry and have the car checked. Something would be wrong with the engine. Yet, it now takes him 10 beers to get to where 5 beers would have taken him previously, but he knows that everything is just fine.

This high tolerance is not without cost. The cells, in adapting to and compensating for the harmful effects of alcohol, have done violence to themselves. They have suffered so much damage that they can no longer tolerate alcohol. Hence, the Jellinek's victim begins to lose his tolerance. He gets drunk on two beers. Where before it would have taken him two tanks of gas to get to his destination, he now gets there on 1/8 of a tank.

WITHDRAWAL

Because the cells feel normal only in the presence of alcohol and because these same cells can no longer tolerate the alcohol that makes them feel normal, the Jellinek's sufferer experiences withdrawal.

Withdrawal means that the cells that feel normal only in the presence of alcohol experience acute distress when the alcohol is removed. This distress takes the form of nervousness, depression, nausea, headache, irritability, hangover. Severe withdrawal includes hallucinations, violence, convulsions, D.T.s.

In ***Under The Influence***, Dr. James Milam calls withdrawal symptoms the "visible sign of addiction" and adds, "The alcoholic is most sick, not when he drinks, but when he stops drinking."

Dr. Jellinek states that withdrawal symptoms "are promptly relieved by more alcohol, but the relief is of short duration and the symptoms recur after a short interval, whereupon the drinker again takes recourse to more alcohol. This process goes on and on . . ."

TOLERANCE/WITHDRAWAL NIGHTMARE

Physical addiction to alcohol is now complete and the person with Jellinek's disease lives a nightmare: He can't get drunk and he can't get sober. His body needs alcohol to feel normal; he can't handle as much as he needs to feel normal so he goes into withdrawal; the only way to stave off the withdrawal is to drink; the drinking isn't working because he can't tolerate it to the same degree that gave him relief before. He is in constant pain, a prisoner to a biochemical imperative he must obey.

He is standing on a seesaw, trying to keep his balance between ***loss of tolerance*** on the one end and ***withdrawal*** on the other. For a while all had been well, but ever so slowly, the board begins to shift. Soon, the ends are flying up and down with reckless abandon as the afflicted person tries to keep his balance, shifting his weight first to the left and then to the right. He can no longer get back to the center, but loses his footing and rolls from one end to the other.

Control has never been an issue. Now trying to regain control becomes the focus of his life. He is a prisoner of his own body's chemistry, pulled and pushed between the polar forces of what his body needs and what it can stand.

MEMORY IMPAIRMENTS

This middle, or crucial, stage in the progression of Jellinek's disease is characterized by severe impairment of the mental and emotional faculties. Vernon Johnson in ***I'll Quit Tomorrow***, considers these impairments as the "gross distortion of the memory system: blackouts, repression, and euphoric recall."

Blackouts are ***chemically-induced periods of amnesia***. Not only has someone with Jellinek's disease lost control over his drinking, but whole segments of time, entire conversations and experiences, are lost to memory.

The person may act normal and go through all the motions of business, social or family life; when he sobers up, he has absolutely no recall. This is especially infuriating to the family or friends who feel that the Jellinek's disease sufferer is lying when he swears he does not recall what he did or said when he was drinking.

Blackouts are like shooting pictures with no film in the camera: The lens aperture is set, the light is adjusted, the exposure meter is correct, the shutter is snapped, but nothing is recorded.

Although frequent blackouts characterize this middle stage, many, many alcohol-addicted persons experience blackouts from the very beginning of their drinking. In reviewing her experiences of blacking out whenever she drank heavily, a woman commented, "Why, I just thought that was part of drinking, that it was normal. I thought everyone drank and then didn't remember. I never knew it was THE sign of alcoholism."

There are few alcoholics who have not experienced blackouts; non-alcoholics rarely, if ever, black out.

While blackouts are chemically induced lack of memory, ***repression*** is a psychologically-induced forgetfulness. This is a common defense mechanism that everyone, alcoholic and non-alcoholic, may experience. When a given incident is so horrible or so shameful, the mind automatically pushes it down, out of the reach of memory.

The alcoholic represses much of his behavior. He must shove it down deep into the hidden recesses of his mind so he can continue drinking. If he were to look at everything he did and said while drinking, he would be overwhelmed. It is as if the disease must protect itself by covering the eyes and plugging the ears of its victims.

And the more bizarre the drinking behavior, the more swift and effective the repression. The results of a continual pattern of repression are depression, nervousness, hostility, and self-pity.

While blackouts and repression separate the person with this illness from his memory, ***euphoric recall*** distorts the memory. Johnson considers euphoric recall "most devastating, for it is the greatest single factor contributing to self-delusion."

The individual who has Jellinek's disease is fast losing touch with reality. It is either out of his mental grasp or it is so distorted that all his warts are beauty marks; the drunken fights are dramatic or comic exchanges; the run-ins with the law are supposedly signs of one's roguish temperament or free spirit; the drunken crying jags testify to one's sensitive or poetic nature.

An alcoholically impaired woman had become intoxicated while at a formal dinner dance given by her husband's company. She had danced wildly, fallen on the floor, insulted the president of the company and his wife, made sexual overtures to younger men in the firm, totally embarrassing her husband.

She had seen herself as witty, charming, graceful–the life of the party. She knew she was a valuable asset to her husband's career–

indeed, he was lucky to have her as a partner, and with her, he would surely go places in the firm.

At the end of the evening, she went to the ladies room to freshen up. Her lipstick was smeared across her cheeks, her mascara had run down her eyes, and a false eyelash was stuck on one eyebrow. She looked in the mirror and screamed. Reality did not square with her fantasies.

In order to truly understand Jellinek's disease sufferers one must comprehend that blackouts, repression, and euphoric recall are not under the jurisdiction of the intellect or of the will any more than are the elevation of acetaldehyde levels. Memory functions reside in the brain; as the cells of the brain become more and more distorted because of the impact of alcohol, they lose their ability to function effectively.

In other words, someone with Jellinek's disease is not lying when he states (or swears) that he does not remember. He cannot remember, and if he does, it is so rearranged and colored that any semblance of reality is absent. Not to understand that he is telling the truth from his vantage is to miss a critical dimension of Jellinek's disease.

LATE, CHRONIC STAGE

At this point in the progression of Jellinek's disease, acute physical, mental, and social deterioration occur. Tolerance has decreased significantly and the pains of withdrawal are a fact of life; constant drinking is the only solution.

Dr. Jellinek articulates what has happened: Marked ethical deterioration and impairment of thinking; alcoholic psychosis; drinking with persons below one's social level; recourse to "technical products" (rubbing alcohol, bay rum); indefinable fears; tremors; inability to perform physical tasks; obsessive drinking; vague religious desires.

The cells, tissues, and organs of the body have long been assaulted by alcohol. At first, the body accommodated and adjusted, then rebelled against it by throwing the person into withdrawal, but now, at this later point, it simply weakens, throws down its defenses, and the disease rampages.

According to a recent American Cancer Society forecast, 483,000 people were predicted to die from cancer; between 9,000 and 19,000 of those deaths were predicted to be directly related to alcoholism. The exact mechanism by which this occurs is not clear, but possible explanations may be that:

1. Alcohol acts as a solvent, facilitating the transport of carcinogens across cell membranes.
2. Because alcohol damages the liver, that organ cannot carry on its repair process, thus promoting abnormal tissue growth.
3. Alcohol creates certain enzymes in the liver that produce carcinogens.
4. Alcoholic beverages themselves may contain chemicals that cause cancer.

Cancers of the lips, mouth, tongue, pharynx, and esophagus occur more often in those with Jellinek's disease than in others. Of these cancers, 34% are fatal. The chronic use of alcohol together with tobacco accounts for 75% of these cancers.

Esophageal varicose veins (varices) develop and many an alcoholic has bled to death when these veins burst. Ulcers and stomach cancer result from alcoholism, as well as irritation of the bowel.

More than 75% of cases of chronic pancreatitis in the U.S.A. occur in alcoholics. Acetaldehyde in sufficient amounts forms pancreatic stones that obstruct the ducts. In a study of pancreatic cancer, 75% of the victims had a history of moderate to heavy drinking.

The first of the liver diseases to develop is alcoholic ***fatty liver***, because alcohol replaces fat as the preferred fuel for the liver; consequently, the unburned fat builds up in the liver, increasing acid levels in the blood which are associated with hyperglycemia (elevated blood sugar).

Alcoholic hepatitis is characterized by the inflammation and death of individual liver cells. This condition is painful; the person may experience nausea, jaundice, and fever. Hepatitis, as well as fatty liver, are reversible.

The liver disease that develops at a later stage is known as ***cirrhosis***. The liver is so plugged with toxic substances that blood cannot flow through and backs up. The blood, in turn, picks up these toxins and carries them to the head where they do further damage to an already damaged brain. This has been called "blood-sludge."

Scar tissue develops in the liver, further cutting off the free flow of blood and further increasing the toxins in the blood since the liver is failing to clear them. Cirrhotic liver is a major cause of death in those plagued by Jellinek's disease.

Upon autopsy, as much as 30% of alcoholic cirrhotics had undetected liver cancer. It is suspected that the reason that so few cirrhotics die from liver cancer is that cirrhosis develops much faster and that liver cancer has not had time to develop.

Nevada, Alaska, and the District of Columbia have the highest per capita alcohol consumption; they also have the highest death rates from cirrhosis.

Cardiomyopathy is a primary cause of death in the Jellinek's disease. It is characterized by chronic shortness of breath, swelling (of hands and feet, the lungs, and the viscera), fatigue, heart palpitations, and bloodstained sputum. High blood pressure and irregular heartbeats are other signs of heart disease connected with alcoholism.

Heart disease is the number one cause of death in the United States. Many cardiac and diabetic patients are alcoholics who are being treated for heart problems and diabetes. These critical medical problems are greatly aggravated by Jellinek's disease, for which they are ***not*** being treated; likewise, their death certificates will not mention the root cause of death, alcoholism.

Myopathy is a disease of the skeletal muscles, long associated with alcoholism. The muscles become weak and cramp painfully. Leg cramps at night are common among alcoholics.

General muscle weakening accounts for many of the falls and mysterious bruises alcoholics suffer. For example, a college girl entered treatment because she would wake up every morning covered with bruises. She had no idea where they came from and did not remember falling. Even when she was not drinking, her legs would give out when she least expected it.

Blood disorders such as ***anemia*** and nutritional disorders of the B complex vitamins such as ***polyneuropathy, Wernicke's encephalopathy***, and ***Korsakoff's psychosis*** occur in the later stages of Jellinek's disease.

Many alcoholics simply do not eat. They get all or most of their calories from alcohol. These are empty calories, devoid of essential amino acids, vitamins, and minerals. These nutritional disorders effect the central nervous system and the brain, resulting in headaches, confusion, agitation, hallucinations. If untreated, irreversible brain damage (Korsakoff's psychosis) results. This is known as "wet brain."

Seventy to 80% of Jellinek's disease afflicted men experience a reduction in the production of the male hormone androgen, which results in impotence and a sharp decrease in libido. The same percentages (70-80%) of alcoholic men show testicular atrophy and infertility.

In addition, men experience an increase in the production of the female hormone estrogen, which results in the enlargement of mammary glands and a general feminization of the alcoholic man.

Women, likewise, experience infertility, loss of sex drive, and a loss of secondary sex characteristics such as breast and pelvic fat accumulation. Cancer of the breast is more frequent among alcoholic women. According to a 1987 study, even women who drink moderately (three drinks a week) run higher risks of breast cancer than those women who do not drink.

DEATHS ATTRIBUTED TO ALCOHOL

Because various diseases exist at the time of death, e.g., stroke, cancer, pneumonia, these illnesses are frequently listed on death certificates as the cause of death. Yet these illnesses may have taken years to develop, growing slowly, unnoticed under the steady onslaught of acetaldehyde, of alcohol.

Chapter Three

The Alcoholic Person: An Inside Story

God tempers the wind to the shorn lamb.
LAWRENCE STERNE

I have been asked to tell you what it feels like to be an alcoholic. First of all, I hate that word. It reminds me of a dark and damp cave with all sorts of horrible things growing on the walls.

Before I start, I need to tell you that I haven't had a drink in years and that I go to A.A. three or four times a week. It is hard to look back on my drinking days, because now it seems pretty far away. As a matter of fact, it seems like another lifetime away. But if I forget those horrible times, I might need to refresh my memory by drinking again. What is that saying about those who do not know their history are bound to repeat it?

I'll try not to bore you with a lot of details. I remember a lot of stuff quite clearly, but a lot is pretty fuzzy. I was in a blackout a lot of the time.

My life was pretty ordinary, pretty boring, I guess, by other peoples' standards. And my name is Anne. I'm now in my forties.

I grew up in the suburbs. My father was a banker and my mother stayed at home and raised the six of us. I was the oldest. He drank as long as I can remember. She started when I was in high school. The youngest was in first or second grade.

There were a lot of horrible scenes, which I won't go into at this time. I just knew that I would never end up like them. I've had a lot of therapy now, so I don't have that rage that I carried with me for so long.

When I had to face my own alcoholism, I had to face theirs. I had to accept the fact that I had a disease; I couldn't accept this until I accepted their alcoholism as a disease. This was harder than accepting it for myself, but I'm getting ahead of myself.

I was a real straight kid. Obnoxiously so. I would have been called the Super Kid or the Hero, if we had used those terms. I went to Sunday School. During high school, I sang in the choir. I took religion very seriously–I was scrupulous. I saw everything in moral terms and just knew that God was there to get me for everything.

I know if I were Catholic, I would have been running to Confession all the time like my girlfriend Mary Jean. At least she got to feel better for a little while. I never did. And I'm sure that I would have been a nun, like Mary Jean.

I did very well in school and hung out with all the smart kids. We were really the snobs. We had a club that we called the G.Q.'s–the Gin Queens. When we'd get together, we'd drink gin and tonics or Tom Collinses. I can remember never getting drunk, like a lot of the other kids. This was proof to me that I'd never be an alcoholic like my mother and father.

I could have graduated from high school after my junior year. There were scholarships available, two to art schools. I have always been able to draw and paint well and the natural thing to do would have been to get some formal training. I guess I figured if I went to college, I'd still be a part of the family, and I really wanted out.

I didn't go to college or to art school. Everyone was very upset about that, but I guess I needed to rebel. I just got a dinky job in a bakery. I met Dave, he was twenty-eight at the time, and I got pregnant. The scrupulous one gets pregnant out of wedlock.

So I had to get married. Just a week before the wedding–the invitations had been sent out and all the arrangements had been made–I had a miscarriage. It was a Saturday night and I was getting ready to go out. I started to bleed and got really scared. My sister took me to the hospital.

No one could find my parents. They called everywhere but no one knew where they were. When we finally located them, they came to the hospital, so drunk they could hardly stand up. My mother was singing and flirting with the doctor and my father was in one of his violent moods. My sister was crying and I was a mess.

We went on with the wedding. Dave was in the Army and due to go over to Vietnam. We lived on base and every afternoon, we'd drink with a group of people just like ourselves.

I was really the life of the party. I could hold so much more than just about anyone else, including the men. I had a lot of blackouts, but it just seemed funny at the time. My husband was busy but I had a lot of time on my hands. I got back to my art . . . until it was time to party.

I should tell you that every time I got drunk, and that was often, I'd tell MY STORY. I'd tell the story about my miscarriage and my parents and all the blood and my sister crying and how I went on with the wedding. I told it hundreds of times, to anyone who'd listen. I just had to tell MY STORY, over and over and over again.

My drinking didn't seem to cause us any trouble. I was aware that I was drinking a lot, but it just seemed natural. That lasted for four years. Dave was discharged and we came back home. I had a baby boy, Matthew. Dave got a good job, something with computers. I never really understood what he did. But he had to travel a lot, often for a week or so at a time, and I was home alone with the baby.

I set up an art studio at home and worked all day. About five, I'd start with my martinis. I'd have some of the girls in the neighborhood in and we'd have a few drinks. Then they'd go home, I'd feed Matthew and get him into bed, and then drink. I just drank. I'd put on some music, turn down the lights, and sit alone and drink.

Dave never called during the week, so I didn't have to worry. When he came home on Friday, I'd have the house in perfect order, a roast in the oven, flowers on the table, romantic music in the background. He was exhausted and wanted to be quiet and I was looking for some companionship. By ten we'd have a terrible fight. I know I would tell him MY STORY, over and over again.

My husband had no experience with alcoholism, so he never suspected that I was in trouble. But then, he was never home. He took another job where he didn't have to travel. We moved to another house and I cleaned up my act. I was very careful about my drinking. He always went to bed early, so I would stay up and do my drinking at night.

It was hard waiting for him to go to bed. By five or six, I really needed a drink, but I didn't allow myself. I knew if I started, I'd be out of it by nine. I just loved to turn down the lights, turn on the music, and mellow out.

When I wasn't drinking, I felt that something was missing in my life. It was just so wonderful to mellow out. The scruples that I had as a kid were always with me and I was haunted by the idea that I wasn't good enough–as a mother, as a wife, as an artist. When I drank, I became beautiful to myself and my thoughts were lovely and pure and mystical.

I'd read poetry, you know, the women–Emily Dickinson, Adrienne Rich, Sylvia Plath. I'd play Joan Baez and Buffy Sainte-Marie and Judy Collins and go with Suzanne down to the river and feed on oranges that came all the way from China. It was all so lovely–my boozy, mystical, drunken nights alone.

I guess Dave knew what was going on. We were fighting a lot–never really about my drinking. It was always about something else–the baby, money, work, the car. I don't know. We were always fighting. I just wanted him to leave me alone. I just wanted to live my life and he wanted me to live his life or something. It is all kinda fuzzy now.

Anyhow, Dave took another job where he was gone most of the time. I was painting a lot and a friend from high school had her own gallery and she wanted to show some of my stuff. I began making enough money through the sale of my paintings to have someone come in and watch Matthew. He was about three. I couldn't manage him and my work.

About this time, I found that a little wine would help me paint. I'd always have it in a pretty glass and if anyone would come in, I'd pour them one. I was starting to feel agitated most of the time and I really needed the wine to keep on going.

But I was working like a mad woman, turning out three or four paintings a day. I couldn't stop the paint, it just seemed to run out of my head, down my arms, and onto the boards. And people raved and wanted to buy more. My pictures were so calm and peaceful and serene.

It was really weird. My home, my clothes, my art was all so lovely, so harmonious, with subtle shades of pastels. I loved to do flowers and gardens and always had flowering plants in my studio. People would comment on the loveliness of my life and my work.

But inside, I was a wreck. I started to feel that I was losing my mind. I'd play Judy Collins and Joan Baez all day, hoping they would calm me down. I got into Zen, and Valium. The doctor was such a pushover. He thought I was just a high-strung artist who needed a little extra help to calm down. To this day, I wish he had seen what I really was.

I still looked pretty good. I'm tall, almost stately. I had good eyes, good skin, good hair. I would wear exotic caftans in the purest shades of blue, with eyeshadow to match. I'd flow around my studio, paintbrush in mouth, wineglass in hand, listening to Judy going down by the river with the oranges that came all the way from China.

I should tell you that I wore caftans because I had gained so much weight that I looked like a pregnant cow in any thing else. And the uglier I became to myself, the heavier was the makeup. I started smudging my cheeks with pewter blues and violets and charcoals.

The wine wasn't working anymore, so I had to drink vodka when I worked. And when I didn't work. I was drinking all the time. I had to drink in the morning, just to get going. Pretty soon, I was waking up in the middle of the night, just to drink. Also, I was pretty good at balancing the pills. I talked the stupid doctor into giving me some Dalmane, just so I could get to sleep. My whole life revolved around the vodka, the Valium, the Dalmane.

I had the prescriptions at three different drug stores so they wouldn't catch on to me. And I'd use different liquor stores or have it delivered by the case "Thank you, Roger, my husband and I are entertaining some clients this weekend. Just leave the box in the garage. My husband will bring it in when he gets home."

I was getting afraid. Of everyone. Including the rubbish collectors. I was afraid they'd see the empty bottles, so I'd sneak off at night and put the bottles in the neighbors' garbage cans. Or I'd save them up and take them to the city incinerator.

I was afraid of anyone who came to the door. I pulled the drapes so they would think I was out or sick. Even when the rubbish men came, I'd duck down beneath the kitchen counter so they wouldn't see me.

I was afraid of the phone. I'd have to talk with people and I couldn't stand to. When those horrible people would call, trying to sell me insurance or carpet cleaning, I'd swear at them and slam the phone down. Usually, I just let it ring.

I was getting desperate. Dave was staying away more and more, and when he came home, there were the terrible fights. Matthew was crying a lot and I'd get mad at the sitter, fire her, and hire another. I needed someone in the house so he would be all right. I just couldn't take care of him.

I'd have terrible crying jags. The manic periods of work, work, work were over. I couldn't work. I couldn't think. All I could do was drink and take my pills.

I was so depressed and confused that I decided to end it all. I had a big drink, took my Valium, and went for the razor. A few good gashes and it would be all over. I had read that Marilyn Monroe's suicide turned her life into a work of art with a message. I'd go out in style, like Marilyn.

I was so drunk that all I managed to do was to shave my wrists. About this time, Dave took Matthew and moved out. I got my pills, my bottles, and my paints and locked the doors. It was a living hell–the lovely pastels turned into ugly shades of black and brown and purple, with red and orange and yellow gashes.

I didn't eat. Or sleep. Or bathe. I'd fall on the floor, pass out, and then come to, throw some paint around, and drink myself unconscious. I vomited a lot, but managed to get the pills and booze down. It was so horrible. I feel horrible all over again now, just retelling it.

This went on for nearly two weeks. I think I was getting ready to die.

To this day, I can't say exactly what happened. I just remember crawling to the phone and calling a friend of my sister's. I remembered vaguely that she had been a terrible drinker and that she was okay somehow. I guess there was just a little flicker of life that refused to be snuffed out. I still can't remember how I made that call, or even how I remembered her name.

She came over with another woman. I think they had to crawl through a window because I couldn't get to the door. They got me into a hospital and that was the beginning of the end. I know if I had continued as I was, I wouldn't be here today.

I'll leave the story of my recovery to another day. I'll just say that I've kept the paintings that I did in that last whatever it was. They are a good reminder of the hell I crawled around in with my pills and my bottle. I never want to be there again.

HOW DOES IT FEEL TO BE OUT OF CONTROL?

What does it feel like to be an alcoholic? How does it feel to be out of control and have to present to the world the facade that you are in control, that everything is cool, that you are the same old person, just going through a little bit of a hard time?

How does it feel to sneak drinks? Hide bottles? Take money for the kids' shoes to buy a bottle? Shout at your host at a party and not be able to stop yourself? Fall on your face? Not remember where you have been nor with whom? Look in the mirror and see a beast? Feel your skin shrinking like a cheap cotton shirt? Write names and numbers and not know what they mean? Open a telephone bill and not remember your drunken late night calls to forgotten friends or enemies?

How does it feel to hear jokes about drunks and know the laughter is at you? How does it feel to hate yourself for being so out of control? How does it feel to stop for a single beer and end up in oblivion? How does it feel to be hated for your weakness and know it's not a weakness, yet you don't know what it is?

In ***Crack-Up***, F. Scott Fitzgerald, himself an alcoholic, describes the nightmare: "In a real dark night of the soul it is always 3:00 in the morning, day after day. At that hour the tendency is to refuse to face things as long as possible by retiring into an infantile dream—but one is continually startled out of this by various contacts with the world. One meets these occasions as quickly and carelessly as possible and retires once more back into the dream."

To be addicted to a chemical substance is to be plunged into the dark night of the soul, to be stripped of that quality that makes one truly human, namely, the ***will***. To be addicted is to be claimed, to be owned, to be lessened. The ancients said that a man loses half his soul the day he becomes a slave; an addicted person is a person with only half a soul.

An understanding of the concept of addiction lies in the very root of the Latin word, ***ad + dictus***, having been spoken for, having been claimed. The addicted person is claimed, owned by a force outside himself. One may be claimed by art, sports, work; such a person is said to be an art or sports addict, a workaholic. And one may be claimed or spoken for by chemical substances and as such is addicted to nicotine, cocaine, alcohol. The alcoholic is one spoken for, claimed, owned by alcohol; propelled, ready to rampage and destroy, his will helplessly dangling. Someone with Jellinek's disease is confused, unaware that he is out of control, suffering from an illness that tells the victim that he is fine, that others are the problem.

It is essence of Jellinek's disease to tell its victim that it does not exist, as if to utter its name would shatter it. Its very existence and growth depend on the confusion it creates, as if the disease itself knows that once it is named, its power shrinks like a tumor under a blast of radiation.

The person with Jellinek's disease plays a game of Rumpelstiltskin, feverishly trying to guess the name of the demon that has laid claim to his soul. Stress . . . depression . . . too much religion . . . not enough religion . . . father's drinking . . . mother's drinking . . . sad childhood . . . because I'm Irish . . . because I'm a rebel . . . because I'm so sensitive . . . because I hear a different drummer.

And the demon dances and sings within the soul of its victim, laughing that the fool still doesn't know his name.

Imagine: a skiff, a light rowboat where one can pull the oars, directing the path across a lake, moving at times faster, at times slower. The sweetness of dipping the oars at will: the mind beckoning the arms, the arms pulling the oars, the oars sweeping the water, the water rushing the skiff, the skiff moving where it is directed.

Imagine: a demon motor, uncontrollable, affixed to the stern, always running, propelling the skiff against the rocks, into the reeds and shallows, sometimes idling but ever ready to churn the waters without notice, to rampage and to destroy. The oars dangle helplessly in their oarlocks and, finally, shatter.

Someone suffering from Jellinek's disease rampages through life, out of control, on a course that is steadied for disaster, not only with his own body, but with his family, with society, with nature. And as he careens from one incident to the next, minor skirmishes or brushes with the law escalate until a major felon stands before a court of law.

The alcoholically impaired is trapped in an insidious moral dilemma: He knows that he is doing bad things (lying, breaking his promises, sneaking, getting drunk) but he knows that he really isn't to blame, he just somehow has to do these things to keep going. Or as one recovering woman described it, "It was all so innocent. I just don't know how I got into all of that. On some level, I was really innocent."

The person with Jellinek's disease is compelled by his body's chemistry to engage in morally destructive behavior for which he truly feels himself to be innocent. If he is not to blame, who is?

Struggling for an explanation for his behavior, so different from his inner picture of himself, so different from the man he really is, his mind lights where it can. It cannot blame him, but someone must bear responsibility: The family, and, by extension, his friends, his neighbors, his coworkers, his deceased parents–an ever-widening circle of those upon whom his mind may lay the onus of his actions.

But the family remains the most guilty of all. They are the closest, their lives are intertwined, they are to blame. And as his disease gains momentum, they grow more evil and mean, driving him to drink by their insensitivity, their demands, their lack of love. They try to make him stop drinking; yet drinking is the only comfort left.

DENIAL: THE HALLMARK OF JELLINEK'S DISEASE

It is said that alcoholism is the only disease that tells you it isn't a disease.

Millions of chemically dependent people run from doctor to doctor, from diet to diet, from one group to another to find out what is the matter. Why is life so horrible and hard? Why can't I cope like I used to? Why has my family turned against me? What is happening to me?

Why is it that a family can be suffering exquisite mental and social pain because of a father's drinking, and the father, basically a good and honest man, assumes absolutely no responsibility for their anguish and goes out to have a few beers with the boys?

Why is it that an indigent alcoholic, forced to have both legs amputated because of frostbite and gangrene, is completely unable to relate his fate with his drinking?

Why is it that an elderly woman whose husband died of alcoholic complications, and whose adult children cannot relate to each other because of their painful childhood, cannot see that she herself has Jellinek's disease, despite incipient diabetes, blotchy skin, puffy eyes?

Why is it that studies show that nearly half of suicide attempts are by the alcoholically impaired? For teenagers, the figures are even higher. In fact, alcoholism has been called "chronic suicide."

Perhaps the single most frustrating, most infuriating characteristic of the alcoholic is his not admitting he has a problem with alcohol even when his family is falling apart, his job is on the line, his drunk driving convictions are accumulating, his liver and pancreas are shot, and his wife is suing for divorce.

The dilemma appears to be that either alcohol has done such extensive damage to his brain that he cannot see the red nose on his face or he is simply a barefaced liar.

And the family continues to bleed to death while the alcoholic goes skipping through the tulips, oblivious of the trail of destruction he is leaving, impervious to cries and prayers that he stop drinking.

And because of the alcoholic's complete and total disavowal of any problem with alcohol, the family either thinks, "Yes, he's right. There is no problem. It's just us." Or they grow to hate him and plot murder in their own hearts because of his cavalier attitude to the monumental family tragedy that he appears to be orchestrating.

Denial is a word endemic to the field of alcoholism. A woman is said to be "in denial" over her alcoholism. Counselors speak about "breaking through her denial system." A recovering alcoholic speaks about "being in denial about my denial."

Although the word ***denial*** has a very specific psychiatric meaning, its sweeping use in describing an alcoholic's inability or unwillingness to own up to his alcoholism often causes further confusion in an already painful enigma.

It is in the ***very nature of the disease that self-awareness is dim, blunted, absent***. Even in recovery, all that is left is a memory of bizarre occasions and of painful, confused feelings. Recovering people, sober many years, suddenly remember a forgotten incident, a buried conversation, something that was seen or said or felt while drinking.

To deny something means "to say not" or "to negate." A two-year-old with chocolate smeared across his face will deny that he got into the ice cream. A teenager with a new driver's license will deny that he was going over the speed limit when he took his mother's car out on the highway to open it up. The diabetic with Hershey bars tucked into her purse will deny to the doctor that she is eating candy and has no idea why her sugar is up.

In these instances, the child clearly knew he was into the ice cream, the teenager clearly knew he was speeding, and the diabetic clearly knew she was eating candy. They negated what they had done, they denied what they had done, but the salient point is that each one was ***lying*** and was aware that he or she was doing so.

There was no mental obfuscation, no hidden cellars of the mind where their true intent and actions fell. They each did something they should not have done; they each got caught; they each lied to get out of paying the penalty.

However, with an alcoholic (as with anyone who is truly "in denial" about something he cannot and will not face), he is not overtly, consciously lying. He truly does not see that he has a problem with drinking, much less that he is an alcoholic. Yes, there may be times when he has a little too much to drink, but not so much as to raise all the fuss.

The wife served with divorce papers, the double amputee, the hit-and-run driver–none of these can make a direct connection between his or her drinking and its consequences.

And it is this very phenomenon that exacerbates the rage of those around them. How can they not see? Why do they lie so? Why do they insult our intelligence by pretending that their drinking is not the source of all our heartbreak?

How this denial happens is highly complex when one looks at the mental gymnastics that produce it; it is utterly simple when one considers the effect of allowing the alcoholic to continue drinking with impunity.

In a recent book, ***Vital Lies, Simple Truths***, Daniel Goleman explains the process of how and why we lie to ourselves about these very painful areas of our lives and experience. He writes that the mind lies to itself to protect itself by 1) turning off; 2) creating blind spots; and 3) lying at all levels of behavior.

TURNING OFF

Primarily, the mind can protect itself against anxiety by dimming awareness, by turning off.

Anxiety is the response we have when the information we receive about ourselves is frightening. The Chinese are about to launch a megabomb on the East coast . . . A dentist is coming at me with a whirling drill . . . the checkbook is registering negative numbers.

Goleman calls anxiety "mental static." When there is static on my radio, I turn it off. When there is static in my mind, I turn it off.

To turn off my mental static, I close it out, think about something else. I don't think about the Chinese but a trip to Hawaii; I stare at the ceiling in the dentist's office, looking for interesting little shapes and pictures so I don't notice the drill; I keep on spending money because if I think of how broke I am, it will only get worse.

And I keep on drinking, just a few little beers or a glass of wine. They keep yelling at me about my drinking and it makes too much static. I might be an alcoholic. I might have to stop drinking and I can't do without it. I'll just drink some more and think about something else. He's overreacting. He's poisoning the kids' minds against me. I don't have a problem.

BLIND SPOTS

Secondly, the mechanism of tuning out awareness creates a blind spot: Goldman calls this "a zone of blocked attention and self-deception."

The term "blind spot" is commonly used in our everyday speech to signify an area at which we either are unable or unwilling to look at. Although we use the term as a figure of speech, it derives from an actual void in our field of vision.

Behind the eyeball, the optic nerve which runs to the brain is attached to the retina. There are no rod and cone cells at this point (cells which register light), therefore, the light coming through the pupil does not register and a blind spot in the field of vision is created.

It is the nature of that blind-spot that nothing within it can be seen and ***it cannot be seen itself***.

Our mental or psychological blind spots are just as real. A mother, confronted with the fact that her son has just raped and killed a 6-year-old, avows, "My boy would never have done that. He has always been a wonderful son, a son any mother would be proud of."

The alcoholically impaired develops her own blind spot. There are no cells where the light hits the psychological retina and no message gets carried to the brain. She looks in the mirror, over her shoulder, and sees nothing. Why is everyone so excited? Everything is under control. She just had some wine with the girls.

This blind spot is the cornerstone of the alcoholic's system of defense. This is what is meant by alcoholic denial.

And in her blindness and denial, the alcoholic's condition worsens as her chemical dependency grows, as her self-image deteriorates, as her ego strength weakens.

Vernon Johnson writes about deteriorating alcoholics: "For many reasons they are unable to keep track of their own behavior and begin to lose contact with their emotions. Their defense systems continue to grow, so that they can survive in the face of their problems. The greater the pain, the higher and more rigid the defenses become; and this whole process is unconscious. Alcoholics do not know what is happening inside of themselves. Finally they actually become victims of their own defense mechanisms."

There is a direct correlation between the progression of Jellinek's disease and the swelling of the blind spot, the burgeoning of denial.

As the person with Jellinek's disease becomes more dependent upon alcohol and her life is becoming less manageable, her denial rapidly spreads to encompass the entire scope of her drinking.

Denial becomes the magician's cape that the alcoholic spreads over her tracks–First you see it, then you don't! It's all gone! There's nothing there at all! But the sick magician loses her footing and gets ensnared in her cape, struggling against her own blindness and suffocating herself in her denial.

LYING AT ALL LEVELS

Thirdly, Goleman writes that these blind spots occur at each level of behavior, from the psychological to the social.

In other words, the alcoholic may experience extensive physical problems due to his drinking, he may lose his job or family and be in trouble with the law, but as long as he needs and uses these blind spots, he is truly unable to see the consequences of his drinking and is precluded from doing anything about it.

How does this actually work? How can someone look down and see himself without legs which had to be amputated because he had fallen asleep in the snow during a drunken binge and say that his drinking causes him no problem? How can an elderly woman with elevated sugar levels, puffy eyes, blotchy skin, and bruises from unknown falls pour herself another drink, completely oblivious to her problem? How does it work?

Psychologists speak of information coming into the mind as a "stimulus." I look into the refrigerator and see a piece of banana cream pie. The pie is a stimulus. It enters the part of the mind where senses are stored and filtered and goes from there into the awareness. I am then able to make a conscious response–I am a diabetic, stay away from sweets, close the refrigerator door, get out of the kitchen.

Let us say that I have a finely tuned defense system with a major blind spot concerning my diabetes. I look into the refrigerator. I see the pie. I know I am a diabetic, that I must avoid sweets, but at this moment, I simply do not want to deal with the fact that I am a diabetic.

I only partly take it in. At the moment, my diabetes does not fully hit my level of awareness, but I keep it stored in my long-term memory. I cannot make a conscious response, because the fact of my diabetes never fully entered my level of awareness. It only can enter my unconscious level.

So I take the pie out of the refrigerator and eat it, because to me I really don't have diabetes. And if later in the day someone asks me how I am getting along with my blood sugar, I would think he was crazy because I believe I simply don't have diabetes.

> ***Denial***: I don't understand. It was a nice night, fun people. I remember wearing my new navy sports coat and drinking a few martinis. I think the Robertsons and the Moodies were there. I think the rest of the night was fine–just a little fun with some friends. I honestly don't know what the hell she is so upset about. Really, I've doubted her sanity for a while now. And she's even trying to make me believe that I'm an alcoholic.

> ***Reality***: I drank last night. First martinis, wine, some Rusty Nails. I made an ass of myself, fell on the floor, fought with the hostess, made sexual overtures to the teenage daughter of the host, ran into a tree coming home. The following morning my wife is enraged. She screams and hollers, saying how mortified she was at my behavior. The car is a wreck, our lives are a wreck, the kids won't speak to me, the dog avoids me.

This is the classic denial syndrome: the blindness of the alcoholic and his blindness to that blindness.

The alcoholic has diverted the facts of his drinking behavior away from his awareness into his unconscious. His wife has taken the same stimulus, his drinking, and reacts differently. She allows her husband's drinking fully to enter her awareness, wherein she has a conscious response to his behavior. She screams and is enraged.

BLACKOUTS

Compounding the barrier of denial are the already mentioned blackouts: Alcoholically induced periods of amnesia. Even if the alcoholic wanted to remember, he could not. Parts of the night are simply gone and the parts he can remember suffer from "euphoric recall"–the nice night, navy sports coat, fun friends.

The alcoholic does not have conscious access to knowledge of the amount he drank, how he drank, what he was like, the effect he had on others, how he looked, how he sounded. It was simply a nice evening and now his wife is all upset. It truly does not make sense to him. The reality of the situation has been blacked out.

SOCIAL REASONS FOR DENIAL

The social reasons for such denial are great. Who wants to be an alcoholic? It is a horrible label and which of us would choose it? Which of us would choose the label "Murderer"? "Rapist"? "Child Abuser"? "Thief"? "Pimp"?

For the same reasons the family denies that there is one in their midst who is an alcoholic. It is just such a horrible label to paste on anyone. And if he is really an alcoholic, he may have to go to A.A., and that would confirm it.

PERSONAL REASONS FOR DENIAL

Apart from the vast negative social connotations, the Jellinek's disease sufferer knows that an alcoholic is one who is out of control, and he ***has*** been able to control his drinking on many occasions. He never drinks in the morning (yet), he never drinks during Lent (yet), he has gone for periods of six months, three months, six weeks without a drink; alcoholics cannot do that. So they cling desperately to the illusion that they are still in control.

If one has lived with and loved an alcoholic, one feels somewhat of an authority on alcoholism. The experience is usually so traumatic, so pervasive, so unique, that the survivor feels qualified to recognize and to define alcoholism with all its nasty ramifications.

Jellinek's disease comes in many shades of gray and the one person's drinking may bear little relationship to the drinking of another. Even within families, there may be three sisters, all alcoholics, but all three may have very different drinking histories, patterns, problems. To know one is not to know them all. This would be analogous to equating a carcinoma on the hand with a malignancy in the brain.

One defines alcoholism by what one knows of the alcoholism of another. This frequently happens if one has lived with an alcoholic whose drinking was much worse than one's own drinking.

If a woman has had an alcoholic husband who beat her and the children while shouting obscenities at the neighbors, it is very difficult for such a woman to see her own quiet slips into oblivion every night as alcoholism. How can she see her own "just relaxing" as the same disease as her husband's?

If a young man had a mother who never moved off her couch and died of cirrhosis of the liver at the age of 40, how can he see his excessive drinking of beer with the boys as alcoholism? He is nothing like her. She only drank vodka, straight. She wasn't any fun; he's the life of the party. The pattern just doesn't fit.

Every alcoholic's definition of alcoholism is subjective, contoured to fit the shape of his own blindness. His standard is highly personal, based on his own history.

Since Jellinek's disease is hereditary, most alcoholics have had intimate knowledge of another alcoholic–a mother, a grandfather, an uncle or brother. But because Jellinek's disease is a coat of many colors, it may manifest itself differently in different members of the family: One may be violent; one may be funny; one may not drink at all.

If one has been affected by an active alcoholic, one cannot help but draw conclusions about alcoholism and about alcoholics. The irony is that making assumptions about alcoholism from another's drinking is an attempt to make order out of chaos while all the while constantly creating more chaos because these assumptions miss the mark.

Vernon Johnson, in ***I'll Quit Tomorrow***, writes, "Very different sorts of people become alcoholic, but all alcoholics are ultimately alike. The disease itself swallows up all differences and creates a ***universal alcoholic profile***. The personality changes that go with the illness are predictable and inevitable . . ."

As we observe real alcoholics (late stage), we see that they are irresponsible, self-centered, lying, impulsive people bent on their own destruction and the destruction of their families. And this is usually true. We feel that all alcoholics are alike.

Ignorant of or unwilling to understand the biochemical pathology that set the stage for the disease and confusing the effects for the cause, we all become experts in the phenomenon we call alcoholism. We know for sure that this would never happen to us, but, God forbid, if it ever did, certainly we would be the first to recognize it.

Denying and misconstruing what alcoholism is all about insures its steady, lethal progression. Someone with Jellinek's disease perceives that there really is no problem and tells himself to take it easy. And if there is a problem, it must be of someone else's making. He just does not see it.

It is the blindness of the alcoholic more than his actual behavior that sets off the deadly rage of the family. The family watches the source of their pain laugh at them, as he goes blithely through life oblivious to the damage he is creating.

As long as the alcoholic cannot see his illness, to speak of recovery and healing is simply whistling in the dark. It is the blindness of the alcoholic that must be healed, as if suddenly nerve cells were to appear at the juncture where the optic nerve meets the retina and the mind is filled with light and color and reality.

Chapter Four

Drugs: The Panorama of Jellinek's Disease

Cocaine isn't habit forming. I should know— I've been using it for years.
TALLULAH BANKHEAD

The air was heavy with pepperoni and onions. Shouts from Papa Joe's Pizza Parlor grew louder as the day grew hotter. The red sign in front of the bank registered 93 degrees. 12:32 p.m.

Jerry Sachs, sitting alone in his second-floor apartment, stared at the television and took another slug of vodka. Sharks, snakes, and moray eels swam over the door jamb. He rested the cheese jar that he used for a glass between his legs. The floor was too far down.

He pressed the channel button. "Days of Our Lives" on Channel 5. "All My Children" on 7. The Cubs on 9 . . . Makeup game with San Diego . . . Wish Steve Garvey would break a leg . . . Screwed us in the playoffs last year.

Yoplait yogurt ad. The girl in the red shorts looks like Lori. Screw Lori. She was no good. No good for me. Better off without her.

Lori refused to move into the single room above the pizza parlor. She had enough. For a long time it was good between them—as long as the money held out. Now he was on his ass and she didn't want any part of him.

A trickle of blood ran from his nose onto his upper lip. He wiped it away with the back of his hand and wiped his hand on his jeans. The bleeding continued.

He stood, knocking the vodka jar on the chair, spilling its contents. Christ Almighty! Goddamn nose.

He went into the bathroom and blew his nose on toilet paper. Streaks of dried blood were on the mirror, shower curtain, door. Drops of blood were everywhere–the floor, the edge of the tub, the toilet seat. Blood was caked on the edge of the sink and along the base of the toilet.

He blew again, washed his face in cold water, rolled a few sheets of toilet paper into a narrow ball, and stuck it in his nostril. He heard her voice again, ***Only a fool falls on his back and bruises his nose***.

Babbi, his grandmother, sat inside his head and whispered her sayings to him all day long. He couldn't get away from her. It was like she had learned all her insane proverbs just to torment him. It was like she pounded them into his head from the day he was born so that they would now come to haunt him in his little streak of bad luck. Anybody could get down. Anybody. ***Who comes to greet the pauper? A cold wind and wild dogs.*** Go to hell, Babbi!

He grabbed a damp towel and went back to the TV. The empty jar was on the floor. Holding on to the edge of the chair, he bent over, picked up the jar, and aimed himself for the vodka on the kitchen table.

On the table were his food stamps and his welfare check. Enough to keep him going until next week. He filled the jar, spilling some vodka on the table. He bent over, licked it up, pushed the toilet paper further up his nose, and went back to the game.

The seat of the chair was wet from the spilled vodka. He threw the musty bath towel on the chair and carefully lowered himself into it.

Second inning. Nettles on third. 0 and 1 pitch to McReynolds. Deep into center field. Deep . . . deep . . . over the wall. Nettles scores, McReynolds trots home. Padres - 2; Cubbies - 0. Jerry snapped the channel button to 26. See how the market is doing.

Gold. Silver. AT&T. Pork bellies. GM. Zenith. Coca Cola. Corn. Cattle. Proctor & Gamble. Swiss francs. British pounds. Yens. Beans–soybeans, soybeans, soybeans.

He drank another long drink, wetting the red toilet paper sticking out of his nose. He shoved it further in, laid his head back, and closed his eyes. Soybeans. Goddamn soybeans.

That's right, Jerry, ***Lie down with the dogs, you get up with the fleas***.

Shut up, Babbi! Just shut up! Give me a break. Give me a break, Babbi.

How did it all happen? What happened? One minute he was on the top of the heap, the next minute, he's out for the count. Slurping vodka over a stinking pizza parlor. In a hole in the wall and no one even cares if he lives or dies. He'd be better off dead, if the truth were known.

I know, I know . . . ***The ugliest life is better than the nicest death.*** But his life was so ugly, so very ugly. How much longer could he go on?

What happened? For years, he never drank. Hated the taste of the stuff. A couple of beers in college when he was expected to drink with the crowd, but even then, he wouldn't finish them. He didn't like drinking. They thought he was a prude. Jerry would always fall back on the line, "Jews don't drink," and they would leave him alone, as if he belonged to a weird species that didn't know how great it was to tie one on. Besides, drinking made you lose control and he knew he had to be on his toes every minute, even with those guys.

After college he tried selling insurance but it was too slow. Trying to scare his friends into investing in life insurance when their only thoughts were to get a job and make money. One of his calls was to a brokerage house and the minute he walked through the doors, he knew that was the life he wanted.

They hired him and soon he was running their operations from the floor of the Board of Trade. On the side he traded commodities, futures commodities, for himself and was soon able to buy himself a seat.

The Midas touch, that's what Jerry Sachs had, the Midas touch. He could turn those damn beans into gold with one flick of the wrist. The first three months he was on his own, he rolled over $350,000, always taking positions, always going for the big win. Scalping was fine, if that was the only way you could do it, but Jerry Sachs had the balls to do it big, and he was big. They called him Jerry the Sack because he needed a sack to hold all his money.

He'd come home from work and hide crisp $50 and $100 bills around the house for Michelle to find. God, he loved her. He loved their life together–the cars and trips to Vegas and Vail, clothes and parties, one on top of the other. They never had time for kids, but talked about it–one day when they were ready to settle down.

He could never really see Michelle settling down to take care of kids. She didn't even like the nieces and nephews. Kids were too dirty and noisy, she'd say. His brother Mark only had one and

Michelle thought it was one too many. And then Babbi would visit them and say, for everyone to hear, "***Having an only child is like having only one eye***".

Michelle kept going, faster than he could. Maybe it was those pills the doctor gave her for weight. Jerry called her his Speedball Queen. Then one night she overdosed and he couldn't wake her up. When the doctor came over the next morning to examine her body, he handed Jerry 5 mg. of Valium, wrote a prescription for Seconal so he could sleep, and wished him luck.

Yes, Babbi, ***Trouble cuts up the heart***. After the funeral, Jerry climbed into the bean pit like a crazy man. He'd scream and shout and buy way beyond what he could cover. His voice was raw, his ears rang, his feet were numb, his hemorrhoids throbbed. He found himself getting careless and confused, not writing out orders promptly and forgetting whom he had bought from.

He started to party right after work. Some girl gave him grass and he was off and running. At first it made him dizzy, but soon a warm glow settled in his gut and his whole body tingled. Jerry the Prude who never touched drugs or booze started smoking pot and relaxing with beer every day. Pot and beer never hurt anyone, and now that he was single again, he might as well live it up.

He started looking different. Lines were starting to form on his forehead and circles darkened his eyes. Babbi put her big arms around him one night, "Dear, dear Jerry, I know, ***The gates of tears are never shut***". She thought he was distraught over Michelle's death, but he hadn't time for that. Life was for the living and he was living it to the hilt.

And every day as he put on his blue smock, straightened his yellow trader's badge, and headed for the pit, he knew this was the day to clean up. He had gotten out of trouble–the boys cover for each other, because you never know when you'll be the one down. But it was only for a time. Jerry the Sack would soon be off and running. He had his Valium to keep cool, his Seconal to sleep, and his grass and beer to relax with.

Then he met Lori. And Quaaludes. She had two prescriptions for one hundred Quaaludes a month. Jerry told his doctor that the Seconal weren't working and he asked the doctor to switch the prescription to Quaaludes since he missed Michelle so much and nighttime was pure hell and he couldn't sleep. He got a prescription for one hundred Quaaludes a month.

Ludes were his love drops. He and Lori would settle in with a jug of Chablis and Ludes. They drew him into a warm, euphoric, sensual world and he and Lori made love anytime, anywhere. Michelle had been funny about sex. If she only had Ludes instead of speed, they would have made it and she wouldn't have had to kill herself.

Then Lori the Lude began taking two and then four at a time, fighting sleep, going crazy all the time. She called it her Lude wars and when it was over, she was irritable and hyperactive. One night she convulsed and Jerry had to call the paramedics. She cut back then, increasing the wine and pot.

After that, Jerry's cousin brought him opiated Thai sticks from Arizona and soon they were all doing sticks and shroms, poisonous hallucinogenic mushrooms dipped in milk.

Jerry would lie in the darkened room, his body heavy as lead, but his spirit soared high above and took on the mind of God. He could go backward or forward in time with the speed of thought, unencumbered by the weight of his body. He was in another plane of life where mere mortals dared not enter. Jerry Sachs became God and he could see where only God could see.

From the ecstasy of the night before back into the bean pit. The clawing and shoving and pushing left him bruised. His judgment was off and his hearing was going. He was down by two hundred contracts, each worth $3,000. He'd make it up. Let the others puke out, not Jerry the Sack. It would be only a matter of time before he'd cover himself, get back on the track.

He always had rules for himself: Never overstay a good market, you'll overstay a bad one; follow the trends; when you go stale, get out for a while; don't trade on rumors; don't go below $200,000. He was breaking all of his rules.

Then the magic day came. Snow fell from heaven. Right into Jerry Sacks' nose. With the first snort of cocaine, Jerry knew that he had found what he had been looking for all his life–in the pit, with women, money, drugs. Coke was the most exquisite thing he had ever known.

With that first blast, Jerry experienced a high to end all highs. Instant heaven. Instant ecstasy. Instant bliss. He was off and running.

It took about thirty seconds to hit and from then on, it was total elation. His nose cleared and he drew his first free breath in thirty-five years. He couldn't stop talking. His arms and legs grew numb, but soon his body and mind were one. He knew everything and felt everything. He was big and powerful, alert, responsive.

Jerry Sachs, the All-American boy! Triumphant, successful, open to creativity and risk, adventurous, wild, on the track with the stars! Jerry Sachs, the Biggest of the Bigs at the Board, Perfect Lover, the Dreamer who makes all his dreams come true!

He could afford it. He'd never have to lie or steal. Jerry the Sack made Big Money and a few thou for some fun over the weekend was nothing.

With every snort he went up, but never as high as the first one. The highs would only last for fifteen or twenty minutes, then he would bring himself down with rum or brandy but carefully, slowly, careful not to crash, just ease yourself down and then you can go back up again. Up, up and then slowly down, up, up, then down. Being down wasn't pleasant, but it was worth the high.

Before coke, he would never leave the floor to go to the bathroom or to get something to eat. He might have missed something. But now, stepping out of the pit for a few minutes for a glorious snort was a good thing. He was running a big half-mil ahead–he had gotten his old stuff back.

In his back pocket he carried a pint of rum to bring him down, but he left the coke in his locker. His nose was running a lot and had even bled on occasion. He'd rub baby oil around inside his nostrils to coat the membranes. Jerry the Sack was in control. You just had to stick by your rules and everything would be okay.

Then it all happened so fast. The bottom dropped out of everything. He couldn't get up as high and the downs were terrible. Bugs were crawling on his skin and his nose was bleeding every day.

He was depressed and his judgment was off. He made some bad calls that he didn't own up to. The only rule at the Board was that you stick by your deal and don't welsh, you don't say that you bought when you sold, you don't say it was for an eighth when you meant a half.

It didn't take long for people to stop dealing with him. Jerry the Sack got sacked. He was alone in the pit, honor gone, and honor was the only thing that held the boys in the pit together.

So Jerry left the Board. He still had loads of money– condo investments, the boat, stocks, his cars, and the gold ring with the one-carat diamond that Michelle had given to him for their first anniversary, with the note, "To Jerry, my favorite devil."

And the last day that he walked through the doors out onto LaSalle Street, he could hear Babbi whispering in his ear, "***Uphill one climbs slowly; downhill one rolls fast***." But he wasn't down; he just needed a rest.

He and Lori holed up. It was going to be one big party. He was entitled to it, standing on his bloody stumps at the edge of the pit for all those years.

The depressions were getting worse. He wanted to kill himself. He switched from rum and brandy to vodka. He was drinking more. He stopped snorting his cocaine and started cookin' it up so he could smoke rocks of crack, eventually he graduated to speed-balling (mixing coke with heroin and shooting it into his veins). Bugs crawled all over his skin and his arms and legs were raw from scratching. His nose was falling off.

Jerry was getting violent and went for the knife. Lori called the police. Money was running out and they had to move. She got a job in a restaurant and they got a smaller apartment. His money was gone and they couldn't afford coke or the rest. Fights were common. She said she couldn't take it any longer.

He moved out and got the room over the pizza joint. He had to go on welfare and get food stamps. There were no more drugs, only the vodka. He got the booze with food stamps and when he was hungry, he would go down and rummage through the black bags that Papa Joe threw out at night. Hard pizza and cold spaghetti and lasagna.

Jerry rested the cheese jar on the floor. Snakes, sharks, and moray eels swam across the television screen. He made his way into the bathroom. He had little control of his bladder left and his pants smelled of urine.

After he went to the toilet, he looked in the mirror. Bloody toilet tissue hung from his right nostril. His beautiful black curly hair was gray and matted. His cheeks were sunken and yellow and covered with two weeks of beard.

The face tells the secret, Babbi would say now if she could see him. Snakes, sharks, and moray eels dipped and dived across the shower curtain and onto the yellow tiles.

And she'd tell him, ***God does not bargain and God does not change***. But Jerry played God – all his life he thought he was God. But then she'd whisper in his ears, ***Jerry, poor Jerry, don't you remember, for every disease, God sends the remedy.***

CHEMICAL DEPENDENCY

In order to understand the widespread ramifications of the nature of Jellinek's disease today, there must be an understanding of the total picture of drug dependency. Drug dependency is a state in which the use of a drug is necessary for physical well-being. ***Physical dependency*** upon mind-altering chemicals is what defines it. While psychological dependency usually accompanies physical dependency, this psychological aspect alone does not constitute true drug dependency.

The drugs of which we are concerned include alcohol as a primary drug, as well as sleeping pills, tranquilizers, diet pills, and painkillers, together with cocaine, marijuana, and other so-called recreational drugs.

Data released by DAWN, the Drug Abuse Warning Network, produced by the Substance Abuse and Mental Health Service Administration, reported that there were 600,000 drug-related ED (emergency department) episodes for 2000, up 450% in 15 years. There were over 1,000,000 drug-mentions, meaning that the patient had more than one drug in his/her system. In descending order, alcohol-in-combination with other drugs accounted for 20% of these episodes, cocaine - 18%, heroin - 10%, marijuana - 10%. 13.6 million Americans use illegal drugs on a regular level.

When the term drug abuse is used, the reference is to a broad classification of chemicals that basically affect and change the chemistry of the brain. Those most frequently abused are ***downers, uppers*** and ***psychedelics***.

DOWNERS

The downers, or depressants, include such drugs as alcohol, and the sedatives and tranquilizers such as Valium, Darvon, Seconal. The opiates, heroin and morphine, are also downers. These drugs slow the transmission of information between nerve cells and act to inhibit behavior, speech, heart rate, breathing and coordination.

When any of these are used in combination with another, the risk of death from oversedation increases greatly, sometimes with effects being as much as fifty times higher than could be achieved with one drug alone.

METABOLISM OF DOWNERS

When neurotransmission is slowed down, the heart rate slows and breathing is depressed. The overall effect is one of calm and peace. Ironically, the person may also feel free, adventuresome, uninhibited, and may do things that he would not normally do.

This is because the transmitters that control behavior and register what is socially and morally acceptable are also depressed; the person ***feels*** stimulated (although downers are not true stimulants). Whereas one would not normally drive down a street where children are playing at sixty miles per hour or go home from a bar with a strange man or woman, he or she might do so when the social controls and judgment faculties are so depressed or inhibited by drugs that these situations appear normal.

Taken further, with the ingestion of more and more alcohol, and perhaps combined with other sedatives, the body may become so relaxed that coma and death ensue. Many inadvertent suicides result from combining sedatives in such a way that the entire nervous system is so depressed that life is virtually snuffed out.

The funny behavior we see when one has had one too many–saying silly things, unsteady gait, slurred speech–is the result of depressed inhibitions and impaired motor skills. Obviously a person in this condition is a danger if he gets behind a wheel or smokes in bed. The most insidious thing about being so intoxicated is that the person can feel that he is acting normally or even better than usual. He will insist that he is in fine shape and may argue about handing over his car keys.

REBOUND EFFECT

When the brain has been depressed chemically, it fights back, struggling for life. It has been chemically slowed down or put to sleep and it comes back with greater activity than before, shooting off neurotransmitters at a great rate. This is called the "rebound effect."

Hyperactivity and anxiety are experienced as the brain rebounds, or bounces back. This frequently means that one has to drink again, or take another Valium, perhaps in the morning or during the night (the hair of the dog that bit me), to quiet the shaking nerves and to reduce the anxiety experienced from increased activity in the brain. In the progression of Jellinek's disease, one is on a relentless merry-go-round: Drink/rebound/drink some more/rebound again/drink more.

ALCOHOL

When any drug is taken into the body, the whole body is affected. Alcohol is metabolized in the liver at the rate of one-half ounce every hour. This is the same for all alcohol: Beer, wine, liquor.

The liver breaks down toxins (poisons) in the system and keeps them from entering the bloodstream. When too much alcohol (a toxin) is introduced, the liver cannot keep up and the poison (acetaldehyde) goes directly into the bloodstream, causing intoxication.

Once the toxin reaches the brain, it has a direct effect on the enzymes called neurotransmitters. These neurotransmitters carry messages between the brain cells, which tell the body how to behave. Normally these messages are transmitted smoothly, but the introduction of these toxins changes the pattern: Downers such as alcohol and sedatives, cause the messages to slow down, with the potential of death if these messages come to a halt; uppers, or stimulants, cause the messages to speed up, with another death potential threatening.

BLOOD ALCOHOL LEVEL (BAL)

An indication of intoxication (toxins in the body) is the Blood Alcohol Level (BAL). One frequently reads that someone was arrested for drunk driving with a BAL of .14 or .22. This is the ratio of alcohol to a certain quantity of blood.

If the BAL registers .02, it is an indication that a person had one drink and is relaxed; .05 means two and a half drinks and the person is suffering from impaired judgment; .08 means five drinks, the person has little or no judgment, and is legally drunk; .20 means ten drinks, erratic emotions, lack of coordination, and the individual has been legally drunk for six hours; .40 means that the person is in a stupor and has no judgment or coordination; .65 means the person may be in a coma and is near death.

Alcohol ranked Number One among drugs involved in emergency room visits. During 1984, there were 21,701 of such alcohol-related incidences. In the year 2000, the number was 204,524 or nearly 10 times as many. Between 20% - 35% of suicide victims were alcoholics. In many cases, no one knows if these suicides were deliberate or accidental.

SEDATIVES/HYPNOTICS

Sedatives are basically those drugs that have a calming, mellowing effect. They reduce anxiety, induce sleep. Some of the more familiar ones are the barbiturates such as Seconal and Nembutal; the non-barbiturate hypnotics, such as Doriden and Quaalude; and the minor tranquilizers such as Miltown, Librium, Valium, Xanax, and sleeping pills, such as Dalmane Ativan.

Liza Minelli, reflecting upon her own chemical addiction, commented, "These aren't harsh drugs . . . I developed a whole new soothing vocabulary, Valium, Librium, Dalmane, all nice sounding names. The people who manufacture drugs use names like that to make it easier for you to take them."

The nonbarbiturate sedatives have been called the ***benzodiazepines***. These are the downers, the tranquilizers, the sleeping pills. Valium is the most frequently prescribed drug in the United States: 65 million prescriptions are written yearly, 75% by nonpsychiatric physicians.

Mixed with alcohol, these benzodiazepines are lethal. Their effect upon the central nervous system is addictive and may be synergistic: That is, the presence of two or more drugs will result in a total effect much greater than the simple sum of the drugs. It means that drugs mixed arbitrarily can provide a multiplier effect: One plus one plus one does not equal three but perhaps six or ten or fifty.

Persons taking Valium or Xanax while drinking run a greater risk of depressing their central nervous system to such a degree that death ensues. Many suicides have inadvertently happened this way. The central nervous system does not know the difference between the depressing effects of booze and the depressing effects of other downers. Together they act to depress not only anxiety and sleeplessness, but also the basic functions that are critical to life.

Xanax, also sold under its generic name of Alpraxolam, is perhaps the most addictive of the benzodiazepines. Ironically, when it was first developed in 1973, it was thought to be the miracle tranquillizer because it was non-addictive.

A young psychiatrist had the miracle drug on his license plate and would shoot around town in his little red Ferrari with his Xanax plates gleaming in the sun. When he began treating his anxiety patients for Xanax addiction, he had the plates changed.

According to the National Institute for Mental Health, 19 million Americans suffer from anxiety disorders, which includes generalized anxiety disorders, panic disorders and social phobia. There were 30 million prescriptions written for Xanax in 2001, up from 24 million in 1997, or an increase of 1 million each year.

In January, 2002, Noelle Bush, the 24 year-old daughter of Gov. Jeb Bush, was arrested in Tallahassee, Florida for impersonating a doctor and calling Walgreens for her own order for Xanax. The Governor, originally opposed to a Florida referendum mandating treatment rather than jail for first and second time offenders, has had a sudden change of heart and now supports the measure.

GBH OR GAMMA-HYDROXYBUTYRATE

Although GBH was placed on the Federal government's list of controlled substances in 2000, this substance remains popular with health enthusiasts, depressed persons and those who suffer from insomnia. Commonly used as a "club drug" and at rave parties, it figures in date rapes and is more deadly than Ecstasy.

GBH severely depresses the nervous system and is highly addictive. It is a white powder which dissolves readily in liquid and can be poured into drinks or drunk straight from a bottle of water. It kicks in within 15 minutes and can last up to six hours.

As with other sedatives, GBH slows the heart and lungs, creates a feeling of relaxation, and interferes with motor control. Overdoses can result in loss of consciousness, seizure, coma and death. The Drug Enforcement Agency reports 5,700 overdoses and 65 deaths due to GBH as of January, 2000.

Despite the fact that it has been declared an illegal drug, it is still sold on the Internet as a cleaning solvent and in health stores, gyms and the Internet as a nutritional supplement. Despite the fact that the chemical compounds BD and GBL frequently appear on the labels of such products, these rapidly convert to GHB when ingested.

In an ironic twist, a 31-year-old body-builder, a Roman Catholic priest from Sheffield, Illinois, was arrested in January, 2002, for making and selling GBH. Rev. Jeff Windy (whom the pastor called "a breath of fresh air") purchased industrial-strength GBL from an Iowa chemical supply company. With two other men, Fr. Windy manufactured GBH in multi-gallon quantities. He sold single gallons of GBH for $440 on the street.

While GBH is used in date rapes to render victims helpless, those who become addicted are not street junkies but athletes and others concerned about nutrition, weight loss, sleep and body-building. Exactly how this chemical effects the brain is not well known, but doctors speculate that it alters levels of dopamine and serotonin, then hits the reward center and "flips the *Switch*" to begin the mad spin into addiction.

ROHYPNOL

Rohypnol is an insidious sedative, ten times stronger than Valium. This premier "date rape" drug produces a drunken state wherein people feel sluggish and experience black-outs after its ingestion. Produced in pill-form, it is dropped into drinks and is swallowed without the person's knowledge or consent. The drinker is disabled, helpless and is unable to resist being raped. It now carries a blue dye to discolor the drink so that the drinker may be alerted to the presence of this drug.

OPIATES: MORPHINE AND OTHER NARCOTICS

One of the oldest drugs known to mankind, opium, springs from the unripe seed of the poppy. Homer, writing in 700 B.C., said that Helen of Troy "threw into the wine they were drinking a drug which takes away grief and passion and brings forgetfulness of all ills." (Odyssey IV, 220)

In the nineteenth century a tincture of opium was known as GOM, God's Own Medicine. The British fought two wars with China during this same time to insure that the opium trade would remain open, as the British had obtained control of opium production in India and had vigorously promoted the use of opium and alcohol in both India and China.

From opium comes ***morphine and codeine***, both highly effective in the relief of pain. Heroin is obtained from a chemical derivative of morphine. Today, synthetic opiates are produced that include methadone, Demerol, Percodan, Dilaudid, and Darvon.

The common characteristic of all narcotics is that they induce drowsiness and sleep (sedative) and that they kill pain (analgesic). Narcotics are highly addictive, and when accompanied with alcohol, prove to be deadly. While the opiates share the sleep-inducing property of the sedative drugs, they also kill pain; sedatives do not kill pain.

It is the extremely pleasant euphoric state that habituates one to the opiates. It is common knowledge that heroin is used to remove mental pain; we have etched on our collective conscience the image of a poor or disenfranchised person, lying in a tenement hallway, nodding in a twilight smile, immune to the squalor around him. In the Eugene O'Neill play, ***Long Day's Journey into Night***, Mary Tyrone, a morphine addict, defends the use of her drug to her son: "It kills the pain. You go back until at last you are beyond its reach. Only the past when you were happy is real."

Although the downers (alcohol, tranquilizers) and the painkillers (opiates) both create a euphoria, they are different classes of drugs. Theoretically, physical cross-tolerance, does not develop ***between*** them. Cross-tolerance definitely, however, does develop ***among*** the different opiates: If one is dependent upon morphine, one is likewise dependent upon heroin, Demerol, etc. Moreover, the National Institute on Drug Abuse categorizes the opiates heroin and morphine under the general category of "Narcotic Analgesics," which includes painkillers such as Darvon, Percodan, Codeine, Demerol, and Dilaudid, Vicodin, Oxy-Contin.

Oxy-Contin is a powerful prescription drug designed to relieve debilitating pain. In California, a physician was ordered to pay $1.5 million to a cancer patient for failure to prescribe Oxy-Contin. It is advertised as safer than other narcotics because of its pain-release mechanism.

However, when crushed, it is quickly absorbed into the body through injection or snorting.

Purdue Pharma, the makers of Oxy-Contin, have aggressively marketed it to doctors, offering promotional cards for free tablets for patients from the pharmacy. In 2000, Purdue Pharma had over $1 billion in sales for Oxy-Contin. In 1999 there were 6,400 prescriptions written for Oxy-Contin; in 2000, there were 10,800. This is an increase of 68%.

According to Dr. David Gauvin, pharmacologist at the Drug Enforcement Agency, there were over 1,000 deaths where oxycodone, the active narcotic in Oxy-Contin, was found upon autopsy. One tablet sells for $80 on the street.

The estimated non-medical uses of Oxy-Contin nearly doubled from 221,000 in 1999 to 400,000 in 2000. More recent data is not yet available, but the present numbers could well be approaching 1,000,000.

However, because the effect of bringing one down, of the slowing down of the neurotransmitters, is similar in both cases, many people have ***experienced*** an actual tolerance/dependency effect between downers and opiates. Many addicted people get the same effect from Valium and Librium as they do from Codeine and Dilaudid. They make no distinction. And those looking for a way to justify the use of opiates will note that they are in a distinct class and may feel free to use them. Theoretically, this may be true; actually, it does not hold up.

The effects of combining an opiate with a sedative (alcohol) are extremely dangerous. Both slow down and depress breathing and the entire respiratory process. Combining the two drugs may easily depress respiration, leading to a coma and ultimately to death.

Methadone maintenance programs (which attempt to withdraw chronic heroin users by substituting methadone, a less powerful opiate but one closely related to heroin), have revealed that patients who drink heavily while on methadone have ten times the death rate as those who abstain from alcohol while being withdrawn. In addition, while on programs, thousands have become methadone addicts. A drug is still a drug.

Heroin has been the latest of the old drugs to achieve "respectability". From the bleak 1955 Frank Sinatra movie, "The Man with the Golden Arm" wherein the poker man, the jazz man shoots up to documentaries of poor addicts writhing in dark corners, screaming with the pains of withdrawal, heroin has been the drug of the lower classes.

Formerly heroin had to be distastefully shot into the veins, muscle or skin ("popping") with needles. With warnings of the transmission of AIDS, Hepatitis and other infections through dirty needles, many stayed away from it.

With the influx of higher quality drugs from South America, heroin, called "China White", can be purchased cheaper and used cleaner and quicker than before. It can be injected, sniffed, snorted or smoked. It is the most abused and most rapid acting of all the opiates. Addicts say it will "steal your soul".

In Hazelden Voice, (Winter, 98), Phil Kavanaugh, a supervisor of men's care, reports that addicts describe heroin use as an unending sexual high. "Alcoholics want emotional ups and downs. Pot smokers and users of hallucinogens want to reinvent the world in their own mind. Heroin addicts want to get rid of the pain. Then life bangs them up until they recover."

It is estimated that there may be 1,000,000 heroin users today. The fashion industry glamorizes "heroin chic", the gaunt, anorexic, strung out, death-like visage of young people. Rock stars who have succumbed to the allure of the white heaven are Janis Joplin, Jimi Hendrix, Jim Morrison, Sid Vicious, Kurt Cobain, Jerry Garcia and Jonathan Melvoin.

The good news is that treatment for heroin addiction is rising, 31% from 1992 to 1997. Of all illicit drugs, heroin addiction accounts for the highest numbers (16%) seeking treatment. Twice as many were males than females and 77% were age 30 or older.

Both alcohol and heroin damage the liver. The combination may lead to sudden and violent liver disease. More than 20% of New York City heroin addicts have shown signs of chronic alcoholism upon autopsy.

Unlike alcohol and other drugs, these opiate pain killers, heroin and morphine, lose toxicity with increased use. However, they can still be overdosed. In fact, most of the overdose cases are among new users with undeveloped tolerance. From January to June 1985, emergency cases of heroin/morphine episodes numbered 6,136. In the year 2000, there were 97,000 cases, or a 1600% increase.

This is in no way to say that the narcotics user is safe. He usually dies from malnutrition, accident, or extreme tissue damage. Up to 50% of narcotic addicts consume large amounts of alcohol, with 25% having a history of alcohol dependency. It must be stressed that narcotics dependency combined with alcohol dependency is lethal; narcotic-related death and insanity are no less common than alcohol-related damage and death.

UPPERS

Uppers are referred to as stimulants and include the amphetamines Benzedrine, Dexadrine, Elavil, and cocaine as well as many other drugs used mainly for diet and weight reduction. Stimulants increase the levels of neurotransmitters at synapses. The heart rate dramatically increases and the body feels full of energy. When uppers are abused the most frequent cause of death is heart failure. Speed Kills, a popular saying in the 60's, means exactly that.

METABOLISM OF UPPERS

When stimulants reach the brain, they cause the neurons to fire off messages too quickly. The person will have increased energy, a lack of appetite, and an exaggerated sense of well-being. He will talk nonstop and sound disconnected as his thoughts run away with him.

When these stimulants (cocaine, amphetamines, etc.) wear off, the person is left with a letdown feeling, with anxiety, and with a heart that beats uncomfortably fast. It takes time for the neurotransmitters to function normally again; in the case of any prolonged chemical abuse, the receptors that receive the messages become damaged.

This is why, even after the body has been cleansed of the offending substances, the person may still have motor-skills impairment and memory loss. Although these conditions may correct themselves with time and abstinence, the condition can be so distressing that the person with Jellinek's disease will return to the drug of choice, that drug or drink that he prefers, in order to feel what he perceives as normal. In other words, a person usually returns to the drug he is most comfortable with, regardless of the side-effects.

AMPHETAMINES

Amphetamines are referred to as speed, those stimulants that rev up the human motor and pour energy into the system.

Many alcoholics and drug addicts first begin using amphetamines as diet pills. Weight problems plague the American people. 90% of Americans think they are overweight; 35% want to lose at least fifteen pounds; 33% of American women, ages nineteen to thirty-nine, diet at least once a month; thirty million American women (1 in 3) wear dress size 16 or above. And 95% of weight loss during dieting is soon put back on. Diet pills are as American as Halloween candy.

Others take stimulants to stay awake while driving or taking exams or competing in sports.

One woman, presently a recovering alcoholic, describing her four years in college on Dexadrine, stated, "I don't remember anything about it. I just ran through . . . It was wonderful."

Another woman, presently in A.A. described her use of Black Beauties (amphetamines): "They were great, my real friends. I could drink more. I could screw around and still do what I had to do. I never slept and never ate. My parents thought I was anorexic." Still another recovering alcoholic described her two-year experience with amphetamines as "Zoom! Zoom! Zoom!"

Aside from the synergistic or multiplier effect of mixing amphetamines and alcohol, amphetamines frequently have more subtle effects on persons effected by Jellinek's disease. Because there is no cross-addiction (they are in two distinct classes of drugs), a person may play one off against the other and still be involved in rearranging one's mood and behavior.

One woman, now recovering, had first become addicted to dextro-amphetamines given her by her boyfriend, a medical student. For over 25 years, she would alternate periods of intense speeding with periods of drinking. When her husband, a physician, cut off her pills, she would step up her drinking until it got so bad that he would allow her to have her pills again. She presently feels that her drinking would have escalated faster and that she would have gotten into treatment sooner if she had not had the pills to pull her in another, equally disastrous direction.

AMPHETAMINES FOR CHILDREN

A specific amphetamine-like substance, methylphenidate, commonly called Ritalin, also deserves attention. Medically, it is intended to work as a stimulant in adults and as a reducer of restlessness, hyperactivity and distractibility in children. An estimated 2.6 million Americans are on Ritalin, most of whom are five through 12 years of age.

When drugs have one effect on adults and the opposite effect on children, this is known as the Paradoxical Effect.

Ritalin is generally administered to children diagnosed with minimal brain damage (M.B.D.) or with attention-deficit hyperactivity disorder (A.D.H.D.) The latter is interpreted to mean a condition that is manifested by those children who daydream or whose attention wanders off in the classroom. In a particular second grade class, 9 out of 22 children were on Ritalin. These children would march to the office every noon to get their smart pill.

To date, there has been no research proving that Ritalin is a precursor of drug abuse in children. However, clinicians are finding ***high correlations*** between teenage alcoholism/drug addiction (particularly cocaine abuse) and the use of Ritalin as a child.

Ritalin is chemically related to the amphetamines, speed. Regardless of its obverse reaction (calming) in children, the wisdom of administering it to children has been brought into question.

In ***The Essential Guide to Prescription Drugs***, the location of Ritalin's action is in areas within the outer layer (cortex) of the brain that are responsible for higher mental functions and behavioral reactions.

In describing how Ritalin works, the book states, "Not established. Present thinking is that this drug may increase the release of the nerve impulse transmitter, norepinephrine. The resulting stimulation of brain tissue improves alertness and concentration, and increases learning ability and attention span. (The primary action that calms the overactive child is not known.)"

There are a myriad of reasons why a child may be inattentive and restless in school: Preoccupation with family problems, sight or hearing difficulties, food or environmental allergies, schoolwork that is either too difficult or too easy.

It is relatively easy to administer a pill to a child who is having problems (and subsequently, causing problems) in the classroom. While Ritalin may be quite effective with some children, its use as an antidote for a child's daydreaming and restlessness is profoundly questioned.

Ritalin is an amphetamine-like chemical that effects neurotransmission of the cortex of the brain. Knowledge and understanding of the chemistry of the brain is still in a relatively primitive stage; more is left to be discovered than we already know. Therefore, the first thing we must be wary of is that what we don't know may truly hurt us at a later date. (Thalidomide was quite effective in preventing miscarriage . . .)

Second, other valid physical or social problems may interfere with a child's behavior in the classroom. These will not go away with the use of Ritalin. The incentive to search out these problems is removed if the child begins improved classroom functioning with Ritalin. It actually masks real problems that do not get solved.

Third, a child learns that a pill can solve his problems. If pills can help you get better grades, they can also help you lose weight, calm down or pep up (whichever way you want to go), mellow out, get friendly, get sexy. Not paying attention in school is of a very different order than having strep throat. At an early age, a child is introduced to the nonphysical illness pill by the medical profession. In other words, he learns it is all right to solve your problems with a little pill.

Last, the 15 million children who have an alcoholic parent are five times as likely to develop Jellinek's disease and other drug problems as those children who do not have such a parent. It is these very children who most likely are demonstrating the abovementioned problems in the classroom. To administer an amphetamine-like substance, about which little is known, to a high-risk population is unconscionable. (It must also be noted that it does not matter to the child's genetic predisposition if his parent is actively drinking or recovering. He has inherited the same genes.)

METHAMPHETAMINE

Closely related to amphetamine chemically, methamphetamine is a white powder that is snorted, smoked, shot into the veins or pressed into a pill. Its street names are meth, crank, crystal, crystal meth and speed. Ecstacy (MDMA) is chemically similar to meth with hallucinogenic properties that is taken in pill form. This is discussed below. Unlike many of the uppers that are sold by pharmaceutical companies, meth is made in illegal labs, frequently in homes where there are children. Initially, one using methamphetamine experiences high energy, is restless and talkative, with dilated pupils.

Prolonged meth use produces loss of appetite, increased mental and physical energy, insomnia, paranoia which can resemble paranoid schizophrenia, compulsive behaviors, high blood pressure and increased heart rate. Meth binges produce paranoid delusions and psychosis. Long term users show some of the same damage as stroke victims and Alzheimer's disease suffers.

Methamphetamine users are those who want to be "up", who need not sleep or be fatigued for work, sports, study. Meth suppresses the appetite so weight can be shed and pumps up the central nervous system to enhance athletic performance. Overdose from meth is to be expected with such a powerful chemical that speeds up all the body's neurological systems, effecting the brain, heart and lungs. In 1992, there were 6,500 hospital emergencies for meth; in 1997, there were 17,000.

Methamphetamine is feared to be more harmful to babies than cocaine. At the Drug Effected Babies Clinic at Blank Children's Hospital in Des Moines, Dr. Rizwan Shah found that 80% of babies born to addicted mothers were now addicted to methamphetamine. When her study began in 1993, 80% of babies were addicted to cocaine. (Chicago Tribune, June 10, 2001)

MDMA - Ecstasy

A recent player in the drug abuse world is Ecstasy. Ecstasy is a derivative of amphetamine. Its long name is 3,4-methylenedioxymethylamphetarnine (MDMA). On the street it has various nicknames such as X, XTC, Adam, M&M and others. Unlike the "natural" drugs like opium and alcohol, Ecstasy and related "designer drugs" are artificially synthesized in laboratories that are illegal and underground. These compounds are derived by altering the chemical structure of amphetamine and during their synthesis are sometimes combined with other compounds like caffeine, ephedrine, methamphetamine and ketamine. Ecstasy is typically swallowed in pill or liquid form and its molecules are released into the blood stream as the pill or liquid is broken down in the stomach. This drug reaches the brain approximately 15 minutes after ingestion on an empty stomach.

Ecstasy has both short term and long term effects on the brain. The neural pathway that seems most effected by Ecstasy is the serotonin pathway. The serotonin producing neurons are located in a region of the brain stem known as the Raphe nucleus. These neurons send long connections to higher brain centers such as the neocortex and the limbic system (amygdala and hippocampus) as well as down to the spinal cord. Serotonin transmission in the neocortex at the front of the brain is involved in regulating memory, cognition and perception. Serotonin transmission in the limbic system is involved in regulating memory and mood and alleviating depression

The short term effects of Ecstasy are via its ability to block the reuptake of serotonin from the synapses. It does so by targeting and blocking the proteins that transport serotonin. When Ecstasy binds to serotonin transporters, serotonin can not bind. Thus, more serotonin is left in the synapse and can continue to signal/stimulate the target neurons.

When more serotonin is in the synapse, the signalling by serotonin is increased because more neurotransmitter molecules are available to bind to serotonin receptors. In some ways Ecstasy works like the newer selective. Serotonin reuptake inhibitors (SSRI's) like Prozac, Paxil, Zoloft and others that have been developed to treat depression.

When Ecstasy is used, the short term increase in serotonin levels that occurs in different brain regions results in greatly elevated mood, feelings of empathy, and other pleasurable sensations. Emerging evidence shows that Ecstasy can also inhibit dopamine transporters and cause an increase in dopamine levels in the pleasure/reward center of the brain. These changes in the pleasure centers are exacerbated by the positive emotional mood effects in the serotonin circuits.

However, there can be adverse effects as well. Among these are sweating, increased heart rate, muscle spasms such as jaw clenching and hyperthermia. These effects are mediated by the descending portion of the serotonin pathways from the Raphe nucleus that projects down to the spinal cord. When individuals take multiple doses of Ecstasy in one night ("stacking"), the adverse effects can be increased to the point of becoming life threatening. The most serious problems are from hyperthermia and irregular heart beat.

One of the big problems with Ecstasy is that it continues to have effects on the brain for some time after the drug is eliminated from the body. These effects appear to be due to changes that take place at serotonin synapses. The after-effects include depression, anxiety, restlessness, irritability and sleep problems.

More serious problems occur with repeated or long term use. In these situations the serotonin neurons themselves become damaged and the density of serotonin transporters as well as serotonin levels are reduced. This has been shown to occur in chronic Ecstasy users subjected to brain imagining by PET scans (positron emitting tomography). The evidence from animal and human studies is accumulating to suggest that serotonin neurons become damaged and their terminals may die after prolonged Ecstasy use. This damage can be long term and perhaps permanent. Because of this loss of serotonin terminals, Ecstasy abusers can suffer from memory impairment, thinking ability, clinical depression and more. These drugs are far from harmless. The National Institute on Drug Abuse (March 27, 2000) News Release warned that Ecstacy irreparably harms neurotransmitters, resulting in permanent brain damage that manifests in anxiety, depression and other psychiatric disorders. In 1993 there were 68 hospital emergencies from Ecstacy; in 1997 there were 637.

COCAINE/CRACK

Cocaine, gold dust, or the champagne of drugs has been the recreational drug of choice since the eighties. Government figures estimate that there are five thousand new coke users daily, that as many as 8 million use cocaine regularly (at least once a month), and that as many as 2.4 million Americans may be addicted to cocaine. In 1984, 604 people died from cocaine; in 1992, cocaine was responsible for 22% of all suicides in New York City.

Just as one can't step into the bright sunlight without casting a shadow, one is unlikely to use only cocaine without another companion drug, such as heroin, amphetamines, Valium, and most frequently, ***alcohol***. The reason for the use of the central nervous system depressants lies in the nature of how cocaine effects that system.

In order to avoid the crash, the coke user learns to bring himself down with a chemical depressant so he can shoot (or snort or smoke) back up again. A major depressant used is alcohol. Others are Valium, heroin (speedballing), or even cough medicines such as Nyquil or Formula 44 which are high in alcohol.

In a 1991 study at Johns Hopkins University School of Medicine, researchers have cloned the protein that pumps dopamine, the neurotransmitter linked to pleasure and movement. Cocaine binds to this protein pump and clogs it, flooding the narrow space between the sending and receiving cells. This flooding causes the euphoric rush or high associated with cocaine.

A recovering alcoholic described his two-year romance with cocaine and alcohol: "The first time I snorted, I went up–a high that I never knew existed. I was off and running. It took 30 seconds to hit–then it was total elation. My nose cleared, my hands and feet got numb. Soon I had no body, no mind. They were one and I was one with the universe. I was up as high as I could go.

"Let's say that first high took me to the maximum, up to 100. Then when I came down, I went to 0, where I had begun. But then, the next time, I went up to 90, but I came down to -10. The next time, it was only up to 80, but down to -20. I kept looking for that Magic Place that I went to the first time, but I never got there again. But I kept going down deeper and deeper.

"I moved from a few drinks a day to a quart, then to a half gallon of vodka in just a few years. You can drink as much as you want with coke. Coke lets you drink ad infinitum. I was about to commit suicide, but I ran out of money and had to quit coke. But I still had my booze.

"I was a scout master, president of the J.C.s, head of the school board, Man of the Year in our community. I won the District Service Award, and was Father of the Year. They asked me to run for mayor 8 times. I ended up selling coke to kids–my own and their friends."

Treatment centers are filled with people hooked on the drug. In addition, the potential for kicking off an addiction to alcohol is high, because alcohol is frequently used to avoid the coke crash.

A 30-year-old man in treatment for cocaine addiction stated, "If anyone ever comes to your home and offers you coke, punch him in the face. If you are at his house, run out the door. I lost $30,000, my business, my home, my wife and kids in 6 months, all because of cocaine. It is so good no one should ever try it."

The classical addiction model requires both a ***tolerance*** effect and ***physical withdrawal*** symptoms. Tolerance means that one needs more and more of a drug to get the same effect. With regard to cocaine, the tolerance effect may actually work in reverse.

Dr. Neal A. Lewin, instructor in clinical medicine at New York University School of Medicine, states that people are taking cocaine "in a compulsive manner in potentially dangerous doses. The end result is very much like what you see with people who are addicted to heroin or amphetamines - a total disruption of their social and professional lives. The chronic cocaine abuser ends up just as devastated."

The marriage of cocaine and alcohol is a ticking time bomb. Cocaine by itself augments the senses. Unlike the alcoholic who slurs his words, shakes, has blackouts, and gets sloppy, the one on coke looks and acts like a dynamo. The coke user visits the Magic Place where body and soul are one.

Jules Trop, a recovering cocaine-addict describes his Magic Place: "In the beginning, I thought I was communicating with God. In the end, I thought I was God."

Because cocaine creates a state of hyper-alertness, one can drink ad infinitum; the usual signs of increased intoxication are not felt; the person who is lowering himself slowly with alcohol is protected from its immediate consequences. However, because cocaine is short-lived, the stimulating effects of cocaine vanish and one is left with a high blood alcohol level.

This is particularly dangerous when one gets behind the wheel. Within fifteen minutes, the cocaine withdraws and another drunk driver is loosed upon the highway.

In a 1991 report, the Center for the Future of Children estimates that each year 4.5% or 160,000 babies are exposed to cocaine before birth. More than 600,000 babies are exposed to some type of illicit drug before birth.

In a 1993 interview, Dr. Ira Chasnoff, an associate professor of pediatrics at Northwestern University Medical School and Director of the National Association for Perinatal Addiction Research and Education, stated that 75% of these babies showed behavior problems and 25% experienced growth deficiencies, brain hemorrhages and respiratory difficulties.

There is little money for prenatal care and drug-treatment for addicted mothers. Dr. Chasnoff estimates that for every dollar spent on prenatal and drug-treatment, we save $10 to $15 in long-term care for drug exposed children.

Cocaine, the fun powder of the eighties, the snow that symbolizes verve, success, power, the drug of the stars and of those who approach stardom, frequently preambles a life of dependency on drugs, on alcohol and a life destroyed for their children.

Historically, cocaine abuse has involved snorting or injecting the powder form of the drug (which is the hydrochloride salt). However, cocaine can also be chemically processed into "free base" and can be smoked. The smokable form is "crack cocaine" and it is exponentially more addictive than the hydrochloride salt form of cocaine. The reason for this appears to be that smoking crack cocaine enables the drug to reach the brain much faster than snorting the drug.

The term "crack" refers to the cracking sound heard when smoked.

The current thinking is that the faster a drug with addictive properties gets to the brain, the higher the probability that it will be abused. After snorting cocaine, the drug travels in blood vessels from the nose to the heart, then to the lungs, then back to the heart and finally to the brain. After smoking cocaine the drug goes directly from the lungs to the heart and to the brain. Thus, the shorter the time between taking the drug and experiencing its brain altering effects in the pleasure/reward centers, the greater the likelihood of its abuse.

Forty hours after forward Len Bias, University of Maryland All-American, signed with the Boston Celtics, he was dead of cardiorespiratory arrest. A bag of crack was found in his car.

The chief medical examiner for the State of Maryland said that in a case like Bias's, cocaine would interrupt brain signals to the heart, causing it to beat irregularly and inducing arrest. Upon autopsy, it was discovered that his heart had not been damaged by strenuous physical activity, as some had anticipated, but that there were signs of previous cocaine use.

The uses of crack and the exchange of sex for drugs have led to an epidemic of sexually transmitted disease's (STD'S). Nearly half of those with various sexually transmitted disease's, including HIV/AIDS report having used sex for drugs.

Perhaps the most tragic effect of the crack epidemic that chokes our cities is the legacy of crack babies, little twisted, jerking souls that will never really have a chance. Crack kills.

PSYCHEDELICS

Psychedelics–LSD, marijuana, mescaline - do not appear to be addictive in themselves, but the attendant, frequent use of alcohol and other drugs is certainly cause for alarm. We must also take into account the deaths, such as suicide and automobile accidents, related to the use of psychedelics. Art Linkletter's daughter made headlines when, under the influence of LSD, she jumped to her death from a 12-story window.

Psychedelics have also been reported to be responsible for psychotic episodes in unstable individuals who, without mind-bending drugs, might have been able to suppress them. Long-term therapy may be necessary to treat the underlying disease which might never have shown itself otherwise.

MARIJUANA

Perhaps the most common entry level or gateway drug, in addition to alcohol, is marijuana. The substance marijuana (grass, pot, weed, joint, dope, etc.) is a mixture of the crushed leaves, flowers, and small branches of the hemp plant Cannabis Sativa. It grows throughout the world and is first recorded as having been used in 2700 B.C.

The primary psychoactive agent of marijuana is tetrahydrocannabinol (THC). At relatively low doses, THC acts on the brain like a mild sedative (such as alcohol or Valium); at higher doses, it resembles the hallucinogens, such as LSD. In addition, high doses do not produce the anesthesia, coma, and death inherent in sedatives.

There is rampant confusion in both the scientific and medical communities regarding THC. This is particularly alarming considering the vast numbers of people, especially the young, who regularly smoke marijuana.

Pharmacologically, THC is classified as "a unique psychoactive drug." This is because little is really known about it. The chemical structure of THC does not resemble any known or suspected neurotransmitter and it is not presently known which transmitters are effected by THC.

According to the US Drug Enforcement Agency, THC level in marijuana has increased from less than 1% in 1974 to 5% in 1997, with levels as high as 17% due to advances in growing methods.

Because of its popularity in the 60's and 70's, myriad studies were conducted on the effects of marijuana. Many of these, in hot pursuit of ready government and foundation research monies, were done quickly, carelessly, and without proper controls. And because of increased national interest, unreliable results received much publicity.

We are presently left with a body of conflicting information regarding the long-term use of marijuana.

What is known is that the tar content of a marijuana cigarette (joint) is seven to twenty times that of an ordinary cigarette. If one smokes 3 to 5 joints a day, it may be considered to be like smoking as much as 3 to 5 packs of cigarettes. This may be compounded if the marijuana smokers also smokes regular cigarettes. Doctors are presently finding young people in their 20's and 30's with pulmonary emphysema, wherein 50-70% of their lung capacity is destroyed.

THC does not dissolve in water, and therefore is not eliminated by the kidneys as alcohol is. It lodges in the white blood cells and reduces their capacity to fight infection. At an adolescent psychiatric hospital in St. Louis, half of which accommodates psychiatric patients and half of which is for chemical dependents, it was found that the chemically dependent patients evidenced ***10 times*** the number of infections as the psychiatric patients. Lowered resistance to infection is a hallmark of smoking marijuana.

The most insidious effects of marijuana are in the brain. Because it is not water-soluble, it stays in the body longer than any other drug. It takes up to seven days to get rid of half a dose of the THC from one joint. The unexpelled THC of heavy, and long-term pot smokers gathers in what Dr. David Olds calls "large globs" in the brain, evidenced upon autopsy.

Pot smokers may experience a distorted sense of time (stoned); they may experience a distorted sense of speed and distance (hallucinated); they may suddenly experience the effects of marijuana even when they are not smoking (flashbacks); they may become sluggish, apathetic, lacking in ambition (amotivational syndrome).

Pot, the great differentiator of the 60's, replaced in the eighties by cocaine, is still the entry level drug of millions of young Americans. It is still the favorite relaxer of the graying and balding Flower Children of the 60's.

A reported 29 million Americans use marijuana; 9 million use it daily. As with cocaine, it rarely stands alone, but is accompanied by the glass of white wine, the cold beer. And while the addictive properties of marijuana are still debated, millions find themselves growing more and more dependent upon the glass of white wine, the cold beer.

In the year 2000, 88.5% of high school seniors stated that they could easily purchase marijuana. A young, seasoned authority said knowing how to get it is like knowing who is the quarterback on the football team. High school bathrooms across this country reek of the "skunky" odor, a metaphor for the big business of drug buying and selling that goes on in our schools.

Marijuana overdoses numbered 96,500 which were registered for emergency room episodes in 2000, up by 43,800 since 1996. Nearly 12,000 deaths occurred in 1999 due to all drug overdoses. According to Carol Falkowski, Director of Research Communications at Hazelden, 200,000 Americans sought treatment for marijuana addiction, half were under the age of 20.

It is of interest to note that students and young people who suffer from undiagnosed or untreated ADD gravitate to the calming, sedating, centering effects of marijuana. We have yet to understand how addictions, anxieties, ADD and learning disabilities weave together. Nineteen million Americans suffer from anxiety disorders; 30% of those with panic disorder use alcohol to relieve their symptoms, 17% use cocaine or marijuana.

Millions began a life of addiction to alcohol with that first innocent drag on a joint, wherein they were introduced to the magic of a psychoactive, mood-altering chemical. THC, so innocent, so up-beat, so camp.

NICOTINE

It is commonly known that tobacco kills 430,000 Americans each year. One quarter of Americans smoke, costing the economy $100 billion in consequential diseases and early deaths.

Two thousand teenagers become new smokers daily.

According to a 1996 article in the Journal of Substance Abuse and Treatment, 80% to 95% of alcoholics smoke, three times greater than the general population. These alcoholic smokers smoke more cigarettes and draw in more heavily that the regular smoking population. Today, 95% of AA meetings are smoke-free.

Until now researchers and clinicians have been stymied by the ferociously addictive power of nicotine. Millions of Americans have struggled with abstinence, only to experience relapse as a matter of course. Perhaps in no other addiction do recovering persons look down upon those "weaker" souls who still struggle with the addiction.

In a breakthrough article in *Neuron* (March 14, 2002), University of Chicago researchers have discovered exactly why smoking is so pleasurable and so addictive. As in so many addictions, nicotine scores a direct hit on the brain's reward center, the nucleus accumbens deep in the ventral tegmental area, and floods the brain with the "feel-good" dopamine.

Dr. Daniel S. McGehee, the author of the study, states "These really important events in our lives have a different quality to them that is imparted by the reward system. What the drugs of abuse are doing is usurping that reward system."

The reward center is in our brains to help a person learn what is good for survival and what is not, e.g., food, sex, fun, sleep, sports, art, poetry, children. Dopamine is dispensed by the brain with great care and moderation. A jolt of dopamine makes a person feel good and lays down a memory of a good experience to be reinforced. Within a few minutes, the neurotransmitter acetylcholine tells the reward center to turn off the dopamine and things get back to normal. If the reward center remained flooded with dopamine and felt high, new learning and subsequent survival would be blocked.

However, nicotine blocks the acetylcholine so the dopamine cannot be reabsorbed back into the system and the brain stays flooded with dopamine. This blocking of the reuptake system creates more mischief, fooling the brain into thinking that nicotine is a proper participant of life, according to John Dami, a Baylor College of Medicine neuroscientist.

One cigarette contains 10 milligrams of nicotine; within 10 seconds after inhaling, 1 or 2 milligrams get into the blood stream and hit the nucleus accumbus (Nac), a bull's eye into the reward center. The average smoker takes 10 puffs with each cigarette; that is 300 hits with 1.5 packs of cigarettes.

At the same time, the nicotine molecules plug into another set of inhibitory neurons, jamming their ability to turn off the dopamine. Dani summarizes this process as "No other outcome than excitation when you've got nicotine in the system".

It is estimated that 30 million Americans try each year to quit smoking and fail. There are millions of dollars spent each year on gum, patches, hypnosis, anti-depressants. Millions shamefully ignore the pleadings from their families, friends, doctors. Years ago, cigarettes were called "coffin nails". Few smokers take pride in their need to smoke, as many are seen hunkering down outside work-places, restaurants, in their cars, out in the garage. All the broad social pressure smokers experience cannot compete with the feel-good dopamine careening deep within the pleasure center of the brain.

DUAL ADDICTION/POLY-ADDICTION

According to a 2000 research up-date from Hazelden, 69% of patients admitted for treatment had a diagnosis involving both alcohol and drugs.

The terms dual-addiction (addiction to two drugs) and poly-addiction (addiction to many drugs) are commonly used to describe the situation of chemically dependent people. In fact, there are therapists and counselors who feel that it is rare today for one to be dependent strictly upon alcohol.

Alcohol appears to be the one constant in all these addictions. There are those who begin with pot and beer, those who mix their diet pills with wine, those who ease themselves down from a coke high with vodka. Some hop-scotch: Valium or painkillers and then, when the prescription runs out, switch to alcohol; when the alcohol gets out of control, back on the Valium.

MIXING

It has become increasingly popular to mix uppers, such as cocaine, with downers such as heroin (speedballing). The heroin and cocaine are taken together by injection to produce a smooth longer-lasting high. The heart rate speeds up and then slows down from the mixture, an action which was responsible for the deaths of John Belushi and David Kennedy. This is like speeding a car, braking fast, speeding, braking again.

Another way drugs are mixed comes from taking sleeping pills at night to rest and diet pills during the day to stay awake. When it is time to sleep again, more of the sedative may be necessary to calm down and accidental overdose can be the result. This is like being in an out-of control elevator: up, down, up, down.

TOLERANCE/CROSS-TOLERANCE

If one has developed a tolerance for alcohol and/or other drugs, it means that more and more of the drug is needed to create the same effect. (This is explained in depth in chapter Two.) Tolerance is usually seen together with dependence, which means that one must increase the dosage of the drug to feel normal, although the altered body chemistry is objectively abnormal. Once dependence has occurred, the individual has no choice but to continue usage or experience withdrawal.

Tolerance to any drug can be seen as an indication of addiction. People with normal responses do not generally take drugs in the amount or with the frequency that leads Jellinek's disease victims to become tolerant to their effects.

CROSS-TOLERANCE

Cross tolerance occurs between drugs in the same classification. If one is tolerant to alcohol, he will have tolerance to all other sedatives, even if he has never ingested any other sedative besides alcohol.

In addition, this cross-tolerance must be seen in relation to where a person is in the progression of Jellinek's disease: If he is in the middle stage with increased tolerance, he will have a higher tolerance to all drugs in the same category; when he loses his tolerance, he loses it to all drugs in that same category.

When the alcoholic takes a tranquillizer, he needs a higher dosage than the non-alcoholic. This is seen when alcoholics (both active and recovering) need to be anesthetized for surgery; they need a greater amount to achieve the same effect.

A woman with Jellinek's disease who had not had a drink in 13 years was undergoing minor surgery. The anesthesiologist could not get her under. As she was finally beginning to fall asleep, she heard him say to the surgeon, "This one must be a drinker." The tolerance that one develops after years of drinking is a permanent bio-chemical fixture, regardless if the person is actively drinking or not.

CROSS-ADDICTION

Cross-addiction works much like cross-tolerance in that the Jellinek's disease sufferer is addicted to all drugs in the same classification. This is why switching from alcohol to Valium or Librium does not relieve the alcoholism, it only compounds it. The body does not know if the sedative is a liquid or a solid; the chemistry of the brain simply slows down and eventually, with enough alcohol and/or tranquillizers, comes to a halt.

Tolerance and addiction do not occur between the different classes of drugs (uppers, downers, psychedelics). However, to go from alcohol to cocaine is still using a chemical to effect a mood; the user will generally go back to the drug of choice or wind up combining the two.

A person recovering from drug and/or alcohol addiction is playing Russian roulette when he uses other depressant drugs. Pain medication is to be done advisedly, and only under the supervision of a doctor knowledgeable about drug and alcohol addiction and of the patient's drug history. In instances of surgery or acute pain, the recovering person must inform the attending physicians (surgeons, anesthesiologists, internists, etc.) that they are drug dependent, although recovering.

Treatment centers are presently seeing people who had been in treatment eight or ten years previously for alcoholism who, ignorant of the wide sweep of Jellinek's disease, find themselves addicted to cocaine. A drug is a drug is a drug.

PROGRESSION OF TOLERANCE EFFECT

When drinking and using drugs first begins, the person goes from feeling normal into euphoria and then back again to normal as the liquor wears off. If he has put too much liquor into his system, he may feel pain and remorse for a while, but eventually winds up normal again.

As the disease progresses, he will drink again during the pain stage but will feel only a mild euphoria and is quickly taken through normal and back to pain. In the final stages, pain becomes constant and the drinking can only produce a lesser degree of pain that is by now perceived as normal. When William Faulkner was asked why he drank so much, he replied, "For the pain."

This increased tolerance demands that someone with Jellinek's disease has to consume large amounts of liquor and/or pills just to maintain a feeling he can live with. Unfortunately for him, alcohol and pills do not lose their toxicity with increased tolerance so that he may drink himself to death before he can seek help. Many of the 123,400 people who died from drugs and alcohol in 1998, would still be alive today if they had gotten help. Only 11% of those in need receive any treatment or counseling. An average of 33.5 years were sliced off each of these people's lives.

EUPHORIA

It is that desirous euphoric state that is the siren's call to a life of addiction. Euphoria–that feeling of well-being or buoyancy or calm that lifts the harassed mother out of her kitchen, that smooths out the jagged edges of the executive's day, that relieves the boredom of the bus driver, that creates a feeling of connectedness for the lonely senior citizen, that empowers the teenager to act out her fantasies.

It may be the incredible being one with the universe feeling that accompanies the hallucinations produced by psychedelics. It may be that of the alcoholic who picks himself up with a snort of cocaine and then drinks a glass of wine to mellow the journey to sleep. It may be that of someone who takes his marijuana with a cold beer, making life seem not so hard, but rather nice and even funny.

Millions begin a life of addiction with that first innocent drag on a joint, that lovely white wine to enhance a meal, the cold beer at the ball park, or the prescription pill to lessen pain or anxiety.

Because these are so much a part of the American way of life, it is difficult, if not impossible, to see the chemical snare into which millions of us are beckoned, held, and finally trapped. It is the destroyed careers, the fractured marriages and broken children, the loss of quality of life and billions of dollars that are the landmarks of that devastation that we once called peace.

Chapter Five

Alcoholism and The Family: Roles and Stages

All happy families resemble one another; every unhappy family is unhappy in its own way.

Leo Tolstoy

Kit stood by the kitchen sink, rinsing egg off the morning dishes. She sank her red hands into the soap bubbles. Her wedding ring disappeared.

She turned to the calendar above the phone. She was due three days ago and her periods were as regular as the clock. Wouldn't it be funny if this were the miracle baby, the stroke of grace that would bring Frank Kelly to his senses? Maybe she'd even call the baby Grace, if she were a girl. But if she were a boy . . . if she were a boy . . . if dreams were horses, lovely beggars would fly, wouldn't they, Kit?

Kit poured herself another cup of coffee. The house was quiet in that first hour after the kids left for school, before Pops was up and while Frank was at work.

Kit tried to read the paper, but she could not concentrate. The outside world of crime and sports and international news was unreal. She clipped a few coupons for coffee and cheese, scanned the obituaries, flipped to the horoscope.

Libra: Relief from present struggle to manifest soon. Finances on the upsurge and unknown family member makes unusual request. Special care in area of health, with spotlight on chronic or reoccurring problem. Aries figures strongly.

With a sigh, she closed the paper and held her head in her hands. With no warning, a wave of rage swept over her, pounding her head, throttling her bowels, flooding her nerves with fire. She trembled as the heat raced through her veins, down her arms and legs and into her hands and feet. God, I'll kill him! I'll kill him! I'll kill that son of a bitch!

And that same fantasy she knew so well flashed in her mind–she was on her knees, plunging the butcher knife deep in his belly as she poured whiskey in his eyes and nose and mouth and he choked and grasped for air and she poured more whiskey down his throat and stuck the knife in again and again and he died in a sweet pool of whiskey and blood and they were all free. And even Frank Kelly would be free. Dead and free.

And there was no sin. She didn't need to go to confession and say bless me father for I have sinned. She would be doing a holy and noble act, putting the son of a bitch out of his misery and freeing them all.

And no one would arrest her, for they knew what her life with him was like. Maybe she'd even be given an award, like a woman in war who saved the life of her child by lying on top of him during a bombing. Kit Kelly, Purple Heart, Medal of Honor, Seal of Good Housekeeping, ***Newsweek*** Woman of the Year.

God, I hate him. And now another child may be on its way, his child, my child. Our child. She closed her eyes with shame as she thought of the night they conceived. There was no love, no tenderness, not even desire. Those things were long gone. It was more like a rape with his drunken hands on her and she lying like she was dead so she wouldn't feel anything, so she wouldn't wake the kids with screams of revulsions. And yet life had begun.

As her rage was spent, her mind rolled ahead to the birth of the new child, healthy, beautiful, perfect and as the child was born, Kit would start to bleed and they couldn't stop the bleeding and she would slowly lose consciousness and die. The sweetness of death with its stillness and peace.

Kit looked into her coffee cup. Her reflection was distorted. Dear Mother of God, Kit prayed, help me, I'm so filled with hatred. I hate myself. God help me.

These fantasies of murder and death were happening more often and becoming more real. She'd slide into them when she was cooking or at church or helping the kids with their school work. She was growing to be a stranger to herself, her mouth taut with rage, as tight little webs of control framed her lips. Michael or Patty would find her scowling to herself and even Pops noticed the angry river furrowing between her eyes.

Goddamn it! Here she was, only 38, and she had the complete responsibility for all of them—her father, the four kids, and her husband, the biggest baby of them all. It was like having five kids, not four. Frank Kelly had long since given up any pretense of being a husband and a father. True, he still brought home his check, but that was the beginning and the end of his obligation.

Frank Kelly, the baby. Kit Kelly, the mama. And the papa. Perhaps if it were only picking up the slack, Kit would not have minded. If Frank had had a stroke, Kit would have had to do many of the things that a normal husband or father would have done, and she gladly would have done it.

Yet with his drinking, it was worse than if he had had a stroke. Kit had to play mother and father: The complete discipline of the children fell to her; attendance at school and church events was her duty. He was simply not around, and when he was there physically, his mind and heart were not with them.

Each time Kit thought of the children, she felt a fresh sweep of anguish. Something was happening to them that wasn't normal. They were all reacting to their father in their own little ways that seemed to protect themselves from the full impact of his drinking. On some level they didn't seem to be like other kids. But weren't they better off ***with him*** that with no father at all?

Kit thought of Margaret, her oldest, only 12. As a baby, Margaret was full of the joys of life, as her mother would say. She was never without a smile or a giggle and went to everyone without hesitation. Life was easy when she was little, but Frank was better and took pride in his little girl who so resembled him. He took her to the zoo and ball games and movies and he was the only one whom she would let call her "Maggie".

Margaret seemed particularly hurt by her father's drinking, as if he had violated a special pact between them. She was growing up fast. Kit wondered what she would do without Margaret, for Margaret seemed to be the 'bridge over troubled waters', the one stratum of common sense in the madness that was their life.

Now Margaret was changing from a happy-go-lucky girl into a worried woman much too fast. Margaret had flashes of anger surpassed only by Kit's, yet she seemed to feel so responsible not only for what went on, but for how everyone was feeling.

Kit told her again and again that things would work out and not to worry so but Margaret wouldn't believe her. Margaret worried about the bills, about her brother Michael and her two younger sisters and about Pops. When she finds out about the baby, thought Kit, she'll be in a tailspin. She did very well in school and was starting to win awards in science and English. And she baby-sat for the whole neighborhood to save up money for college. She was worried about paying for college at 12.

Margaret seemed obsessed by the idea that Kit ought to get a divorce. She would go into a rage when Kit would try to explain to her that she had her vows and had promised God that she would stay with Frank Kelly for better or for worse. Kit really didn't believe it and she knew that Margaret was right, as usual. It was just Pops–he would never for one second stand for it. And Frank's brother, Tom, was a priest and there would be the scandal. Divorce was completely out of the question.

Four children and now she was bringing another one into the world to join the madness and sadness that was theirs. Perhaps the excitement of a new baby would make Frank's drinking seem less important; the whole family was now centered around his drinking, his behavior, his moods. The kids and herself and Pops were all second fiddle to Baby Frank and his drinking. Maybe now it will be different.

If it were another woman, thought Kit as she poured herself another cup of coffee, I could compete. I'd win, hands down. I can't compete with the bottle. It holds him, enchants him, captivates him as I can't. No woman could. It holds secrets and magic that I don't have.

As she finished her coffee, a shudder went through her. I can't take anymore . . . I just can't take any more. She thought again of the birth of her new child and her own life slipping away as she approached the purity of oblivion and the integrity of death that would reproach the lie of her living death with Frank Kelly and his bottle.

THE SLEEPING BEAR:

Imagine any street in any town or city in America. Brick and frame and stucco houses stand beside each other. Trees and bushes are banked by ivy, fern, flowers. Bicycles, big wheels, wagons, and strollers block the sidewalks as dogs and cats compete with children for space and attention.

Imagine the interiors of these houses: families, large and small, whole or fractured, living out their lives to a somewhat predictable, rhythmic beat. They go to work, cut the grass, correct children, sweep floors, butter bread, make money, make love, grow older, take a rest. A nuclear family, an extended family, a family of one–each living its own life to its own beat, doing the tasks common to all, sharing the values and culture of American society.

Imagine one of the homes, perhaps stucco, perhaps with flowers and baby strollers and bikes and dogs and children. It is not unlike the many other homes on the same street, except in the front room sleeps an 800 lb. ***ursus horribilis***, a great grizzly bear with a large wedged head, a thick black snout, and a heavy coat of gray-brown matted fur.

He is not hibernating, only dozing. The steady drum of his snoring rumbles through the house. They know only too well that with the slightest noise, he will open his black marble eyes, stretch his mighty legs, and flash his knife-claws in their direction before he begins another mad rampage, growling and roaring and thundering as they watch in terror, knowing that it is only a matter of time before he destroys them entirely.

The worst part of their lives is not the sheer terror that the presence of the grizzly imparts, but it is the fact that they must keep his presence secret, that no one must know of the madness and horror that dwells within their walls.

Neighbors are not invited in, friends cannot come to call, people are cut off at the door; no one must ever guess the shameful secret that abides within the otherwise normal stucco house with flowers and bikes and children. The family must keep the raw stench, the ghastly sounds, the ugly scenes to itself.

The family is united in hiding the truth from the world, for they feel they are responsible, that they have somehow welcomed the bear into their midst and now they must live with the consequences.

While the family must never let on to the world that a grizzly bear lives in their front room, their life within the home is erratic, chaotic, hysterical, as each member of the family learns his own unique way of acting when the bear is sleeping and when he is awake.

Their timing becomes intuitive, for they know when the bear goes into a deeper sleep, they may get a respite for a few hours. Yet they can never let down their guard, for the bear can break out of a dead sleep and begin its terror when they least expect it. And when he has been sleeping for a while, everyone grows uneasy, knowing that in a few moments he will awake and strike.

When the rampage begins, they each go into their own act to neutralize the effects and to feel that they have not lost control entirely.

In a desperate attempt to pacify the bear and to maintain control, each member of the family learns a special and unique way of acting, determined in large part by his position in the family and his individual temperament.

Members of the family become as actors in a horror film and each becomes locked into his own role. Members of other families on the street act in accordance with their own personalities and with each incident or issue that evolves; they are more or less free to develop within the constraints of their own history, talents, and opportunities. Members of the family with the bear in their front room become fixed in their individual behaviors at an early age and never are free to know honestly or to respond honestly to how they feel and want to act; they continue to try to pacify and control the bear long after the bear has died and they have moved away.

ROLES

What are these roles or behavior slots that are common to all Jellinek's diseased families? Why do these roles persist long after their function is no longer needed? Why are they so destructive? How can families living with Jellinek's disease break out of these locked in, predictable ways of behaving and begin to function in more healthy, open, creative ways?

Sharon Wegscheider in ***Another Chance: Hope and Health for the Alcoholic Family*** delineates the roles or behavior slots for members of an alcoholic family: the Dependent (the Jellinek's diseased), the Enabler (frequently the spouse), and the children: the Hero, the Scapegoat, the Lost Child, the Mascot. (These roles of the children will be delineated in the following section, Chapter Six.)

THE DEPENDENT

The ***Dependent*** is the person in the family who is chemically addicted. Frank Kelly's body chemistry was dependent for its normalcy on alcohol. As he lost more and more control over his behavior because of the demands of his body, he wielded more and more power over his family.

The Dependent is as powerless over his disease as the rest of the family, but as he is sucked into the vortex of his illness, he pulls the rest of the family with him.

The entire family life centers around his drinking. Healthy families are centered around the growth and happiness of each of its members; issues such as vacations, school problems, a change of job or residence, a pet, an investment all move in and out of the family's attention, yet the family is centered on its own healthy development. The alcoholic family is centered on the drinking, and all other issues are either not dealt with or are dealt with peripherally.

The Jellinek's diseased must protect his supply of liquor at all cost: lying about it, hiding it, squirreling away fresh bottles for an emergency, jiggling the family's finances to buy it. One woman became the active good neighbor and would take in mail and water plants of people who were vacationing; she did this to steal liquor to keep her supply replenished. An alcoholic cannot be without her supply.

Likewise, the family of the alcoholically impaired must keep the supply down. They throw it out, hide it, water it down, and then lie when questioned by the alcoholic. The Jellinek's diseased is playing a role and the family are playing roles. Everyone eventually ends up doing the same things, perhaps in reverse, but basically the same.

The Jellinek's diseased is dictated to by his disease. He is driven to do things he would not ordinarily do simply to pacify the cells within him screaming for relief. He is dependent upon a chemical to assuage the pain within, but at a great price. And as he grows in his dependency, the dictates of his addiction become more and more urgent and accountability toward his family become less and less compelling. There are others to take over, to pick up the slack.

THE ENABLER

The ***Enabler***. He or she is the one most closely tied to the Dependent. He or she is most probably the spouse, but an Enabler may be a parent, a child, a friend, an employer, anyone who stands between the Dependent and the consequences of his drinking.

The very term enabler has an almost insidious ring to it, as if the person who assumes this role secretly wants the drinker to continue drinking. Unfortunately, the term does not have within itself the pain and nobility and self-sacrifice that motivates the Enabler. Nor does it contain the ever-widening ignorance and misunderstanding of Jellinek's disease that binds the Enabler to his role.

The Enabler straddles the gulf between the Jellinek's diseased and the family, the neighborhood, the place of employment, society at large. He or she is the middleman, the go-between, the boundary spanner.

The Enabler translates, explains, rearranges, modifies, and interprets the bizarre behavior of the Jellinek's diseased:

> Father - "Mom is on the kitchen floor because the floor was just waxed and it was too slippery for her." (Mom was drunk and fell, but you don't have to deal with that now.);
>
> Wife - "Frank won't be in today. We've all been hit by the flu." (Frank has a hang-over, but he might lose his job and where would we be then?);
>
> Nurse - "Dr. Hamilton felt that you were confused about the nature of the surgery he recommended." (Dr. Hamilton was in a blackout and didn't remember what he told you.)
>
> Child - "My mom couldn't help me with my book report because she had a very bad headache last night." (Mom couldn't see straight);
>
> Mother - "Peter did not mean to lie about the substance in his locker. He didn't understand what you meant." (Peter was afraid of getting kicked out of school and blamed another kid for the grass.)

The Enabler is on the firing line and has assumed the major responsibility for absorbing the shocks of the alcoholic's behavior, for interpreting the bizarre behavior in the context of normalcy (waxed floor, flu, headache), and for presenting the alcoholic and the alcoholic family to society as being no different than others. A family perhaps with a little bad luck, or with a little more creativity than most, but basically no different.

And all the while, the Enabler, acting out of love for both the Dependent and the family, begins to feel more and more put upon. The stress of the monumental task grows as the alcoholic, gradually freed from responsibility, drinks more and more and with less and less impunity. The Enabler, like a clown juggling a dozen balls, worries when an itch or a sneeze will be too much and the balls will crash to the ground and he will stand in shame and failure and everyone will know the truth.

The Enabler has signed a contract to do the impossible and grows more and more resentful as the burden increases and takes its toll. The Enabler functions as both mother and father, controlling the finances, controlling the mood and emotions of the family, knowing that it is only a matter of time when he will have to drag the sun up from the East and shove it down in the West.

"I was fighting alcoholism with the weapons of ignorance and self-pity," admitted one woman who had mobilized her children against their drunken father. Together they would conduct 'search and destroy' missions, looking for bottles squirreled throughout the house. She even controlled the natural feeling of love they had for their father and would belittle them when they sided with their father. The children eventually grew to regard their father as a cross between a clown and an idiot. The Enabler could not allow feelings of sympathy for the alcoholic to surface. She was the one holding it all together, and if there was any extra sympathy, she was the one to get it.

The Enabler assumes super-human dimensions, doing many jobs, wearing many hats, deflecting the hand of fate and softening its blow. The Enabler keeps the family from self-destructing, makes the world believe that things are just fine, but all the while he or she is consumed with primitive feelings of rage and revenge that life dealt such a nasty blow.

MARRIAGE ADJUSTMENT TO JELLINEK'S DISEASE

The marriage between the Dependent and an Enabler (it does not matter which is the man and which is the woman) revolves around the drinking. There are seven basic stages common to these marriages as outlined by Joan K. Jackson in "The Adjustment of the Family to the Crisis of Alcoholism."

PRELIMINARY STAGE

Drinking is basically not a problem and incidences of drunkenness are treated simply within the context of 'over-sociability' or having a good time.

In effect, the couple who begin a relationship that ends up as an alcoholic marriage are no different from other couples, except that one of the partners is most probably in the early, hidden stage of

Jellinek's disease and drinking is not a problem; there are few signs of the chaos that is to come as the biochemistry of the early stage alcoholic grows more and more dependent upon alcohol.

STAGE I

In this early stage, both parties pretend that there is nothing wrong. Incidences of drunkenness are either ignored or dismissed as insignificant, simply a part of adjustment to a new marriage. It may well be that the alcoholic is sufficiently controlled not to cause any overt scenes; perhaps the alcoholic is clever enough to hide traces of inordinate drinking from an unsuspecting spouse.

The spouse is reluctant to speak to either friends or relatives at this point. The drinking is not really out of control, but it has come as a surprise (perhaps to both . . .). The spouse struggles for an answer: Maybe when the period of adjustment is over; perhaps if I hit upon the right formula (a little something to eat before we go out, not going out with certain people, less red meat, more sex, less sex); there's probably something the matter with me and he is just too kind to say–I must be driving him to drink.

If there are fights and arguments over the drinking, they usually end in an emotional stalemate, both parties hurt that they are not understood, that the other is doing something untoward and is basically an insensitive person, and that there has been a radical mistake in choice. Doubts about the marriage and doubts about a self who could have blundered so in the selection of a mate begin to gnaw at both.

Early on, the dynamics of control, guilt, and rage are beginning to rear their ugly head. Neither party knows what is happening and flails about for control over the drinking and over each other.

STAGE II

This begins when the drinking causes social isolation. The wife begins to dread a party; she sees her husband dressing, glass on the edge of the sink; he shaves deliberately, as if he is putting on warpaint for the battle to come. She soon refuses invitations, saying nothing to him. She has been embarrassed too many times, has lost too many friends because of his Jeckyll/Hyde behavior. If she accepts the invitation, he would only start a fight, become loud and obscene, fall in the bushes. Enough. They'll just stay at home.

The wife begins to realize what she secretly knew all along, but pretended not to know. Her husband is a drunk. His carefree, crazy behavior before their marriage, and even his wonderful unpredictability in the early days of their marriage were all signs that she should have paid more attention to. He's now a husband and father and becoming less and less predictable. He's dangerous.

The night he came home late from an out-of-town business trip. She was in bed, nursing the 3-month old baby. He fell on top of them, passed out cold. The baby would have suffocated if she had not been able to shove him off. He spent the night on the floor, reeking of liquor, snoring and snorting and mumbling incoherently. He's dangerous.

She finds herself becoming more and more anxious. Time that should have been spent otherwise is spent worrying about him, about them. But then he throws her a curve. He stops drinking. Life begins again. She doesn't say anything: It might embarrass him; it might jinx him; it is none of her business.

Maybe she made this all up. He really never hurt anything or anybody. He had such a bad childhood–it will just take him a little longer to mature, but he's worth waiting for, with all his other wonderful qualities. She always was such a worry-wart. Calm down. Be grateful. Things are now on the right track. As a matter of fact, they are great!

He's been five months without a drink. They are a typical American couple, happy, close, another baby on the way. He's outside painting the lawn furniture they bought at a garage sale. Their two-year-old is asleep. A can of beer would taste so good. Its hot. And he could never paint without a can of beer. Besides, he's got the problem licked–five months with nothing to drink, and he really didn't miss it. He can handle it. All that fuss over nothing. He begins drinking again.

Within days, his drinking once again becomes the focal point of their lives. Everything else is secondary.

Pregnant or not, the wife has to pick up the pieces or the whole thing will fall apart. She is starting to hate him. (He has hated her for a long time.) Their relationship is strained, each fearing to draw too close. Is another betrayal waiting around the corner?

He feels that she is a bully, a ball-breaker. She only wants to boss him around and to sit on her mighty throne and pass judgment on him. He'll be damned if some woman is going to dictate to him. He's the captain of his own ship and if he wants to drink, by God, no one can stop him.

She feels he is selfish, weak, only interested in his own comfort. She feels put upon–she has complete responsibility for the children, the house, the car, the bills. She watches him slowly withdraw from their life together. His heart is somewhere else. She feels cheated. And very angry.

STAGE III

At this point, the family is becoming fractured. The Dependent is firmly established in drinking and the Enabler is firmly established in holding things together. Animosity between them is constant and the children become pawns in the struggle for power between their parents.

The Jellinek's diseased accuses his wife of turning the children against him, of poisoning their minds; she laughs bitterly and tells him that he needed no help, that he did it all by himself.

There are still little pockets of peace when he goes on the wagon and swears off drinking for a diet or for Lent or for a bet, but mostly to prove to himself and to his family that he is not an alcoholic, that he is indeed in control.

(Note that these times are times of dryness, not of sobriety. Dryness simply means not drinking; ***sobriety means not drinking and at peace***. Hence, the alcoholically impaired may be said to be on a dry drunk which may be worse than if he were actually drinking. He has all the characteristics and behavior he had when he were actually drinking.)

At this point, he may even go to some A.A. meetings to get them off his back. He will sit and feel superior to the poor drunks that need that sort of thing. He may pick up some of the A.A. slogans and learn some names. Things seem to have calmed down–the wife isn't nagging so much, the kids aren't so hostile, he's got everything under control. And he still is dry, not sober, despite the fact that he is not drinking.

Because the Jellinek's diseased could not admit that he was powerless over alcohol and that his life had become unmanageable, because there was no willingness to change, much less a commitment to change, he will inevitably drink.

And that little pocket of peace that the family was so tenuously enjoying bursts with that first drink. Hope that was once thought to spring eternal is dashed to the ground. Trust which cements a family together disintegrates and distrust grows like weeds between cobblestones.

No one can trust anyone. They've all been duped again by the con artist. Their sense of betrayal is profound, for they've been betrayed not only by the alcoholic, but by their own emotions which were so easily seduced into a false peace.

The family is outraged. Never again will he pull one of his dirty little tricks on them. As the ashes of the false peace smolder, open war breaks out.

What was formerly nagging or quarreling escalates into screaming, throwing things, physical threats, physical violence. Violence rumbles under the floorboards, beneath the rafters, in the chimney.

The screaming stops abruptly and a deathly silence creeps over the family. They stop talking. They do not look each other in the eye. They sleep in separate beds.

Doors slam. Food is thrown on the table. Cars tear in and out of the drive, over bicycles and dolls left in the way. The grass is not cut and the hedges grow up and over the windows.

An iron skillet is kept handy on the stove for defense. An older child keeps a knife under his pillow. Relatives are growing concerned as the family runs to them for safety. The police may have been called in (but most probably not, for this is the family's own problem).

The children are told, "What goes on within these four walls stays within these four walls." They nod and throw up on the way to school.

The spouse, the Enabler, is going down fast. Rage and revenge have become a way of life. Self-pity is her vocation. Physically, she can no longer keep up her appearance. Migraine headaches, ulcers, nerves. She gets a little pill from her gynecologist to calm her down because her kids are at that age. She may begin drinking – If you can't fight 'em, join 'em!! She has little to give to the kids beyond the necessities for her ONE BIG BABY needs all her energy. She's ready to throw in the towel. Her Codependency is likewise in the late-stage.

STAGE IV

At this point, the family pulls together and tries to stabilize itself in spite of the drinking. The Enabler feels that she has been asked to stand up on the seat in the lead car on a roller coaster, blindfolded. She can do it, once she gets the rhythm, hears the clickity-clack of the wheels, feels the wind in her hair. She can do it. She is the codependent ***par excellence.***

Yes, it is unpredictable, but so is life. One quick dip that she wasn't ready for and it's all over. But she can do it. She has to do it. She promised God that she would stick it out. For the kids sake, if not for her own, she'll make it. They'll all make it.

The Enabler has moved into a new level of control. She has taken the dimensions of her husband and has found him wanting. Where the gap is, she moves in, squeezing him out of the family circle ever so slowly. Emotionally, financially, socially, they don't need him.

On one level, he is losing the power struggle. The kids begin to patronize him, pity him, mock him. He begins to realize the degree of his isolation. He has lost face and the kids are getting too old and too smart to be conned. He is told to leave. His clothes end up on the curb.

By definition, Jellinek's disease is an illness of extreme social and mental isolation. This is exacerbated by the family freezing him out of their lives. He becomes terrified that he is losing everything. He wants back into the family nest and will get back in by whatever means are at his disposal.

There may be the money games where the family gets bribed to open up and let him in. There may be the sex games -threats or hints of other women, fondling of the children, accusations of misbehavior on the part of the wife. There may be more serious violence and the lives of the family members are threatened, for if he can't get back in by being nice, he will have to smash his way in.

The family appears to have achieved a modicum of stability. The Enabler is no longer afraid of the roller coaster and can even peek through the blind-fold on an upward climb. Some people outside the family ***know***, so that has taken off some of the pressure to keep quiet. They all know what they are dealing with and there are few surprises left. They know all his tricks.

It all looks a little bit better on the outside. But on the inside, they are constantly bombarded with blasts of ambivalence: I love him/I hate him; he is evil/he is sick; he needs help/he needs to be whipped; I hope he gets better/I hope he dies; he is my husband/he is a stranger; I am a noble wife/I am a bitch; my kids are strong individuals/my kids are going crazy; this is my cross/this is my crown.

At this point, the Enabler may be forced to seek help outside the family. The stability they have achieved is only an illusion; they are in real trouble and she knows it. She doesn't know where the roller coaster is headed, but she can no longer manage to bounce around blind-folded. The mixed-feelings are driving her mad. She is losing it. Everyone has advice. No one can help.

She may approach her minister or doctor. She may see a psychologist or a psychiatrist or go to the local mental health or family services center. If she is lucky, she may even find her way to Al-Anon, the family component of A.A.

STAGE V

Definite attempts are made to escape the problem. If the spouse has become a member of Al-Anon, she has learned that her husband indeed has a progressive, terminal disease. ***He*** has no power over his illness; ***she*** has no power over his illness. Nor over her own Codependency. Their lives have become unmanageable.

In a paradoxical way, as she realizes, accepts, and surrenders to her own powerless over her husband's illness and her own disease process, she receives the strength and wisdom to detach or to let go of the behavior and drinking of the alcoholic and separate them from the person.

She knows that things can't go on as they have, that a decision must be made. With help, she begins to sort out the issues. Before all her worries seemed to have the same weight; now she will learn to make distinctions between what is important and what only ***seems*** important; between what they ***want*** and what they ***need***; between what she can ***accept*** and what is ***unacceptable***; between what she can ***change*** and what is ***beyond her power to change***.

However, it would be ideal to think that once a spouse gets help then everything falls neatly into place. Jellinek's disease is fraught with ambivalence, paradox, regression; anyone who partakes of it, even at a distance, becomes sucked into the dizzy vortex of contradiction. More than likely, when a spouse begins to receive help, things ***appear*** worse than before.

If a husband senses that a wife is making plans to terminate the marriage, he may become increasingly violent, even menacing. Her life and the lives of their children may be on the line. Or he may stop drinking and put on his best behavior.

While the wife may sort out the critical moral, financial, and physical issues related to separating from her husband, she may find herself addicted to the addict. She may be unable to detach from and to release the alcoholic. She is simply stuck in her own Codependency and is either unwilling or unable to choose anything different.

The children and others in the family, perhaps even good friends, contribute to her painful ambivalence. They may want her to leave him so they can all be free; at the same time they send signals that she ought to stand beside him if he is ever to recover. How can you leave the sick? For better or for worse . . . in sickness and in health . . . or at least until it is inconvenient.

And besides, she is certain that they all secretly blame her for the condition he is in. They think she is the well one. Why did she let this happen? And to the degree that she does not understand her powerlessness over his disease and to the degree that she has not accepted this powerlessness, she will feel responsible. And ***guilty***, for hasn't he told her a million times that if it were not for her, he would not have to drink. She'd just better stay put and reap what she has sown.

This is the time of crisis for the Enabler, for the spouse. She is bottoming out in her Codependency.

She may not find it within herself to make a drastic change in her own behavior. She may not have heard that she is not alone, but that there are others who have faced the same issues before her and who are with her. Her investment in him may seem too great; she simply cannot risk throwing it all down the drain for a simple thing like peace of mind.

She does not hear that unless she takes that first step into recovery, the rest will not take their first steps and they will continue in their sickness. She cannot see that she is as sick as he is. She thinks she can go on. Perhaps if she had another child. Perhaps if he changed jobs. Perhaps if they moved. Perhaps if she got more Valium from the doctor. If she chooses to do nothing, they will all remain stuck.

If she chooses to resolve her ambivalences, they may begin to heal.

STAGE VI

Prior to this, in Stage V, an actual physical separation may have occurred. (If he hasn't left, they are so separated emotionally, that he may as well have left.) The husband puts pressure on the children and on the wife to take him back. Problems of the past seem to pale. The concept of his illness plays on the wife's guilt for having made him leave the house.

If he simply comes back with more promises to stop drinking, the family will not recover and recommits itself to the life they had with him before the separation. He will not be able to abstain from drinking for too long; essential family problems of communication, trust, and openness have not been addressed; the destructive family roles have not been understood so they will continue to be played out against the backdrop of the progression of the family disease.

Many families get to this point and go no further. They sign a truce with Jellinek's disease and Codependency. They are willing to go along with things as they are; they do not see that things do not have to be this way. They may feel that this is the cross that they have to bear.

The Berlin Wall goes up within the family: The Jellinek's disease victim is in the east and the rest of the family is in the west. And on some level, they accept that this is the only way it can be.

This is the critical juncture. They have another choice besides signing a truce. They can sign a peace. With help, they can make the condition for his rejoining the family be that he enter a treatment facility, regardless of the length of the stay, and that he join A.A. upon being released. (This process, called Intervention, is dealt with in Chapter Eight.) The codependent may likewise need hospitalization. All must begin their individual recoveries.

STAGE VII

This stage is entered only if sobriety has been achieved, regardless if there has been a separation or not. The recovery of the Jellinek's diseased and the entire family is a slow, painful process. The roles that have been played out so well and so often have to stop.

The family in the latter stage of Jellinek's disease may be compared to a person suffering cancer. The period of treatment is similar to a drastic surgical procedure, whereby the tumor is excised and signs of spread are determined.

However, the cancer victim is rarely cured by surgery alone and must follow up with various therapies, diet, exercise, rest, and periodic check-ups. Likewise, the family is not cured simply by the husband/father having taken part in a rehabilitation program and by their active involvement in family sessions and family counselling aspects of the treatment program.

The family recovery has only just begun.

The drinking has for so long been the focal point of the family's life. When this is removed, family members stand like the survivors of Hiroshima, unable to comprehend the magnitude of destruction before them. The center doesn't hold.

The Dependent needs to recapture his place in the family. The Enabler has assumed most of the ***responsibilities*** for the children, the finances, the general operation of the family, and consequently, holds most of the ***power***.

The Dependent wants his power back. The Enabler either does not want to relinquish what she worked so hard for or does not know how to give it up. If she lets him share in the running of the family, will he dump it back on her when she isn't looking? Will he blow it again? Who will she ***be*** if she isn't managing things?

It has often been said that ***the alcoholic recovers more quickly than the family***. There seems to be a basic injustice in this, because they have all suffered so much at the hands of the alcoholic's disease (which they did not ask for . . . yet neither did he).

Yet, the picture does not have to be bleak. With treatment and recovery for not only the Dependent, but for the entire family, hope and health is on the horizon. (These issues are treated in depth in subsequent chapters.)

There are an estimated 18 million people who suffer directly from Jellinek's disease. There are an estimated 15 million children who presently live in alcoholic homes. In a 2000 study, approximately 1 in 4 children younger than 18 live with alcoholism in the family. More than 1/2 of American adults have a close family member who has or has had alcoholism.

One could confidently say that there are 100 million people or nearly one out of every three Americans who live with a grizzly bear in their front room.

Millions of us lived with the grizzly bear in our childhood and who, as adults, are still locked into their childhood role of trying to placate the bear with whom we may no longer live. Or perhaps we have found a new bear all of our own.

Jellinek's disease is truly a family disease.

Chapter Six

Children of Alcoholics: The Walking Wounded

The fathers have eaten sour grapes, and the children's teeth are set on edge.

JEREMIAH: 31.29.

Margaret's stomach was churning as she walked steadily past the barber shop, the shoe store, the deli. The dark glass of the tavern contrasted with the brightness of the other shop windows and in the center of the glass was painted ***The Old Well***. The gold letters were outlined in black and were old and beautiful as the letters in her grandmother's prayer book. Under the writing was picture of a stone well with a wooden bucket resting on the ground.

Margaret stood on her tiptoes and shielded her eyes from the glare of the glass so she could peek through the big, gold ***O,*** past the venetian blinds, and into the dark saloon to see if her father was there. He was on a stool, his broad back arched over his drink.

The smell of stale beer and sweaty men mingled with the rattle of ice and the din of men's voices. The bartender in a white apron carried on his mysterious gestures like a priest at Mass, pouring and swirling and setting up drinks, washing and wiping the glasses, slapping the cash register and drying his hands. He leaned across the bar, listening and nodding and giving absolution with a smile of forgiveness and understanding.

As he saw Margaret close the screen door, the bartender nodded to her father. Frank Kelly signaled for a Coke and greeted his daughter, helping her up on the bar stool next to himself.

Margaret tried to drink the Coke, but it would not go down. She felt sick to her stomach. He had that look again, the one he wore every time he drank: His eyes blinked faster, his nose turned into a bright red tomato, his voice flattened and fuzzied, and he had that silly guilty smile that would soon be twisted in rage and violence.

Margaret slid off the stool, landing behind her father. She curled her fingers into the space between his thick black belt and his pants, steadied her right foot on the bottom rung of his stool, and pulled at him to leave. The men seated at the bar turned and laughed. Ignoring the men, Margaret pulled harder. She had to get him out of there while he could still walk.

"Daddy, please! Come home! The dinner is ready. Please, Daddy!"

"Okay, Margaret, okay. I was just havin' a little drink before dinner."

"It's going to start it all up again. You know that, Daddy. Please let's go home!"

Frank stood, finished his beer, wiped his mouth, checked his service revolver in his shoulder holster, and put on his jacket. The bartender winked at him, acknowledging the terrible power of women.

"See you soon, Lieutenant," nodded the bartender as he wiped up the cigar ashes from Frank's place. Margaret glared at him, knowing that if he weren't so friendly, her father wouldn't be there. Besides, all they saw was his nice side and they treated him like a big shot, calling him "Lieutenant" or sometimes "Frankie," as if he were a boy instead of a man, but he liked it. Her mother never called him "Frankie," just "Frank," as if she expected him to act like a man, not a boy.

Margaret and her father walked down the street in silence. Margaret felt like the parent; her father felt like the child. She was only twelve, but she knew that she had to hold everything together—she had to keep her mother calm so she wouldn't scream at him and make him mad. Then he would get violent and Margaret would have to step in the middle so he didn't kill everyone.

There was the night Margaret took the gun away from him when he threatened to kill everyone. And the night Margaret ordered her mother to go upstairs to Pops because Margaret could feel that her mother would antagonize him and he might kill them all.

The world was strange and crazy and things weren't really what they seemed. Lieutenant Frank Kelly, decorated for heroism. Lieutenant Frank Kelly, solving murders and robberies and apprehending dangerous criminals. Lieutenant Frank Kelly, crazy alcoholic who threatened his own wife and children, much more dangerous than some real criminals. And the world thought he was so great, but Margaret knew the great trick he pulled on everyone. Except her. He couldn't fool Margaret.

So often after prayers in the morning before school began, the nun would add a special prayer for the safety of Lieutenant Kelly and the seventh-grade boys would smile enviously at Margaret and Margaret would close her eyes and ask God to let her father get killed so they didn't have to live the way they did. He would still be a hero and no one would ever have to know what a phony he was. The policemen would march and the mayor would hand her mother the flag from her father's casket and his shield would be placed forever at police headquarters and all the kids would feel sorry for them but they would be at peace.

The one Margaret really felt sorry for was Pops, her mother's father, who lived upstairs of them. The house was really his, paid for by his forty years at St. Mary's College. Pops had been a teacher of history and philosophy, and he was still called Professor Foley by the people in the neighborhood.

There was a sadness about Pops, despite the games he played and the tricks he pulled. He was like a soft rainy day without a rainbow. Grannie had been dead for years and he never seemed to have gotten used to being without her. He was broken-hearted because of what was going on downstairs.

He felt that it was really all his fault, for if he hadn't gotten the young rookie policeman who was taking his advanced philosophy course together with his only daughter, Kit, the whole thing would never have happened. "Now, Kit," he'd say to her, "I want you to meet this Kelly lad. He's bright and ambitious and he's going places in the department. And the Kellys are good people with all those priests and nuns. And he was in the seminary himself for a number of years. You just can't go wrong with young Kelly, Kit."

But Kit did go wrong with Frank Kelly, despite all the priests and nuns. There were four kids right in a row, and although Frank Kelly came out first in the test for sergeant and went right into the detective bureau and was on his way up in the department, there never was enough money. Kit and Frank moved in with her parents. Her mother died soon after and Pops was left alone to look after his mistake.

Margaret could tell by the heavy look in Pops's eye that he worried about them. Pops had a bad heart and Margaret worried that he would die before her own father and then there would be no one to take care of them.

Kit would come back downstairs after being up with Pops and her eyes would be red and she'd have some money stuck in her apron pocket. She wouldn't look at Margaret but would tell her to go and fold the clothes or take the baby for a walk or peel the potatoes. Then Margaret would picture Pops upstairs holding his chest and saying his rosary and she would hate her father even more.

Pops never criticized Frank. They'd go to a ball game together once in a while and Frank saw that Pops kept up with the latest gossip about the city, but Margaret could see that they acted funny with each other. If her father had really been bad, he'd stay away from Pops and Pops would stay upstairs until things settled down. Until the next time.

Pops never let the kids say anything about Frank. He'd shake his head and say simply, "He's your father and you're to love and honor him and that's all there is to it. I won't have you criticizing him in my house."

The same thing with her mother. Pops would pat her on the back as he held her in his arms and say, "Kit, Frank Kelly is a good man, down deep, he's a good man. Now I've seen his type before, and there's none better than Frank Kelly. One day he'll come around and you'll thank God that you stuck by him. For better or for worse, Kit, for better or for worse."

It was certainly worse, for all Margaret could see. And then, when you least expected it, they'd act like nothing had happened and that everything was fine and her mother would smile and they'd hug and kiss and laugh. Her mother really was a stupid woman–didn't she know that this wasn't going to last forever? It wouldn't even last until next week, but she had been taken in by him again.

That was the difference between Margaret and her mother: Margaret was never taken in by him. The thing that was the hardest to take was the change Margaret began to feel in her mother. There had always been a special closeness between the two. Margaret had been named after Kit's mother and she wanted to look like Kit.

More often people told her that she was the "picture" of her father, but that only made her mad. She didn't want to have to carry that face around with her everywhere she went. One of those faces was enough in the world.

But her mother. That was a different story. It seemed that her soul had actually left the family and was somewhere else. Her body was there, but that was all. When Margaret spoke to her, she didn't hear. When Margaret told her something that had happened in school, Kit didn't respond. It was as if her father was draining out her soul and all that was left was Kit's thin body in the thin flowered housedress.

Well, if she was just too absorbed with him to pay any real attention to Margaret and the other kids, then Margaret would just have to take care of herself and she wouldn't bother her mother anymore with silly stuff from school. Kit could just spend all her time worrying about his drinking. Margaret didn't need her mother's involvement anymore.

Margaret felt that her mother had withdrawn not only from her life, but that she wasn't much of a mother to the other kids as well. Margaret knew that her mother was trying to be a good mother, but she just wasn't able to be the mother she used to be to them.

And if Margaret did not fully understand her own withering relationship with her mother, she certainly did not comprehend her mother's relationship with her brother, Michael, and with her sisters, Ann and Patty. Margaret did not know how her mother saw them—or even if she did see them at all.

Kit did see them, all of them, and she felt equally inept in stopping what was happening to them individually and as a family. Kit saw that while Margaret was so much older than twelve, Michael was so much younger than eleven. Poor Michael, poor Michael, as if that was his name, Poor Michael. He was hurt and angry, too, but in such a different way than Margaret.

He was a disaster waiting to happen. Michael was having problems in school and had taken to lying to cover his tracks, just like his father. Not a week passed that the nuns didn't call about Michael's behavior, Michael's language, Michael's friends, Michael's report card.

The nuns would always say so sweetly, "Now, I'm sure if Lieutenant Kelly spoke to Michael . . ." and Kit wanted to scream, "Lieutenant Kelly is Michael's problem, Sister! Do you want to speak with Lieutenant Kelly and see what you can do?"

There was a new look of defiance and sullenness that had settled in Michael's eyes. Michael had been born gentle, as Margaret had been born happy. That gentleness had all but left Michael, and behind the defiance and sullenness was an incipient cruelty, as if he had a need to abuse others because he was being abused himself.

Kit would find knives in his room and scraps of paper with obscenities and drawings of murder and rape and drunks lying in the gutter. It was more than just a preadolescent expression of awakening glands. It frightened her, but what could she say to him, with her own dreams of violence and revenge.

Michael's shoulders were growing thick with defiance and his head was cocked at a dare-me angle that intimidated her. He would do nasty little things when he thought he was unobserved, like crushing flowers with his heel or pushing the younger kids or breaking glass in the street.

Michael's father was a cop and his uncle was a priest and his grandfather was a professor. Michael had to create himself into the opposite of all they represented, but most of all of what his father stood for.

Kit closed her eyes and tried to dispel the image of last week with Frank going after his son with the gun when Michael hadn't jumped at Frank's drunken command. And Margaret pushing Michael out of the house and taking the gun away from her father.

Frank hated Michael's black leather jacket and blamed Kit for getting it for him. Michael bought it with his own money and Kit did not want to tell him to take it back. One morning Frank came home drunk and tore the jacket into shreds and left it on Michael's bed. When Michael came home from school and found the jacket, he put it into a paper bag, slammed the door, and did not come home until late.

When he came in, Kit could smell liquor on his breath. She screamed at him and slapped him in the face. Michael grabbed her arm, smiled drunkenly, and said, "Like father, like son, Mama. I'm no better than he is. Isn't this what you like?" He released her arm and went into his room.

Kit knew that she was losing her son and there was nothing she could do about it.

Ann, thin, dark Ann with the dark eyes, was a different story. How could children of the same parents, growing up in the same house, have such different ways, Kit would wonder as she'd survey her children pulling away from her and the pain she represented to them.

While Ann wasn't the help that Margaret was, she wasn't the problem that Michael was. Ann just sort of went along, absorbed in her own little world, seemingly immune to the storm around her. Ann created an island for herself in her own mind, where she was more at home than in their world of violence and drunkenness. Although she was only nine, she had developed a look and style that elevated her above her own family, and there she stayed, impregnable, aloof, detached.

Whenever Kit thought of her daughter Ann, she felt a special heaviness that she had pulled away from them so soon. While she could not admit it to herself, Kit was grateful for Ann's asthma and allergies that forced her daughter to turn back to her. It made Kit feel more of a mother and less of a shrew whenever she held Ann in her arms or dashed her off to the emergency room in the middle of the night.

There was something almost healthy about dealing with Ann's illnesses. The doctor would give her a shot or oxygen and she would have to rest and then she would get better. It would be over without all the mental twists and turns that Kit was doing with Frank and now Michael. It was just a straight fact: A sick girl and her mother. Kit needed Ann's asthma to feel like a good mother, to reattach to her elusive daughter, to feel normal.

Margaret, Michael. Ann. Kit's heart grew anxious and heavy each time she concentrated on them, each time she could snatch a few seconds from her grand obsession with Frank Kelly and his drinking. But then there was Patty, blond, chubby, laughing, standing on her head, making angels in the snow, climbing in bed with Kit when Frank was hours overdue. Patty would pretend she had a nightmare, but all the while she simply wanted to snuggle next to her mother and make them both feel good.

By far, Patty appeared the healthiest, the most normal. She either ignored her father's drinking and her mother's tirades, or she actually did not know what was going on. The older ones could not distinguish what she knew, but they were grateful for her crazy ways, the tricks she'd pull, her imperviousness to what they were feeling. Perhaps she was just too young or too dumb to catch on, but she made them all feel good, or at least normal, for a while.

But then that horrible Saturday in April when the jonquils and daffodils were just beginning to show and Patty brought home a fat little black puppy from a school friend of hers. Patty sat all afternoon stroking and petting the puppy and had lined a little box with newspapers for the puppy to sleep in.

Patty put the puppy in the old baby carriage and walked him around the neighborhood like a new mother. She held the puppy close so he wouldn't miss his mother and he would understand that he had a new mother who would take good care of him.

That evening Patty fed the puppy fresh ground beef and milk and set him in his box for the night. She put a clock beside the box so the puppy could hear the ticking and think it was his mother's heart. The puppy was whimpering, but Kit told Patty to get to bed and that the puppy would be all right. She would hold him if he started to cry.

The children had just gotten to sleep when Frank came home in a rage. Kit started screaming at him and the puppy began crying. He grabbed the puppy and shot out the back door. He came back an hour later without the puppy, patted his service revolver, and tripped up the stairs to bed.

The next morning Patty awoke to find the puppy missing. Kit simply told her to ask her father where the puppy was. When Patty asked Frank, he told her he didn't know about it and then burst out laughing.

Patty ran into the bedroom she shared with Margaret and Ann and locked the door. She came out an hour later and went out and rode her bike. Kit disposed of the box. The incident of the puppy was never again discussed.

For someone so young, Margaret knew many things. She knew things about adults and being crazy and violence and what that did to kids. But most of all, she knew all about alcoholism. She knew the signs: Gulping, sneaking, lying, not being able to stop, becoming a different person with the first drink. Hiding full bottles, hiding empty bottles. Blaming, blackouts, guilt.

That was on the outside. The real thing about alcoholism was that you were just a really twisted, creepy, selfish person. You simply chose your own pleasures before anything else–your family or your job or your life. You turn in on your own little world of booze and fantasy and the rest of the world can't get at you. And when Margaret heard about wonderful Lieutenant Kelly and that the nuns prayed for brave Lieutenant Kelly and the men at the ***Old Well*** called him "Frankie," Margaret wanted to gag.

Margaret was indeed wise for a young girl and in her wisdom she knew that she would never, never, never turn into a twisted, creepy, selfish alcoholic like him. She just knew too much and had been through too much ever, ever, ever to get caught in that ugly snare.

ENABLING ROLES OF CHILDREN

The children of alcoholics learn roles; each child within a family learns a specific role that gives him or her an illusion of control. While these roles are not unlike the roles played by children in a non-alcoholic family, they tend to be more pervasive in the alcoholic family. These roles intrude into all facets of the child's life and follow him more doggedly into adulthood.

One insidious aspect of role-playing is that, while lending a measure of predictability to utter chaos, they lock a child into a pattern of behavior from which he cannot escape. He is expected to act in a particular way; he knows how he will act and others depend on him to act that way. He becomes a prisoner to these expectations and to these behaviors and remains so long after they have served their dubious purpose.

In the story related at the beginning of this chapter, Kit, the mother, assumes the role of the Enabler. Actually, she is the prime Enabler, the one who most allows her husband to continue his drinking because she stands between him and the consequences of his drinking. She picks up the pieces, lifts up her chin, is brave, and gives him free reign to carry on.

However, Kit does not occupy this position alone. Her father, Pops, Professor Foley, also ***enables*** his son-in-law, Frank Kelly, to continue drinking. He has basically taken away much of Frank's responsibility: He provides the home, gives Kit money and emotional support, creates an illusion of fatherhood that cannot be criticized by his grandchildren, punishes Frank (when he is bad) by withdrawing his presence and rewards him (when he is good) by going to ball games and gossiping, and pressures Kit into staying in the marriage, literally rendering her unable to do anything. Pop's Codependency just looks different from his daughters.

THE SUPER KID/HERO

If Pops, in his noble, self-sacrificing way enables Frank's disease to grow, so does Margaret, the ***Super Kid***, the ***Hero***, the ***Responsible One***. Margaret, at twelve, has become a little adult. She runs interference for her mother–dragging her father home, scolding him, protecting the family when he becomes violent, being the voice of conscience, or at least, of reason for her mother (get a divorce), worrying about the entire family's welfare, and praying for the resolution to their problems (let him get killed).

Usually Super Kids are the oldest and shoulder a great part of the responsibility for the care and stability of the family. They become the family Heroes, deflecting any potential for disgrace by being outstanding in their studies, conscientious in their baby-sitting or grass-cutting, altogether dutiful, serious, mature. They are the ones who save for college.

They see their mother's compromises and interpret them as seductions. They see the mother becoming more and more absorbed in their father's drinking and less and less involved in the family; they pick up the slack and begin to discipline, scold, and manage the younger children's lives. Their own childhood slips away from them. What is ahead?

A picture of the world as chaotic and violent begins to emerge for them. They see themselves as special, charged with talent and intelligence and responsibility; they learn at a young age the meaning of control. Their Codependency sends out tender roots.

Control. The very sound of the word resonates with authority, power, order. He (Frank) is out of control . . . She (Kit) is losing control . . . Pops has little control of the situation. Margaret, the typical Hero, is learning how to control, how not to be controlled by her father's drinking (she thinks). Margaret is coming into her own–knowing when to be direct, when to confront, when to be silent, but, oh, so strongly silent; when to take action; when to bide her time, hold back, then . . . wham! strike!

As Margaret becomes more comfortable with the subtle configurations of control, people in authority shrink in her mind. She blames her mother for allowing the situation to have degenerated to the level it has; she blames Pops and her uncle the priest and her dead grandmother and the bartender and anyone at all who might have had the slightest chance of heading off the swelling tidal waters. She blames herself for not being a little older and for not having been born a boy, for if she had been, this simply would never have happened.

Heroes pour themselves into their schoolwork. They are beginning to be noticed as quite exceptional: Studious, yet not geniuses; serious, yet fun; responsible, yet not a drag. Actually, they love school–the entire package. It is quiet, ordered, controlled. Even the noise is controlled, allowed only at certain times, in certain places, for certain reasons.

The adults in the school are dependable. They show up, do their jobs, are in control. Not like home where everything is out of control.

Heroes are driven. Everything they want to accomplish, they accomplish. Awards, office, grades–it is all there for the taking, as long as they strive. They become perfectionists: Rigid, unrelenting, single-minded. They must keep moving, one step ahead of the demons that are after them. If they falter for one instance, they will be overtaken and will fall back into the murky chaos from which they have emerged.

But the bitter irony of it all: They conquer so much with relatively little effort, but the one thing they are really after–being able to make a parent stop drinking–eludes them. Gladly, they would relinquish what they have accomplished if only they could find the key to the One Great Problem.

And the fact that they cannot stop the drinking gnaws at them. They begin to feel basically inadequate–as persons, as daughters and sons. They grow to understand that although the mother and the rest of the family really cannot stop the drinking, they, of all people, ought to be able to find the key.

They grow frustrated, angry, restless. All their victories are hollow. They feel flawed, defective, shamed. They can't figure it out. They are wanting. They feel guilty. Inadequate. They start to get sick: Headaches, colitis, colds. They have accidents with bikes and cars.

Haunted by an awareness of their own inadequacy to make the parent stop drinking and to bring peace and normalcy to the family, they look to greener pastures where they can expend their enormous talents, commitment to others, ability to care and effect change. Where they can control, where they can yield a little power, where they can exercise authority, where they can make people or institutions change.

Perhaps they contemplate medical school so they can cure and heal and control disease that tear apart bodies. Perhaps law school so they can right the wrongs heaped upon the poor and indigent, so they can be elected to Congress and pass laws to regulate the lives of others.

Perhaps they will be nuns or ministers or Peace Corps workers, relinquishing all earthly delights, walking through the ghettos of

Calcutta, Chicago, Watts, in the company of Mother Theresa, alleviating misery, bringing joy and comfort to the suffering, to the least of God's creatures. Or teachers or social workers, listening with that third ear to the most subtle hint of hurt, salving hidden wounds with a tender smile, a wise word.

Then, maybe God will hear and the Heroes, single-handedly, will win the grace for their parents to stop drinking. The sacrifices and merits of the past have not been enough. The greater the problem, the greater the solution. There is no such thing as cheap grace.

If there is some hidden economy in the universe, some latent law of positive and negative energy, then Heroes will dispel the negative with their positive commitment to others; then the alcoholic will stop drinking. Whatever the rationale, they have to get out of there and fast. Heroes leave home early, prematurely, and rarely come back. It is just too much for one person to handle alone.

Heroes need a big arena for their commitment, for their need to control and effect change and manage the lives of others. Besides, they learned at an early age that one-on-one relationships are dangerous. The one man in Margaret's life, Frank Kelly, her very own father and friend and the one she truly loved and understood, had betrayed her. He loves his drink more than he loves her. That is all there was to it.

You just can't trust people, you can't ***really*** get involved, you can't take people seriously. They'll just betray you, not measure up, leave you alone with your stupid heart in your hand and you'll feel like a fool all over again. Just never take them seriously, and then that won't happen. Love many, trust few, always paddle your own canoe.

THE SCAPEGOAT

As Heroes carve out a special niche for themselves in the family by being good, others carve out another niche by being bad. Michael is the Scapegoat, the Acting Out Child, the Bad Kid. The Scapegoat may be either a boy or a girl.

In the Mosaic ritual of the Day of Atonement, two goats were chosen as part of the rite: One goat was sacrificed and the other one, the scapegoat, would have the sins of the people laid upon its back and would be sent into the wilderness. This scapegoat was innocent of sin, yet chosen by lot to publicly bear the sins of the people.

In a family living with the bizarre consequences of Jellinek's disease, which it struggles to hide from the outside world, one child may act badly in public while the Hero performs well in public. In one way, this child is more honest, for his attitude and behavior more truthfully reflect the chaos within.

As the scapegoats of thousands of years ago, they wear on their backs the sins of their fathers for all the world to see. In a very real way, they draw the focus away from the all-encompassing problem of the father's drinking and allow the spotlight to fall on themselves. And all along, they too are enabling the father's illness to progress by deflecting the concern from the major problem of drinking to their own.

The scapegoat is the child who acts out, or dramatizes the hurt, rage, and confusion that are endemic to the alcoholic family. As with Michael, he does not study, is belligerent to teachers, begins using drugs and alcohol, and becomes sexually active at an early age.

He basically needs to carve out an image for himself that is in sharp contrast to the Hero's. And yet, as he seems to be withdrawing more and more from the painful family circle, he is the one most in need of care and affection and the one least able to receive it. His identity with the alcoholic (Big Bad Guy/Little Bad Guy) is set in the minds of the family and the punishment that eludes the father falls on the son.

As the Hero is set on a course of behavior to save the world, the Scapegoat's destiny is one of self-destruction: Trouble with the law, bad marriages, unsuccessful careers, drug addiction, an early death.

However, because this child is so overt in his attitude and behavior, he may draw sufficient attention to himself that he will receive the help he needs. If the person providing the help (school counselor, minister, social worker) is competent and sensitive to the symptoms of Jellinek's disease as a family disease and understands that the Michaels of these families are simply lightning rods who draw attention and help to the pain within, then recovery may begin.

In being the first in the family to move out of the circle of the family's illness, the Scapegoat may be the one to break up the chain of enabling, thereby opening the way for the family, himself, and even the alcoholic to receive help.

Statistics of juvenile delinquents suggest that many, if not most, come from alcoholic homes. The histories of criminals accused and/

or convicted of heinous crimes inevitably contain a violent, alcoholic parent. Violence begets violence.

A great irony of Jellinek's disease is that in many families the role of Scapegoat is not fully developed. The control of the non-alcoholic parent (Enabler) may be so consummate that there is no room for the Bad Kid, the Scapegoat. Everyone has to get in line and march, march, march . . . not missing a beat, not calling attention to the family, because if someone starts to look, they might see the grizzly bear.

There are degrees of acting out: Not doing homework or insolence may be to one child from one family what overt acts of stealing or drug taking are to another child from a different family. If professionals who are charged with the care of children develop a heightened index of suspicion, they will pick up the more subtle modes of acting out and will not minimize these behaviors because they are not as blatant as others. Therefore, the Scapegoat child may draw not only attention, but may be the springboard of the family's recovery.

THE LOST CHILD

In a family where the positions of blatant success (Super Kid) and failure (Bad Kid) are taken, another child simply withdraws. This is Ann, the sick daughter, elusive, enigmatic, apart. Sharon Wegscheider calls her the Lost Child, the Forgotten Child, the Sick Kid. The Lost Child may be either a boy or a girl.

These children come to terms with the family situation by not coming to terms with it. They leave it, as they lose themselves in books, hobbies, imaginary friends, pets. The raving father, the coping mother, the successful brother, the troublesome sister all fade. They lose their power to hurt and confuse. The lives of such children ultimately become simple, immune to the dynamics of the family illness that seems to pass over them.

Ann wraps herself in an invisible garment that neither allows the family to get to her nor allows her to impact the family. This protection serves her well and, despite her allergies, she seems to emerge the most normal, the best adjusted, the one least stigmatized by her father's disease. However, as all the other devices that human nature employs for dealing with the unpleasant facts of life, Ann's protection is not a loose garment that she can draw tightly to herself or unbind at will. Her protection becomes a straightjacket that isolates her emotionally.

Ann is doomed to pursue an illusion of normalcy as feverishly as Margaret seeks perfection and Michael seeks excitement. Ann will have many people in her life, but few, if any, intimate friends.

Friendship is not only based upon mutual attraction but also upon mutual disclosure. One cannot reveal one's deepest thoughts, fears, and dreams if one has been fleeing from introspection and intimacy from an early age. These children will seek those who make few demands on their psyche. Their choice of a mate will be one given to superficial compatibility who will be content pursuing normalcy with the same single-mindedness as Ann.

Material possessions with the right labels and styles will take on paramount importance, for these are all the emblems of the super normal life. Any deviance or lack of normalcy in their children will be denied, overlooked, or swept under the bumpy rug where all other hints of irregularity are carefully hidden.

If emotional isolation removes the Lost Child from the family ring, physical illness brings her back. It is as if her body seeks the support and attention and nurturing that her mind does not allow her to pursue. Allergies, asthma, earaches, stomachaches, fatigue, sleep disorders–the body driving the lost child back to the parent for emotional closeness and intimacy, perhaps in the form of seeking medical help, administering medicine, or even rocking her to sleep or sitting up with her throughout the night.

Perhaps more than any of the other family members the Lost Chid remains lost, psychologically driven from the nest sooner and perhaps more prematurely than the rest, although she may physically stay around longer than the Hero or the Scapegoat. She of all family members will not discuss the problem and by pretending that it does not exist, she also ***enables*** the drinking to continue with impunity.

Concerning such bizarre family configurations, who is to say which child is the most profoundly hurt? The most abused? The most stigmatized? The most driven? Which child will most probably be immune from assistance or future counseling? Which child will feverishly chase the illusion of normalcy all her life, as if in some retroactive way she will remake her childhood and will have been the All-American girl from the All-American family–mainstream, normal, just like all the other kids on the block?

THE MASCOT

Being the youngest in any family is problematic; being the youngest in a Jellinek's disease family sets one on a course of behavior that may immobilize or stunt emotional growth for many years.

The behavioral slots of good, bad, and sick are taken. What is left? What is needed? The Clown, the Mascot, the Sarah Bernhardt. And these, as the other roles, may be held by either a girl or a boy.

Life has grown heavy, nasty, even hateful for the family. The entire family, one way or another, has been sucked into the whirlpool of alcoholism and its members are struggling for their sanity. Enter Patty, the youngest–lighthearted, funny, free of the hysteria the others live with. Dear Patty, skipping in right on time, providing just the right amount of comic relief so that they can go on.

By the time the youngest child arrives, the family's energy is gone. The attention and discipline that the older ones received when they were young has been spent. Both parents are older and as drug dependency consumes the time and energy of both the Dependent and the Enabler, there is little left for parenting.

Things that were important when Margaret was young–a bed made, a good report card, an orderly meal–these things pale in light of the crisis that flames daily. The older children become Patty's parents and Patty feels that everyone is her boss, yet there is no one to take responsibility for her. There is much to do in an alcoholic family: Family members must carry out their roles so that the dependent can continue drinking, while all along seeing to their own survival and maintaining their own illusions of control.

Patty was born into the family when these roles were already well established, yet she, too, has a right to be there and deserves her full share of the attention that Margaret is attracting by being so wonderful, that Michael gets by his hostile behavior, that Ann receives because of her asthma.

Mascots can do it by making people laugh and forget their problems. They help them remember when they were all younger and free and happy. And when the Mascot receives this kind of attention, it costs little to the family, much less than the Scapegoat or the Sick Child demands. All they have to do is laugh.

But the family has greatly deteriorated. Frank is drinking daily, staying out nights, acting violent, obscene, dangerous all the time. Kit is taking Valium and is beginning to drink. Pops is depressed and rarely comes downstairs. Margaret is making plans to save the world–she has one foot out the door already–and Michael is getting worse. Ann is in a world of her own and emerges for meals and medicine.

Patty pulls them all together, although it is only momentary. Things roll off her back and nothing can touch her, for like the court jester, she is turning somersaults and cartwheels and juggling balls and making funny faces and singing crazy songs and the world loves her.

She doesn't do well in school and the nuns are complaining that Patty isn't working up to her potential. But if the truth be known, they aren't too worried, either, because she has such personality and will always get by. Margaret has taken care of the accomplishing for the family and besides, when Frank is sober, he tells Patty not to work too hard because boys don't like girls who are too smart.

Kit enjoys the flash of levity that her youngest brings but she feels somewhat guilty about school. She simply doesn't have the energy to clamp down on her the way she did on Margaret and Michael. Kit mentions to the doctor that Patty is always fidgeting, daydreaming, and can't concentrate on her work.

The doctor puts Patty on Ritalin, a nerve calmer that works in some wonderful, mysterious way to help her concentrate, sit still, stop fidgeting. The doctor told Kit that it was safe and that in no way would Patty become hooked. True, it is a stimulant, like an amphetamine, an upper, but only for adults who are depressed.

Kit did not tell the doctor that her husband had Jellinek's disease, and Patty certainly did not tell. Kit did not tell the doctor that she herself was on 20 to 40 mgs. of Valium every day and was beginning to enjoy a few glasses of Chablis in the late afternoon, when all hell often let loose. She didn't tell the doctor that Michael was smoking pot and drinking. She didn't tell the doctor that Pops was on 40 mgs. of Elavil for his depression. And the doctor didn't ask.

Nor did he tell her that over a period of time, Patty might develop a tolerance for the drug. That means that her body would become accustomed to it and would need more to get the same therapeutic effect. That also means that she would probably become dependent upon it and would have to be taken off it slowly so that she would not become depressed or erratic in her behavior.

Nor did he tell her that the ***Physician's Drug Manual*** warns against administering this drug to children "where there is a history of drug dependency or alcoholism." He did not ask whether there was any family history of addiction. He had no reason to. The Kellys seemed to be just an ordinary family. So Patty the Clown is put on Ritalin, adding to the family's chemical dependency.

Patty is not taken seriously, even when she wants to be. And because others do not take her seriously, she does not take herself seriously. She develops a nervous laugh that releases tension and helps others laugh along with her.

But she also laughs to cover up deep and scary feelings that clowns aren't supposed to have. And sometimes when she is laughing really hard, she starts to cry and that frightens her even more.

People grow to expect Patty to laugh and the neighbors call her "Giggles." She wears a smile on her face all the time and smiles even when she knows that it isn't the time to smile. She just can't help it. When the teacher scolds her, she smiles; then she is accused of being bold and not caring. She cares deeply, but she just doesn't know how to show it.

Patty is as locked into her role as the rest of the family. Patty's clowning and giggling and mirth demonstrate to the world that the Kellys are a fun-loving, happy family, which they want to believe themselves. Are things really that bad if they could have such a bundle of sunshine in their midst? Are they all just overreacting, making much of nothing.

In her own little way, Patty is enabling her father's disease to progress with further impunity. Like Margaret with her success, like Michael with his antisocial behavior, like Ann with her asthma, Patty draws the focus away from the agony the family is in and helps them to pretend that all is well.

CHILD ABUSE

There are 28.6 million American children who live with a mother and/or father who drinks. This is the central fact of their young lives. These children are abused every day of their lives.

This abuse may take the form of physical violence or sexual assault. This abuse may be the constant bombardment of their mind and soul with the behavior of a drunken parent.

How many kids tiptoe around their homes, fearing to wake the grizzly bear, and then hop on their bikes with a toss of their head so no one will suspect what goes on?

Some family problem specialists categorize those children as being in double jeopardy who 1) live in alcoholic homes and 2) experience child abuse. All children who live in alcoholic homes are abused. There are no children in a home where a parent suffers from Jellinek's disease who are not abused.

According to a 1990 study by the Children of Alcoholics Foundation, the total health care cost for a child of an alcoholic is 32% higher, with higher hospital costs and longer hospital stays. A 1991 article in the American Journal of Diseases of Children describes the failure of pediatricians to recognize family alcohol-related problems. At the Johns Hopkins Children's Center in Baltimore, only 1 out of 22 children from homes with alcohol-related problems was properly identified by attending physicians.

There may be child abuse without alcoholism, but there is no alcoholism without child abuse.

Besides those younger children, there are the millions upon millions of young adults who no longer live at home, the young and middle-aged who are raising families of their own, the elderly–all of whom have experienced the violence of living with an alcoholic parent when they were young–and it is safe to say that many millions of Americans of all ages bear within themselves the lesions of their childhood.

Violence comes in many shapes:

- "My father used me for a punching bag."
- "She used to touch me when she thought I was asleep."
- "He was a vegetable . . . We called him `The Vegetable'. . He just sat and drank . . . He was a vegetable."
- "I'd sit in school and get diarrhea because I knew he'd be home and they'd be fighting."
- "I could never bring anyone home. She'd be passed out. Or if she was awake, she'd be nasty."
- "He'd say we'd go somewhere–to a game or out for dinner–and then he wouldn't come home. I'd be excited, but he wouldn't come home. I stopped hoping.
- "I'd hear them fighting and know that he was hitting her. I couldn't stop him. I just held my little sister so she wouldn't be afraid. I'd put my hands over her ears so she wouldn't hear. But I'd hear.

The essence of child abuse is that the integrity and innocence of a child are assaulted by the very person or persons charged with his care.

A child's integrity means that the child is safe, that his body and mind and soul's life are nurtured, that he grows neither too fast nor too slow, that he understands trust and laughter and knows that there are a few people in the world who truly care. It means that he is whole and that gaping wounds are not inflicted on his body, his mind, his soul.

A child's innocence means that he is introduced to the world only when he is ready and that the world, with its guilt and violence and shame, is not allowed to assault him too early, for he is protected. He is treasured, not beaten and burned and raped. He sleeps quietly and hears no parents shouting beyond his walls.

Adults can abuse a child in many ways. They can do it overtly, like striking him or putting his hand on a stove. They can do it passively, like not feeding or bathing him. They can do it sexually, like touching his body or making him touch theirs. They can do it insidiously, like being a vegetable or breaking promises or being nasty and unpredictable.

Child abuse means the sure, steady numbing of young and tender emotions. It means that a child has no time for dreams, only nightmares, and that the future is only going to get worse.

Child abuse means that a young girl or boy learns that the world is basically ugly and violent and that there is really no one to trust. Only yourself. Keep people at a distance and they can't hurt you.

They learn embarrassment, then shame, and finally guilt. They learn to split the world into good and bad with no maybes; black and white with no grays. To be abused as a child means to live in a state of chronic shock and to learn a set way of behaving that keeps the shock level bearable.

The millions of children who presently live in an alcoholic home and the millions of adults who grew up in an alcoholic home are victims of child abuse, regardless of the type or level or degree to which they were assaulted.

Child abuse is as much a part of Jellinek's disease as drinking and blackouts and hangovers. Perhaps more so, because one can stop drinking; health can be restored. Or one dies from drinking and that is the end.

But a child remembers. As he grows and enters his own adulthood, he bears memories that can stay fresh and painful as long as he lives. Unless he does his work to get better.

Very few children of alcoholics receive treatment; estimates are about 5%. It is said that these children show the same anxieties, depression, and confusion as men who fought in a war. And 95 out of every 100 of these children are thrown out into the world with no help, no hope, no healing.

Patty. Michael. Ann. Margaret. Abused kids. Maybe someone, somewhere will look beyond the veneers and see a boy or girl doing his or her very best to cope with something they do not understand. Maybe a teacher or a neighbor or a priest or a doctor will reach out a hand, touch their hurting souls, and draw them out of their hurt into their healing.

Chapter Seven

Codependency: A Whole Lotta Holes

Gotta whole lotta holes in my life
If you stack 'em all together
You can fall through 'em forever.
Kathy Mattea

The red buttons flashed on the phone - line 6, line 3, line 4. Call waiting, No, Mr. Norris was still not in, would you like to leave a message, line 12, busy signal, another call.

Rita took another little bite out of the inside of her mouth. Line 8 flashed. Can I help you? Can I help you? Of course I can help you . . . that's the only thing I can do . . . the only thing I have ever have done. She looked at the stained note from Peter that she had stuck under the waxy rose paperweight. He hadn't even bothered to use a pen. "Dear Mom. I need some help. I'll be sure to pay you back as soon as I can. Some guys owe me money and I'll give it to you then. Love. Peter."

Another line flashed and Rita felt the ropes tighten across her chest. The boss opened his office door and Rita smiled her best I've-got-everything-under-control smile. He nodded severely and made his way to the coffee pot. Black sludge covered the bottom of the pot. He slammed the pot back onto the heating plate and, wounded, hurried back into his office.

Rita's stomach knotted. She inhaled quick and shallow little puffs of air as she put the phones on automatic pilot and ran to make fresh coffee. No one ever said she was responsible for making coffee, but everyone just expected Rita to do it.

The coffee was baked in, so Rita had to dig it out with her nails. If she were careful, she could loosen the sides and it would come out in nice, thin layers of black lace. Rita felt light-headed as she squeezed her hand through the narrow neck of the coffee pot to begin her delicate task.

Ever so carefully, she scrubbed the pot with hot suds and ran the cold water to make fresh coffee. As she began filling the scooper with fresh coffee, the boss walked past her with his head down. He was going downstairs to buy himself coffee from the luncheonette on the ground floor. He'd be in a bad mood for the rest of the day and it was all Rita's fault. His secretary shot Rita a dirty look.

That was the story of her life. Bad stuff was always happening and it was always her fault. Always. She had trained herself to be careful, to check and double-check, not to let stuff fall through the cracks. How could she have ever forgotten the coffee? It was so unlike her. Rita, the double-checker-upper, just didn't let things like that happen.

Rita was losing it. She found herself listening to the race of her heart as she felt the ropes grow ever so tight across her chest. She noticed her hands and how they would quiver and how she had to steady them in her lap when she felt someone was looking at them. She was eating all the time and couldn't face the doctor after she had promised him for the ninth time that she would cut out the salt and fat. Rita just ate all the more.

Last evening when she couldn't sleep, she flipped on the TV and Jay Leno had a guest who kept saying, "Get a life!". Rita stared at the TV. She didn't know what they were talking about so she poured herself a bowl of grape-nuts.

Get a life? Whose life? She had been trained not to think about herself, to take care of others, to be sure that everyone around her was ok and that somehow, she would be ok if they were ok. That was how it worked. But she ended up chewing off the ends of everyone else's life and somehow, she had no taste for her own.

If she lined up all the people she had tried to take care of in her life, they'd fill a football field. First it was her mother and the pills; her father and his rages at the pills; her aunts who came to criticize; Emily, Albert, and William, the little kids who needed protection from the pills and the rages; her grandmother who worried and fretted about all of them and who needed to be lied to.

Then there were her five miscarriages. Rita even found herself telling her doctor that it was ok, that she knew he had done his best, that she must not be meant to have children.

When Ed began shoving and punching her, Rita felt she had it coming. She couldn't carry his children. He had his frustrations at work and with his mother. He had hit her before they were married, but he always seemed so sorry and resolved never to do it again. It made him feel better and they always got closer after one of his fights/pouts/make-up sessions. It wasn't all that bad, not compared to what a lot of other people had to put up with. He just needed to let off steam and she was his wife. He could have been worse.

The other women were another thing, but Ed just seemed to need them. Rita understood and, of course, she forgave. She was lucky just to have him. If Rita had been married to herself, she would have played around. It could have been worse.

She was finally able to have a son and they called him Peter. He treated Rita like his father did. Rita didn't blame him. She deserved what she got.

When Ed finally left, Peter was all she had left and she would do whatever she had to do to make his life happy. Regardless of what it cost. If Peter was happy, then she would be happy.

Rita had no life. She only had the lives of other people: her mother and father; her brothers and sister; her aunts and grandmother; Ed and Peter; the people in her prayer group; the people she worked with; the once-a-week bridge group; all the people she had collected in her 57 years who reflected back to her who she was. She needed them more than they needed her. When they were ok, she was ok; when they hurt, she hurt; if they did not exist, she did not exist.

Rita sat in the dark, the blue glow of the television filling the room. Her jaws ached as she frantically chewed the hard pellets of cereal, trying to fill that hunger deeper than any food could reach. Get a life. Get a life. She didn't understand what they were talking about. Her hand trembled as she reached for the remote to silence the ideas that she could not afford to entertain. The picture faded and Rita closed her eyes, listening only to the tired thump of her heart as it pounded against her chest.

CODEPENDENCY: A DISEASE OF ITS OWN

Experts say that 96% of the American population are codependent. Our institutions, our organizations, our families are rampant with Codependency. It has been described by some as the spiritual illness of our time and by others as simply an empty hoax by pop psychologists, the cure for 20th century snake-bite.

Despite innumerable titles on this subject, the client still asks her therapist when and where and how is she being codependent. Or if she is codependent at all. Others rest secure that they could never be codependent because their fathers never drank. Questions abound. The answers tend to be shopping lists of codependent behavior or so woven with psychoanalytical theory that we feel that the questions are better left unasked.

THE HISTORY OF CODEPENDENCY

Alcoholics Anonymous was founded in 1935. In those early days, most of the designated drinkers were men. The women stayed at home with the kids, suffering.

A short time later, Al-anon was founded by the wives of the men who founded A.A. They wisely felt that they had to have their own program of healing, one separate from the alcoholic.

More and more people grew to understand alcoholism not simply as an individual problem, but as a ***family disease***, since all the members of the family were affected. However, despite this extension of language, for all practical purposes, the alcoholically impaired would either die or receive treatment and begin a life of sobriety. The spouse and children, not appearing as bad as the alcoholic, were expected to snap out of it and to be grateful that he finally got some help. Think of all the people who were still drinking. He, at least, had stopped.

But the family was left with deep ruts in the winter of their psyches. Hurt, rage, guilt, shame, brokenness, anxiety, depression, their own addictions and their own unhealthy ways of coping. The spring rains of the alcoholic's merciful death or miraculous recovery did not have the power to fill in the ruts; sometimes it only made it worse.

To exacerbate the woundedness of the family, experts started calling them the enablers, the ones who enabled or made it easy for the alcoholic to drink. The family wounds were gouged more deeply.

However, in most families, people did what they had to do to get along and to exist despite the presence of active alcoholism. The wife got an extra job. The kids did extra well in school or ran away. The grandfather wrote an extra check, the neighbors plowed the snow, and the teachers made allowances. Everyone had to pick up the slack and keep the family moving as best as it could. Yet they were branded as the enablers, as if they all should have gone on strike until the alcoholic came to his senses.

Lou, the wife of a violent, moody alcoholic who could not hold down a job, clipped coupons, baby-sat, stitched clothes over and over for her three boys and saw to it they played sports, got jobs, stayed in school. She worked hard to hold the family together while caring for her mother with Altzheimer's. Enraged at being called an enabler, she screamed, "What did I do to deserve that on top of all the hell I've been through? Did I pour it down his throat? What else could I have done?"

Such families have been called dysfunctional. But they did function - they went to the store, school, church, the bank. Some families ***functioned*** quite well and some not so well, but they all were in distress, in agony, in pain most of the time.

Because they themselves showed many of the signs of active alcoholism – fears, black-outs, rages, unpredictability, other addictions – they were called "co-alcoholics", like the co-pilots who fly beside the pilot and crash with him when he goes down. This term was used in the late 70's.

However, the term "co-alcoholic" was short-lived and in the early 80's, it was extended to codependent, meaning anyone who was a "co" to one suffering from any chemical dependency whatsoever. In those early days of the use of this term, it was still understood to be intrinsically connected with drugs or alcoholism.

In the 90's, as we studied the codependent's life, thoughts, feelings, actions, we observed a universal pattern that was not unique to alcoholism. People who lived with depression, poverty, instability, religiosity, incest, and the million other ways that families suffer simply develop ways to survive and minimize the pain. There is no choice. We saw that people act and feel and live in ways that are similar to the way that alcoholic families live. And we called it Codependency.

Terry Kellogg in ***Broken Toys, Broken Dreams*** lists the adult symptoms of Codependency that flow from unresolved, untreated childhood abuse:

- relationship problems: clinging, abuse, inability for intimacy, enmeshing
- physical ailments: arthritis, allergies, stress, headaches
- boundary issues: inability to set limits, doing for others what we will not do for ourselves
- identity problems: absence of self-awareness, goals
- shame and guilt behaviors: belief in our own worthlessness and badness
- seeking external validation: letting others define us to ourselves and to others
- caretaking, enabling: removing harmful consequences from the behavior of others.
- intensity issues: needing excitement, creating a crisis and chaos, feeling alive only when things around us are falling apart
- anxiety: fears, hyper-vigilance, phobias which control our lives
- low self-esteem: we feel flawed
- hyper-cautious: timid, refusing to take risks
- colluding: enabling violence, offending behaviors
- victim role: feeling as if we have no choices
- offending behaviors: hurting others, violating boundaries
- passive aggressive: not expressing anger directly, but in covert ways, cynical, sarcastic, withdrawn
- being stuck: acting helpless so others take care of us
- sainthood/martyrdom: being perfectionistic, arrogant
- tolerance breaks: tantrums, falling apart
- problem orientation: life is a problem to be solved
- obsessiveness: ruminating, spinning thinking
- pseudo maturity: pretending independence and experience
- emotional pain: depression, constant hurting

ROOTS OF CODEPENDENCY

A child comes into the world whole. BodyMindSpirit are one. If the child is wisely nurtured, properly nourished, consistently protected, he will grow in age and strength and knowledge and become the mature person he was meant to be.

However, many parents, wounded by their own childhood or addictions, are unable to provide for the physical or emotional needs of the child and do not adequately protect her from whatever is present in the family that has the potential to wound.

The child is not free to remain a child and stay with the natural rhythms of growing from girlhood into womanhood. Critical stages of growth will be leaped over in the rush to adulthood: Forever she remains the Adult Child, caught in that twilight zone of inexperienced life, of bearing burdens too heavy, of never really knowing what childhood was and what adulthood truly is.

The classic response for someone caught in a situation he can not handle is fight or flight. However, the child in such families is too small to fight and too young to flee; he must stay. But he improvises a way to both stay and leave: the child splits - his body stays but his spirit leaves. In Hakomi therapy language, the child sends her spirit into exile, because she knows it is not safe for her spirit to remain.

It is not safe to remain whole, connected with feelings, with the natural flow of pain and joy, to plunge headlong into the excitement of life. She seems to be there, but on a more profound level, she is split in two like a tree struck by lightening.

Look at the faces of children in Somalia, Rumania, Iraq, El Salvador. The wizened eyes stare like the eyes of a fish. They have wisely sent their spirits away, for life is not safe.

This splitting is called ***dissociating***, the opposite of associating, or coming together. If the dissociation is severe, the child actually develops other personalities, as in the famous cases of Eve, Billy, and Sybil. When the boy or girl is severely and repeatedly abused, the split deepens and widens and other personalities are created to carry the abuse and to protect the individual from total annihilation.

This split is deep and profound: The child disowns or divorces her emotions from herself. This essential wrenching apart is called the ***Codependency Split***.

As the spirit leaves, there remains only a wounded child, seeking safety like a dying animal, hiding herself deep in the woods so she can shield herself from more pain or wait for death with peace and dignity. Knowing, however, that she cannot allow these open wounds to be exposed, she develops strategies to survive, to deflect her attention from herself, to lose her outer self so her deeper, truer self will not die. These survival strategies are what keep her alive.

These strategies are another name for ***Codependency***.

A PSYCHOLOGICAL/SPIRITUAL PERSPECTIVE

The central task of life is to become an individual person while connecting to others. Aloneness and togetherness. The very words are replete with the tension implied in the task. What is too much aloneness? Too much connection? When am I too close or too, too far from others? How can I stay connected, yet have my own self? At what point do I begin to disappear into another? At what point do I begin to disappear because there is no one around me?

Beginning with the bloody cutting of the cord at birth, these issues need to be resolved over and over again. The two-year-old, running from his mother at a mall; the 5-year-old, sick each morning so she doesn't have to go to school; the 11 year old, packing up to run away; the 16 year old, failing his driving exam: each attempting to resolve the alone/together paradox.

The success of this delicate task depends on how safe and secure we feel - we don't sail onto the high seas in a leaky boat. We feel safe and secure if we have had parents or guardians to protect us, to shield us, to be there so the world doesn't seem so big.

In families where parents themselves have never been safe and have never had the protection that they needed, where abuse, addiction and pain have been handed down with the family photo album, where no one's needs were acknowledged, let alone met, then the child is not invited to begin her life's work of being separate/being connected. There is no safety net beneath her and she cannot venture forth; it is too dangerous. And how tragic, for these issues are not resolved without mistakes, without freedom to explore and to touch the limits of freedom without an unspoken contract that the base from which she ventures out will not move on her, let alone turn on her if she doesn't do it right.

THE MANY FACES OF CODEPENDENCY

The essential element of Codependency is that we seek meaning and value from people, processes and substances outside of ourselves because we are not at home to selves. Our spirit has been sent away so we replace ourselves with a stand-in. Some of the signs of Codependency are if you:

- are an Adult Child
- rage
- fear abandonment
- neglect yourself
- feel God can't be trusted
- can't relate
- are always on your toes
- feel that the other shoe is about to drop
- guess at what normal is
- let others define you
- look for a quick-fix
- feel like a victim
- don't know when to quit
- listen to everyone's problems
- keep your own problems to yourself
- chase inner ghosts
- have no boundaries
- tell all
- ride an emotional roller-coaster
- get involved in sick relationships
- can't stop thinking in circles
- put yourself last
- take abuse
- can't focus your mind
- come from a distressed family

The exquisite pain of Codependency is that the split within us grows deeper and deeper. Our spirit has been in exile so long that we are strangers even to ourselves and the pretend self we drag around is devoid of our essence, like a car running on fumes rather than a full tank of gas.

The separation/connection task is never successfully accomplished, so we do not truly develop into a rich, abundant maturity but become hostage in that never-never land between adulthood and childhood. We become Adult Children. We are little kids playing dress-up.

THE ALCOHOLIC AND CODEPENDENCY

Unresolved Codependency/Adult child issues are perhaps the single most important block to a peaceful, contented, comfortable sobriety. Codependency keeps shame on a low boil, bubbling away even the most courageous attempts to elevate our feelings of self-worth. Shame and Codependency are set-ups for the Dry Drunk, for Relapse, for feeling crazed without the relief of a drink.

Liz, a 63 year-old factory worker, had maintained a 37-year sobriety filled with rage, an inability to pray, with no real peace. Life had abused her; she could only relate to her family and few friends by abusing them.

In great torment and on the verge of picking up a drink, Liz went to a therapist who herself was recovering from Jellinek's disease and Adult Child issues. Liz began to attend Adult Children Of Alcoholics together with her AA meetings.

She started to get better. Her humor lost the edge and became gentle; her prayer was less rote and was filled with peace and surrender; she began to live in her wisdom and not in her fear.

"If only I had dealt with this other stuff earlier in my sobriety, it could have been so much easier, so much easier," she says with a smile. I was an abused kid - what did I know? Its all part of the same package, somehow. Anyhow, I don't do abuse no more. I don't take it and I don't give it out. No more!"

RECOVERY FROM CODEPENDENCY/ADULT CHILD ISSUES

The surest, quickest and most gentle way to begin this work is to invite the spirit of our Inner Child back to ourselves and to begin to nourish that Little Girl or Little Boy who learned at an early age that life was not safe, but extremely dangerous.

To begin to listen to our Inner Child who is the keeper of our dreams. To trust the wisdom of our Inner Child as she tells us when we are being abused, when we need help, when we need to be alone or with others.

To begin to trust our feelings and not to dodge them through addictions, depression, rescuing and controlling others. And to begin to feel that maybe its even okay to have a little fun.

Chapter Eight

Intervention: Getting the Job Done

One thing I know, that, whereas I was blind, now I see.
JOHN: 9:25

As the brass doors slowly opened, the art deco filigree disappeared in the slot between the elevator and the wall. Leslie walked through the lobby, her burgundy briefcase hitting the fern as she hurried to her cab.

The doorman tipped his hat and held the door. As Leslie headed toward the waiting cab, a thin young man with red shorts and a red headband ran in front of her, knocking her briefcase to the pavement. "Goddamn joggers!" she muttered to herself as the doorman picked up her briefcase, opened the door of the cab, and smiled apologetically. Leslie nodded to the doorman. He closed the door and the cab pulled out, heading south on Central Park West to Sixty-fifth. The driver turned east on Sixty-fifth through Central Park.

An early October breeze brought the scent of changing oaks and elms and hawthorn berries from the park. It was a kaleidoscope of burnt orange and burgundy with patches of green that refused to yield to the dying time of autumn.

Leslie closed her eyes, bit the inside of her cheek, and gripped the handle of her briefcase. Christ Almighty, another day like this . . .. In a flash, she saw herself jumping out of her skin, her spirit free at last, floating over the tops of the trees, caressing the leaves as they touched her. Her old self left in the backseat of the cab, imprisoned in her charcoal gray suit and her crimson hysteria.

Jesus Christ, I'm losing my goddamn mind, my goddamn thirty-five year-old mind. She twirled the tiger's eye ring around her finger, a Captain Queeg spinning a tenuous sanity. The cab turned south onto Fifth Avenue and as it made its morning run past the elegant apartments and duplexes overlooking the park, every muscle and nerve in Leslie's body cried out for comfort.

She pressed her head against the window and tried to hold back the tears that came so often. Fancy shops, and hotels blurred as she pressed a tissue to her eyes to stop the flow of mascara. Suddenly, she remembered the Valium in her purse and a wave of anticipated relief swept over her. Leslie placed the small yellow tablet in her mouth and smiled as she swallowed it.

Leslie had worked out a system: Pills for the day and booze for the night. She could not be sitting at her desk with a bottle at her feet. The pills were so discreet and if she really got in a jam, she'd double up on them.

It was socially acceptable to have alcohol on your breath after lunch, especially if you were entertaining a client, but not before. And she had to get through the morning.

Despite her system, Leslie was getting careless taking a pill right before lunch and then drinking. Sometimes she'd fall asleep at her desk after lunch and she was beginning to smell of booze all the time, even in the morning.

Thoughts of her 11-year-old daughter continued to haunt her. Leslie could not avoid the blazing eyes and quivering lips that were becoming a fixed part of Jennifer's expression.

Leslie knew that Jennifer was growing to hate her. She would catch Jennifer looking in the medicine cabinet at her prescriptions: Valium, Dalmane, Elavil, Percodan. And when Jennifer would ask her about them, Leslie would smile weakly and explain, "Just trying to smooth out the wrinkles, Sweetheart."

Leslie knew that life was no better for Jennifer since the divorce. She thought everything would be different, even better, but things were far worse.

Leslie used to take long walks with Jennifer and go to movies and shop. Jennifer would sit on the top of the toilet when Leslie was taking a bath and they would talk "girl talk" about everything from nail polish and shaving legs to boys and having babies.

They shared little now. Even when Leslie was home, she wasn't there. Not really. Leslie was never home before seven, and it was usually closer to ten. Leslie would be drunk and laughing loudly or crying. And on the rare evening that she was not drunk, she had little to say to Jennifer.

Leslie was growing to hate the kid for just being around, then she hated herself for these feelings. She was not interested in her daughter's schoolwork, her friends, her plans for the future, her life.

Whenever Jennifer had asked for more time or attention from her mother, Leslie tore into her: Who was going to take care of the clients, who was going to pay the rent or put food on the table, how could she do everything, wasn't Jennifer old enough to take responsibility for herself. Then the attacks would begin on Jennifer's father. Leslie would always win because Jennifer could not compete with her mother in a fight or in anything, so she would slip out the door as Leslie made herself another drink.

What would Leslie do without her Valium, the little magic that would smooth out the jagged edges when she was unable to have a drink? In just a few minutes, she'd be ready to handle anything, ready to cope, ready to stand on her head if she had to.

How did this all happen? It all started out so well and so promising. Leslie was "young, gifted, and black." She had the world at her feet, and now after ten years of analysis, she was going nowhere, fast. Maybe another doctor.

That seemed to be her pattern: two or three years with one psychiatrist, then another. They could not get off the race issue–the rage and impotency she ought to feel at being a black woman, discriminated against, castrating all the black males in her life, the devastating hidden effects of two hundred years of slavery washing up on the shores of her psyche.

The cab headed downtown, past the Plaza, St. Patrick's, Rockefeller Center. What a far cry from Michigan, Leslie thought. I was young, gifted, and black. Now I'm dried up, like a raisin in the sun. A colored girl at the end of the rainbow. This colored girl now goes to Park Avenue psychiatrists, one after the other, trying to find out what the hell is the matter with her. God Almighty, what is the matter with me? I feel like I'm coming apart at the seams.

Leslie was the oldest of three daughters. The Jordan family was a quiet, loving family, active in their church, in the school. For thirty-five years, Leslie's mother was an aide at the hospital and her father was a city worker. The three Jordan girls had all excelled in school and Leslie's sister was the first woman from their town to be admitted to law school in the early seventies.

Their grade school had been predominantly black, with a few whites. When she got to high school, Leslie competed with everyone and made excellent grades. Her freshman English teacher took a liking to her and encouraged her to go beyond the small Michigan town. This was the north in the late sixties and Leslie was smart and not afraid to work hard. Her family was behind her and was willing to make any sacrifice to see that she got ahead.

After high school, it was on to Ann Arbor on full scholarship. She majored in business and communications, and after four years, she won another scholarship, to the Columbia School of Journalism. She was smitten by New York and after graduation, she landed a copywriting job with a progressive ad agency.

Leslie would never forget that first Christmas back home after she was a working woman. Her parents and sisters met the train as it pulled into the small station. She would always remember the look on their faces, the look of sheer and exquisite pride that their Leslie was going to be Somebody. Someday.

And all their friends had come to the small house to welcome her home and to share in their pride. They brought their own daughters, hoping that some of Leslie would rub off on them. She was young, gifted, and black and it was a new world, a big world, and anyone could make it, if they were willing to work hard and get along with people.

If they could only see her now. All the digging by the psychiatrists came up with nothing. She was simply falling apart and needed to drink and take pills to stay together. There must be a reason, but they couldn't find it. Thousands and thousands of dollars later, and all they could say was it was because of the color of her skin.

How she wanted to bring them home and show them that things were beautiful in Michigan. Yes, of course, there were hard times. There was little money, but they all worked hard and loved and supported each other. They weren't rich, but neither were most people. The home was clean and simple, and out back her father grew his vegetables and rows and rows of nasturtiums and dahlias and begonias. And inside, it was always filled with flowers and books and music.

She wanted to bring them home and say, "It's simple, but it's lovely, isn't it? Just please tell me what's the matter with me now!" She wanted to introduce them to her parents, to her teachers, to her minister who was as proud of her as if she were his own daughter.

She wanted to take her psychiatrists by the hand and walk them around and say, "You tell me what's the matter. It can't be my people. It can't be my town. You tell me what is the matter with me."

She wasn't stupid. She wasn't lying. She did not really feel that the psychiatrists were right when they blamed her problems on her being a black woman. She had been nearing the top of her profession before she started to fall apart. She had been the right person at the right time, and if the truth be known, she probably wouldn't have gotten as far and as fast if she had been white or if she had been a man.

True, the marriage had fallen apart, but so did the marriages of most of her friends. Leon, her husband, was the right one for her when they met, but they seemed to grow in different ways and soon they had little in common.

They were bored. Careers and marriages didn't mix, and neither was willing to put the energy into saving their marriage. She still had some things to work out about Leon, some deep and hurtful things, but she couldn't get a handle on them. Everybody has marriage problems to work out and it just didn't seem right to blame it all on the fact that she was a successful black woman.

"I'm also a person," she wanted to scream back at them, "and goddamn it, can't you help me? I'm a person, a flesh-and-blood human being who is going crazy! Why can't you help me? I'm just Leslie, a person, not Leslie, a statistic. My skin is black, but my nerves are human-colored and please, Doctor, I'm losing my mind. Can't you please help me?"

Inevitably, the prescription pad would come out of the desk drawer and the solution to all her problems would be scribbled before her. They simply could not or would not deal with whatever it was that was driving her to the brink.

Oh, to be young, gifted, and black. I'm almost middle-aged, losing my mind, my job, my daughter. Please, Dear God, can't someone help me? I don't know what's the matter. I really don't know, but I can't stand it much longer.

The cab turned left onto Forty-eighth and stopped at Madison Avenue. The meter registered $7.25. She threw a $10 bill onto the front seat, slammed the door, and hurried into the building. She was late, thirty-five minutes, but everything was OK. The Valium was kicking in and she was smoothing out. She could make it until lunch, until she got a drink.

As Leslie made her way into the office, her secretary told her that there was a meeting in Mr. Turner's office and that he would like her to come when she arrived. Bud Turner was Leslie's immediate supervisor, a man who was being groomed to take over the vice presidency for marketing. Leslie was in line for Turner's job.

Turner's secretary announced Leslie's arrival, and Bud Turner met her at the door of his office. Seated at an oval table in the corner of his office was Mildred Walsh from the personnel department. She greeted Leslie warmly and the three took a seat at the table.

Turner stated that although Leslie was not due for her annual review of work, a review was in order and, because of special considerations, he had requested Ms. Walsh's assistance. He then presented a picture of deteriorating work: Three of Leslie's accounts had been lost to the company because of her neglect; she had been assigned no new accounts for nine months; fellow employees did not want to work with her; she had contributed nothing to accounts shared with others.

He then presented her with a documented record of her time and attendance: Frequent absenteeism on Mondays and Friday afternoons; late arrivals and early departures; extended coffee breaks and extended lunches; unexplained absences in the middle of the day.

Leslie turned to Mildred Walsh for support. Girls against the boys. Mildred continued to follow the documentation before her as Turner continued. If it weren't for the Valium, Leslie would be out the window.

As if that weren't enough, Turner then began to detail the specifics of her work performance: Deadlines not met; appointments not kept; sloppy, careless copy; rudeness and insensitivity to clients; complaints from secretaries and the art department.

Leslie held her face in her hands. She could not believe her ears. She had been so careful, so circumspect. How did they know what was wrong? The damn doctors didn't know. She herself didn't even know.

Turner closed the file, looked at Leslie, and said simply, "Leslie, we have reason to believe that you are dealing with alcoholism and with drug addiction. You have appeared in the office intoxicated on occasion and you frequently smell as if you are drinking."

"Your work has deteriorated to the point that we will have to let you go if something is not done about it. We don't want that to happen, Leslie, because you have been one of our most gifted, talented, hard-working people. We think you have a future here with us, Leslie, if you are willing to do something about your problem."

Mildred Walsh began speaking about the company's policy for treatment: There were places to go to get help ***if she wanted it***; insurance would cover the treatment; her job security and promotion possibilities in the future would not be jeopardized; the matter would be treated with complete confidentiality. There were others in the company, many of them in supervisory positions, who had received help for chemical addiction in various treatment centers nearby and as far away as Tucson. The average stay was approximately twenty-one to twenty-eight days. The recovery rate was about 75%.

Bud Turner and Mildred Walsh looked directly at Leslie. She looked at the table and then out the window. They continued to look at her.

"Do I have a choice?"

"It's treatment . . . Or you're out."

Tears filled her eyes as she looked at the two people who had finally confronted her. She began to cry, for her horrible secret was finally out in the open.

"And I thought no one knew," she whispered, "I didn't even know myself . . ."

INTERVENTION

What Bud Turner and Mildred Walsh did in making Leslie face the hard reality of her life is called intervention, the coming between the alcoholic and his disease to facilitate recovery.

Intervention is the logical step to be taken by those who love and care for the alcoholic. Once the nature of the disease and the magnitude of the denial are understood by others in the alcoholic's life, the logical outcome is for those caring and responsible people to step in, blow the whistle, and propel the afflicted individual into treatment.

Intervention means ***creating*** or ***recognizing a crisis*** in the alcoholic's life and then maximizing that crisis to get the Jellinek's disease victim into recovery. Intervention is a clearly planned process of confrontation with the alcoholic.

There are certain assumptions shared by those planning the intervention; there are definite, well-articulated steps to be followed prior to and at the time of intervention. There is a specific, tangible goal to be achieved within a specific time-frame.

ALTERNATIVES TO INTERVENTION

In the stories in this book, all the family members, however well-intentioned, stood between the individual with Jellinek's disease and his recovery. They were the well-meaning but ignorant buffers who prevented the alcoholic from accepting the consequences of his drinking.

In Chapter One, Paul avoided confrontation with Helen by working late, providing a housekeeper to look after her, allowing her the freedom to drink. He even carried her to bed so although she was drunk, she would be warm and safe.

In the narrative of Chapter Two, we saw and experienced Steve's crisis in detail. Rather than allow Steve to feel the consequences of his drinking, the family rescued him, bailing him out of school and out of his legal and social problems. In their protection of Steve and of their own image, they stood between him and his recovery.

Although misdirected and counterproductive, they were involved in action (reaction) that gave them the illusion of doing something, yet they were never conscious of the real damage their protective posture was doing.

In Chapter Four, the women in Jerry's life walked out and his supervisors fired him. They left him alone, missing many opportunities to get him into treatment.

In Chapters Five and Six, the entire Kelly family, from Pops on down to the youngest child, was so oriented that Frank Kelly, the father, had no need to stop drinking. He was protected, enabled, coddled–practically given a free ticket to destroy himself and his family.

THE "HITTING BOTTOM" FALLACY

A more subtle and yet more painful position a family may take is to stand and wait for the dependent person to "hit bottom," as if there were some magic floor to the bottomless well into which he had fallen. The terms "high bottom" and "low bottom" have frequently been used in the past to designate how far one must fall before coming to one's senses.

The major problem with this idea is that the family does not in fact stand by passively, peering over the edge of the well, waiting to hear the welcoming splash of water when the person with Jellinek's disease finally hits bottom. They are tumbling in there with him, perhaps falling faster than he is. And there are no bottoms in sight.

The Jellinek's disease sufferer will go to any length to drink and to continue drinking. He must. The dictates of his family, his business and social responsibilities, even his dreams, his ambitions, his goals become less and less imperative as his body's chemistry becomes the motivating factor for his actions.

Controls the non-alcoholic has on his behavior do not work for someone with Jellinek's disease; the cells of his body are in control.

To apply the Hitting Bottom Theory to the slow, tenacious workings of the alcoholic's body chemistry is to sit in a burning house–flames leaping from the walls, smoke curling from the basement, children screaming, beloved objects in ashes–and to wait before an hourglass, each little grain of sand falling to the bottom, before one calls the fire department. It makes no sense.

Waiting for the alcoholic to hit bottom is illogical if one comprehends the metabolic factors involved. It is irresponsible if one perceives the magnitude of destruction his drinking is having on him and on the many people in his life. It is unconscionable if one believes in the power of recovery.

As rescue has been proven to be counterproductive and waiting is suicide, ***intervening*** between the alcoholic and the progression of his disease is the one safe, responsible course of action that may cut through his denial and precipitate his recovery.

THE INTERVENTION PROCESS

The early steps to a successful intervention occur when a family member, frequently the spouse or an older child, seeks help for this purpose outside the family. Family members often seek help, but not necessarily with intervention in mind. In fact, some doctors and psychiatrists prefer other solutions that may actually delay treatment.

Help may be from a minister, a school social worker, an alcoholism counselor, a psychologist. Great care should be given that the right person is sought. The helping professional must be well informed as to the nature of Jellinek's disease and its effects on the family. The professional must either be trained in the techniques of family intervention or be willing to refer the family to one who is so trained.

Alcoholic treatment centers frequently have one or more counselors skilled in the process of intervention. Employee Assistance Program (EAP) counselors in business and industry are trained in intervention. The intervention for Leslie was conducted by the EAP counselor from the personnel department of the ad agency that employed Leslie and by her immediate supervisor.

Once the counselor and the prime family intervenor are established, the intervention group is chosen. The group members are those persons who are closest to the person with Jellinek's disease and who have been most effected by his drinking. This usually means family members, but it may include a business partner, a doctor, a friend or neighbor who is directly involved.

If this is a worksite intervention, it will include the individual's immediate supervisor and other members of management on levels above the sick person. An individual who may be extremely distraught over the drinking and whose emotional stability is unpredictable ought to be excluded from the intervention group.

SHARED ASSUMPTIONS ABOUT INTERVENTION

Once the group is selected, it meets with the intervention counselor. Prior to the actual preparation for intervention, certain critical assumptions must be held by all group members; if there are any members who do not wholeheartedly share these assumptions, they must be excluded because they will dilute the focus and energy of the group.

These assumptions are:

1. The Jellinek's disease victim is suffering from a ***bona fide disease*** that is killing him and is destroying his family.

2. ***Denial*** is a basic part of his disease; the purpose of the intervention is to pierce his denial so that he will see the reality of his disease and seek treatment.

3. Because Jellinek's disease is chronic and progressive, no goal other than that of ***total abstinence*** from alcohol and other mood-altering substances is acceptable.

4. Most importantly, all concerned must acknowledge that Jellinek's disease is the ***primary cause*** of the alcoholic's condition. Financial, marital, health, and other problems are the effects of untreated Jellinek's disease; they have not caused the drinking.

5. ***Treatment*** at a specific rehabilitation center is a must. Time has run out for trying it alone.

PREPARATION FOR THE INTERVENTION

Once it is certain that all members of the group are in agreement over the nature of the problem and the nature of the cure, actual preparation for the intervention may begin.

The first job that group members have is to prepare a written list of specific instances in which the behavior of the individual with Jellinek's disease either endangered life, caused embarrassment, or created other problems. The list must be specific as to time and place and must accurately describe the drunken ***behavior*** and its direct effect.

In a sense, the group is preparing evidence–cold, hard facts. Where there is uncertainty as to time or place, the group has to do its homework; the data must be accurate. The alcoholic is a master at covering herself and one sloppy bit of information will allow her to slip through the net and reaffirm her control of her drinking and will result in a loss of confidence by the group.

Generalizations are not effective because by this time she has heard them over and over. The evidence must be specific, unrefutable; the effect the drinking has on various members of the intervention group is obviously personal and subjective.

While the intervention group is presenting the effect of the alcoholic's behavior, it must be careful to avoid making moral judgments about this behavior. The intervention group is not a judge or jury; that will eventually be the role of the alcoholic herself. The group is the prosecuting attorney, presenting hard evidence in a non-judgmental, compelling way that will allow the weight of evidence to speak for itself.

THE TONE OF INTERVENTION

The person must be presented with the "burden of proof" in a loving, caring, direct manner. Look her in the eye. Tell her you know she is hurting. Tell her that you love her. Tell her that the old insanity is over for everyone.

She must be presented with evidence, not accusation. She must hear and see and feel not only the reality of her drinking behavior, but the reality of the support she has from her family and/or her coworkers and company. The fun and games are over. Yet, an intervention is not a hanging session, but a focused effort to harness the energies for recovery that lie within the grasp of the one with Jellinek's disease and those whom she has hurt.

The following statements illustrate the type of data that ought to be presented during an intervention:

- "On Christmas Eve you fell into the tree, smashing the ornaments. The children were frightened and locked themselves in their bedroom. I felt hurt and enraged because I had worked so hard to make Christmas a beautiful time for us all. You are my husband and I want to be a wife to you. I want to help you, Don, but, you have to help yourself. I can't do it for you."
- "At the Tangley Woods Restaurant on March 3, you had four martinis and insulted John Mathias who had been a client for six years. He withdrew the contract that afternoon. I am angry because I had worked hard to get that contract and you blew it in one afternoon. You have always been a major part of this firm, Esther, and we want you back as you were."
- "Dad, you came to see me in the hospital six weeks ago. You were loud and yelled at the aide when you couldn't find my room. You smelled of whiskey and your eyes looked glazed. I wish you hadn't come. I was embarrassed and felt that I had to apologize for my father's behavior. I love you, Dad. I just want you to get better."
- "Kent, you have had three heart attacks and bypass surgery and at that time you were warned against further drinking. Your liver is cirrhotic, your skin is yellow and in three months you will be dead if you continue your drinking. As your physician, I want to help you, but you have to do your part."
- "Over the past six weeks, your lunch hours have averaged two and a half hours. Yesterday you were out for three hours and ten minutes. I have had complaints from every member of your division. I will not defend you any longer, Karen. I want you to get better, come back and be part of the group. It is your choice now, Karen."

The following remarks will serve no purpose except to raise the alcoholic's defenses and to deflect the focus of the intervention. These are all value judgments which can be debated by the person on trial.

- "All you do is drink, drink, drink. All you think about is your damn self!" (Response: "I haven't had a drink in three days.")
- "Your work has gone to hell." (Response: "You don't give me enough time.")
- "You look like a damn fool with your red nose and stupid look and your shirt hanging out." (Response: "You've gained thirty-five pounds.")
- "If you loved me, you wouldn't do this to me." (Response: "If you loved me, I wouldn't have to drink.")
- "All you have to do is turn on your will-power. I can stop drinking anytime I please and so can you. All you have to do is want it enough." (Response: "You can't stop smoking and I haven't had a cigarette in three years.")
- "You used to be such a sweet person. I don't know why you've let yourself go like this." (Response: "You used to have hair and now you're bald.")

HOMEWORK

Because an individual with Jellinek's disease will be presented with limited alternatives on the beginning of his treatment, arrangements must be made ***prior*** to the intervention. This involves knowing what type of insurance he has, what type of treatment it will cover, and the length of time it will cover it.

The group must also know the availability and quality of treatment centers in the area. It must be ascertained if the person needs to be detoxified prior to treatment. If the person with Jellinek's disease has already been through a three-week treatment center at a local hospital, it must be agreed that he needs longer care and the place for this care must be carefully chosen.

If there is a question of time needed away from work, this must be worked out with his employers beforehand so no excuses can be given. Concerns for child care or other personal responsibilities also must be addressed prior to the intervention.

CHOOSING A TREATMENT PROGRAM

1. Get in touch with A.A. in your area. A.A. members have contact with the local treatment centers and know which ones are the best and which ones to avoid.

2. Call your local hospital to see if they have a chemical dependency unit or if they can recommend one.

3. Speak with your physician. If he regards alcoholism as a ***primary disease*** and not just as a symptom for which tranquillizers might be prescribed, he will know the location of the best rehabilitation center.

4. Be sure that the program or institution is approved by the Joint Commission on Accreditation of Hospitals. This assures the quality of the program and may effect insurance coverage.

5. Make an appointment with a counselor at the treatment center. The counselor will interview the Jellinek's disease sufferer and/or his family to determine the progression of the disease and the extent of damage suffered by the patient and family. The counselor will then make a recommendation as to the type of program best suited to the needs of the alcoholic.

6. Check on your insurance coverage. In most states, alcohol and drug addiction are recognized as primary disease and insurance companies are required to cover the cost of treatment. However, there may be technicalities that you must be aware of: There are centers that are attached to or contained within a hospital building and others that are separate from a hospital (free-standing). Some policies do not cover free-standing centers. There are other aspects of the insurance issue that the counselor will be able to answer for you.

DIFFERENT TYPES OF PROGRAMS

1. Outpatient: These programs last for six weeks and may be conducted under the auspices of the hospital inpatient program or by individual organizations that are not associated with a hospital. These programs are for those unable to attend an inpatient program and/or it is determined that they do not need the twenty-four-hour environment of a hospital.

2. Inpatient/Short-term: This is a three to four week program within a hospital. It is most often preceded by a careful detoxification process.

3. Inpatient/Long-term: These programs last three to six months or as long as necessary. They are usually conducted in an environment not directly associated with a hospital, although there are medical staff available if problems occur.

These programs are for those who have been through a regular three to four week inpatient program (or perhaps more than one), but are unable to maintain continuous sobriety.

Some people who are reluctant to recover may require more than one treatment in a long-term program. Usually, the center is committed to the patient long after he returns home; counselors are available to speak with the patient on the phone and the patient is welcomed back for shorter periods of time if necessary.

SPECIAL PROGRAMS FOR SPECIAL NEEDS

There have long been special treatment centers for priests, such as Guest House in Michigan and the center run by the Servants of the Paraclete in New Mexico. There are also special places for nuns, although many priests and nuns have chosen to be in treatment in non-church oriented centers.

In addition, there are programs which address the special needs of professionals such as doctors, lawyers, and business executives. As in all programs, confidentiality is mandated by Federal law.

Two recent developments in the area of special needs are on the increase: those that serve teens and young adults and those that serve women. The unique needs of both of these groups may be better met in these distinct settings.

AFTERCARE

This is the very important follow-up program offered by various treatment centers. All persons who successfully complete any of the other programs are strongly recommended for this one. It is not hard to maintain sobriety in treatment, but reentering the real world after treatment can be most difficult. A good aftercare program assists the newly recovering person through this transition and may well prevent a relapse and a "going back out" (resumption of drinking).

CAVEATS

1. Beware of treatment centers which make unrealistic promises:

   a. Teaching the alcoholic to drink "normally."

   b. Resolving all of the family's problems. Some of these unrealistic attitudes are conveyed through TV advertising: A family is shown in pain and crisis and then in exquisite harmony after treatment. It doesn't work that way.

2. Aversion therapy. This has been described as "teaching someone how to vomit for $10,000." The patient is given a substance called Emetine, is forced to drink an alcoholic beverage, and then vomits. This is supposed to turn the alcoholic off alcohol. Electric shock treatment is also used. A person who needs to drink will drink, aversion therapy to the contrary.

3. Antabuse medication. This is medication that produces a violent reaction if a person drinks. This is not true ***sobriety*** and works to produce ***dryness*** only as long as the person takes the medicine.

THE CONFRONTATION

After the necessary preparation is completed, the group meets with the person with Jellinek's disease. If this is done in a worksite, the logistics are relatively simple, for the person is present on the job. If this is done by the family, it is advisable to do it in the counselor's office.

By this time, the alcoholic may have a feeling that something is up and will be anxious to defend himself from outsiders who are interfering with his life. Or he may smell a rat and become unavailable.

A divorced woman, drinking heavily, became aggressive when she sensed her business partner withdrawing because of her drinking. She often called her partner, asking her what the matter was and why she was acting so different. The partner knew that the drinking was the cause of the estrangement but could not "accuse" her of being an alcoholic.

When the partner learned of the metabolic nature of Jellinek's disease and the fact that her friend could not stop on her own, she began the process of intervention. Nothing was said, but the alcoholic sensed that something was up and became unavailable to her partner.

The woman doing the intervention attempted to hold a meeting and was finally able to set a date. When they met, the partner expressed in a caring but direct way what she perceived to be the negative effects of the drinking on the business and on their friendship.

Reluctantly, at first, the alcoholic finally agreed to seek treatment. As her partner was leaving, she said, "Why did it take you so long to say something to me? I was ready to kill myself."

If the intervention is to be conducted at home, strategies must be carefully planned–such as the family gathering on a Sunday morning or another time when the person with Jellinek's disease is at home and has not been drinking.

The session begins with a statement by the counselor on why they have gathered and then each of the participants–family members, friends, coworkers–presents his documentation on how the alcoholic's behavior has effected their lives. Love and concern for the one with Jellinek's disease are stressed, but a sense of finality pervades the encounter.

The person is then told that his continued drinking is no longer an option and that he must seek treatment. There are no alternatives. The place for treatment has already been determined. All the arrangements have been made.

If he refuses treatment, then he is informed about the course of action that the family or employer will take. This may be the loss of his job, loss of marriage, his loss of privilege of living at home.

By the time the group reaches the point of intervention, they have become well enough to know that they themselves ***cannot and will not*** live with the alcoholic's behavior any longer.

This must be communicated by the strength of their words and by the clarity of their attitude. If he senses that this is just another ploy and that they can be conned if he takes a few weeks off for "good behavior, they will be in a worse spot than before.

He may ask for time to do it by himself. He may point to periods of being "on the wagon" or to instances of when he stopped smoking or lost weight. The group must acknowledge that they understand that he has actually been trying to control his drinking all along but that he and they know that it has been to no avail.

It is critical that the group be ready to act quickly. If he agrees, he is on his way. (The suitcase has already been packed and if necessary, air tickets purchased.)

If he refuses, he is fired on the spot by the employer or the spouse begins immediate legal proceedings to get him out of the house and to dissolve the marriage. At this point, there can be no more buying of time, for time has run out.

The intervention group need not worry that the treatment won't take if the person enters a treatment center under duress. A 1980 study (Freedberg and Johnson) showed that the success ratios are the same regardless if one seeks treatment voluntarily or under threat of disciplinary action. In other words, it is necessary simply to get the alcoholically impaired into treatment; his attitude upon entering treatment is inconsequential. Let God and the professionals work on his attitudes.

THE HIDDEN DYNAMICS

It is important for the intervention group to understand that, despite whatever the alcoholic may say to the contrary, he is in a living hell from his drinking and does not know how to get out of it. His pride and denial may seem impregnable, but his pain and self-hatred are chinks through which they can be breached. He hurts so much that he is probably thinking how he can end it all.

Vernon Johnson writes of the "mating call of the suffering alcoholic". He is hurt and wounded and is hurting and wounding those he loves most. He does not want to do this but knows of no other way.

Those who love him must reach beyond their own hurts and listen, not to his words, but to his wounded cries for help. Those who love him must have the courage, not to fall into the bottomless well with him, but to point the way to healing and recovery. Those who love him must continue their own shaky, unsteady path toward wholeness with forgiveness and understanding.

One Saturday morning, a neighbor phoned the man next door to see if he could borrow a tool for his garden and asked if he would mind bringing it over. When the man walked into his neighbor's house, there were 14 people sitting in the living room: his ex-wife, his sons and daughters, two men in his law firm, his physician, his minister, other neighbors.

After he had heard what they all had to say about his drinking, one of his son's handed him a letter from another son who was unable to attend the intervention. In the letter, the son told the father how important he had been in his young life, coaching his soccer and baseball groups, helping with homework, buying him a puppy, and how much he missed him now that he had withdrawn from him because of his drinking.

The man was so deeply moved that people cared and had taken the time to come to him that he left that afternoon for a treatment center. To this day, that recovering alcoholic cannot tell the story of that Saturday morning without tears of gratitude welling up in his eyes.

Or, as it says in Isaiah:

The eyes of the blind shall be opened,
And the ears of the deaf shall be unstopped.
Then shall the lame man leap as a hart,
And the tongue of the dumb sing.
35:5,6.

Chapter Nine

Treatment: Prologue to Recovery

The condition aimed at in treatment is "mental sobriety" or "comfortable sobriety". Just being dry was just being in hell.

JOHN BERRYMAN, Recovery

My name is Ed and I am a recovering alcoholic. Before I go into detail regarding rehabilitation, I would first like to qualify myself. When asked to define my alcoholism, I simply say I have a disease of the attitudes, drank too much, and I could not stop. God knows I tried, but I couldn't. I didn't always view alcoholism as a disease. Like most, I viewed it as a sign of moral weakness. Alcoholism was for skid-row bums, not for a father of four who held a responsible position in the business community and had all the material things that led everyone to think I was a responsible person.

This type of thinking only helped to fortify my rationalization and denial of the fact I was an alcoholic. Obviously this type of ignorance had to be corrected and it was suggested that I go into an alcoholic rehabilitation program to learn about my problem. In 1978, I, reluctantly, did just that. I was driven more by fear that I was going to lose all the meaningful things in life if I didn't do something.

Looking back, I can honestly say that I went to a rehab in New York out of the fear of losing my family and job. I also went hoping that the professional help would disqualify me as being an alcoholic and would tell me my problems were due to stress in the home and on the job. When I was home, I blamed the job for my attitudes and on the job, I blamed my home life situation for my less than acceptable job performance. The real problem was me, but I couldn't be honest enough to admit that. I went to rehab for all the wrong reasons. I went for everyone else but me.

Though my first rehab did not help, short term, it was well worth it in the long haul, for it was a beginning. Today, I can say honestly, it was the cornerstone of my recovery and well worth my discussing it with you. With this sketchy background, I would like to tell you of my experiences with alcoholic rehabilitation.

In May of 1978, I entered my first rehab stone sober, which should have been the first tip-off to my eventual failure, but my denial and false pride wouldn't allow me to go drunk. Also recall that I wanted these people to disqualify me, as being non-alcoholic.

I spent the first two days in detox for precaution. Here I didn't have a drink for three days prior and they wanted to detox me. What nerve! Didn't they know who I was? After detox, I was introduced to my counselor whose name was Irene. She was a tough cookie and let me know it right away. I went to classes directed by her and had several one-on-one sessions as well. With time, we got along pretty well.

At this stage of my alcoholism, I was in good physical shape. Spiritually, I went to Mass on Sunday. Don't all Catholics? Mentally, I was screwed up, but still had enough presence of mind and superb bullshit techniques. I think Irene started to feel that if I had a problem, it was in its early stages, and I thought she started to side with me against my wife.

This rehab was a good one–the program was solid and the people were excellent. I learned that alcoholism is a disease, never to be cured, but it can be arrested. I learned that it is an insidious disease that continues to tell you that there is nothing wrong. I was told that to stop drinking was not enough, that recovery continues after rehab for the rest of your life. I learned that I had to change my attitudes and life-style.

With this information, I left to join the outside world. I became a regular A.A. meeting-goer. In ten months, I attended five to six meetings a week. I had a terrific sponsor who was in constant contact with me. I was doing all the things that were suggested, but I couldn't change me. Like they say, "If you don't change the drunk that you brought in, you're going to walk out with that same drunk."

Well, that is what happened to me. I didn't change, except I hadn't had a drink in ten months, so the inevitable happened. I got drunk and stayed drunk for four years. The things that I had been told were "yets" started to happen. Up to that point, I hadn't lost anything yet. Soon I lost my job and wife. For a while I lost the privilege of living with my four sons.

Still, I didn't want to accept my alcoholism. That is the insidious part of the disease. My life and, unfortunately, those of others around me were falling apart, and I still thought I was fine.

The four-year drunk I went on was a living hell. The disease is progressive and it got worse and worse. In spite of myself, I kept a good job and had two of my four kids back living with me. I viewed this as "I'm okay," but, in fact, I was worse than ever. I was drinking more and more, having blackouts regularly, becoming increasingly hostile, even violent.

My oldest son, Jim, who was studying to be a Jesuit, came home between Christmas and New Years in 1982. I tried to bullshit him about my problems but it didn't work. He told me straight out that I was an alcoholic. He said that he could only pray for me.

Perhaps because none of the boys had ever used the word "alcoholic" with me, Jim's words stung. Whenever my sons would be upset with me they would withdraw and I'd get them back by giving them money or by taking them to a ball game.

Jim was different. I couldn't co-opt him. He looked me straight in the eye and I knew I couldn't buy him off. It was almost like he was older or wiser or stronger than I was. And he was telling me a truth that I didn't want to hear. Or on another level, maybe I was just ready. Maybe I just hurt enough. I know I had hurt them enough. It was at this moment I was ready to accept unconditionally that my life was unmanageable and I was powerless over alcohol.

Jim made some phone calls and the next thing I knew I was being visited by his best friend's father. Not planned, and no coincidence, but predetermined by the Man that gave me the Gift of Life. This time I entered rehab with changed attitudes and I was willing to go to any length to stop drinking. I was dead spiritually, mentally, and damn near physically.

I entered Pine Valley Hospital January 2, 1983, drunk and beaten. I was finally able to reach out and say, "I need help." I knew I belonged in rehab and I was happy to be there. I don't recall much of the first couple of days, due to the booze in my system and the

Librium that they were detoxing me with. The doses could have slowed down an elephant.

I met a medical staff of eight nurses and two doctors. A couple were recovering alcoholics and the rest were qualified to handle alcoholics and treat them. My first thought was that these people care and it was their hope that they could help me. I latched on to this hope, for if they offered hope for me, who was I to turn my back and run again. I was too tired to run anymore.

For the first five days, I was classified as a detox person, which meant I could not attend rehab classes. I spent my time being cared for physically by the nurses, whom I loved and trusted.

I started opening up and listening and to my pleasant surprise, I had a calm about me I never had before. I felt good. Toward the end of those five days, I was getting antsy. I wanted to be allowed to enter rehab, but I listened to people who knew what was right and the impatience subsided.

What I didn't know then was that there was a Higher Power who was preparing me for the important initial stages of recovery. Until I unconditionally surrendered, ***nothing***, including rehab, was going to work.

I can remember the first day of rehab before I went to my first class, I found myself on my knees, saying, "Okay, Big Guy, you got me this far, don't let me down now!" He didn't!

I spent the next five weeks in the initial stages of recovery. I was lucky to get the chance, lucky to have so many people who cared, and lucky for the first time in my life that I was able to share my feelings and listen to others. No matter what I was told to do, I did it; I knew if I didn't, I was going to screw up again.

I wound up with two counselors, Tom and Wendy, both recovering alcoholics. As much as they were teaching me about myself, they also shared their own experiences and that gave me more trust in what they were telling me. In addition to Tom and Wendy, there was a Ph.D. psychologist named Don who came twice a week. He was terrific.

I'll never forget the time when it was another patient's turn on the Hot Seat, the one who is focused on during the group therapy sessions. Alex was a rugged, athletic guy. A real pussycat underneath with a real macho exterior. He told his story and I cried. Don asked him what he noticed and he answered, "Ed is crying." We were the two biggest guys in a room of thirty and here we were crying.

Well, I learned right then that I had feelings and could feel mine through other people. What a powerful experience! It told me I was alive and if I would listen and learn from other people's experience, I could get better.

Day in and day out we had lectures, meetings with staff, A.A. people, and just peers. This was great for I no longer felt alone. I could talk about me, the real me, and I could listen and have feelings for others. What a nice feeling, I could start caring about myself and others. Wow!

During the evenings we would go to A.A. meetings, watch TV, talk, shoot pool, but we always had homework prescribed according to our needs. We would be responsible the next day for expressing to our peers what we had done and what it meant to us. If we were honest, that brought us into contact with our own feelings and it helped others.

During the second week in rehab, it was my turn to sit on the Hot Seat. The topic which was given to me was to write a letter to my mother, who had died two months before. I fought this, saying let me write a letter to my ex-wife and I'll show you anger and resentment.

They wouldn't buy it. So I wrote the letter to my mother. In it I explained I was an alcoholic, which she knew, and I was sorry for the pain I had caused her. I asked her for understanding and forgiveness.

The day I was on I knew the letter by heart and I told it like a story. Early on, I brought my ex-wife into it, and Don the psychologist, sitting next to me, leaned over and said, "Cut the ex-wife crap and get on with the topic."

Two things happened: The get-honest lamp went on and I stopped blaming my ex-wife for my problems. I had to start pointing the blame at me, no one else, and my anger and resentments were there long before my ex-wife showed up. The resentments and anger were deep-seated and had started growing some time in my early years.

Things started making more sense.

Not only did I have an insatiable appetite for booze, I also had lousy attitudes. I was once told by my original sponsor that alcoholism is a "disease of the attitudes" and that "if you just take the bottle away from an alcoholic, you've just got a sober son of a bitch." Those two quotes mean an awful lot to me today.

The disease of the attitudes helped me understand what they were teaching me in rehab. I wasn't losing my mind (though at times I thought just that), I was physically, mentally, and spiritually sick from my attitudes and from booze. Just to get sober physically was not enough. I had to get sober mentally and spiritually as well.

The latter two categories, they told me, I would have to work on the rest of my life. They told me if I didn't drink I improved my chances, but I had to continue my recovery and A.A. is the only chance I would have to do so.

I believed them. That's what I do today. A.A. is a continuance of the gift of sobriety that I was given by God and the hope, love, and understanding I received in the hospital.

The tradition at Pine Valley, like other rehabs, is that when you are to leave, you address your peers. Well, that was one of the most emotional moments of my life. I babbled and cried my eyes out.

Over a five-week period, I had come to love forty people and their problems. I also learned to love and trust the staff–nurses, doctors, counselors, and even a tiny cleaning woman from Haiti.

I left Pine Valley with a whole new outlook on life. My attitudes were still there, but I saw things differently. I saw good instead of bad; I saw love instead of anger; I saw trust instead of cynicism; and most of all, I saw hope and faith for me. I owe it all to the people of Pine Valley.

However, I couldn't stop there. I believed them and I went that very first night to A.A. in Lake Commons. Here I met people, like me, who were decent but who had drunk too much. They welcomed me with open arms and minds and to this date have kept me well.

I should point out that at the nine-month mark, I was asked to take over a meeting at Riverview Hospital. It is an A.A./Al-Anon meeting that includes people in the rehab program and their families and friends. This is a real experience, for I see a piece of me in every newcomer.

The lying, denial, and half-heartedness in some are things I can relate to. I can see the pain and the agony of the non-alcoholics much clearer today. All of this has enhanced my own program. Like we say in Step 12–we give it away to keep it. If we don't, well, it would be hell for me down the road.

I am grateful today because I am free of alcohol, but also I am learning a new life that has bumps, but the bumps are few and far between. I have people I love and who love me. I was once told that a practicing alcoholic can't love. Today I believe that! I was incapable of loving others. I was too damn busy worrying about me.

Today I have four sons whom I love very much. They are four super reasons for my gratitude today. They give me love, warmth, and enjoyment–beyond my wildest dreams.

Add that to my non-A.A. friends–social and business–and I am very lucky. But now, you add my A.A. friends and I am the luckiest guy on earth.

Four months ago, I lost a very special friend–her name was Irene–who loved me back to health while I was in rehab. She was tough, but could she teach faith, hope, and love. I feel every friend I have is special, but Irene got me on the right track. I love you, Irene!

What more can I say about rehab? I am alive and that wouldn't have been the case if it weren't for Irene and the rest of the Pine Valley staff. My rehab continues, thanks to all my friends in A.A. and the love and support of my sons.

I love you all for what you have and still give to me– a day at a time.

THE ROAD TO RECOVERY

It has been said that a journey of a thousand miles begins with a single step; for many people treatment is that first step to recovery from Jellinek's disease.

Treatment, or rehabilitation (rehab), is a process of therapeutic medical care to facilitate the recovery from Jellinek's disease. It begins with detoxification. It is conducted with certain goals to be obtained, under the auspices of professional persons trained in the biochemistry and psychodynamics of alcoholism.

DETOXIFICATION

Intoxification means putting toxins (poisons) in the body; detoxification means taking them out. When the body begins to do without or withdraw from alcohol or other drugs, it must go from what has become a natural state to an unnatural state of being free of those chemicals to which the body has become so well accommodated and well adjusted.

A man was taken by his family into the emergency room of a hospital. That day he had only had two beers, a fact attested to by his family. However, the results of a blood test showed that his B.A.L. was .375, nearly four times the amount required to be legally intoxicated. People have died at .30. It took five days to rid his body of alcohol; if he had attempted to do this at home, he could have endangered his life.

In withdrawing, the body rebels, sometimes with great fury. It likes, needs, wants what it has grown accustomed to and punishes the person for stopping. The person becomes nervous, sweats, can't eat, can't sleep, can't think. He may convulse and suffer the dreaded D.T.s: Delirium tremens–shaking insanity.

The mortality rate of untreated persons suffering D.T.s is 20% to 25%; this is 40 times higher than the withdrawal fatality rate for heroin. In some instances, D.T.s may cause a massive coronary, brain hemorrhage, or respiratory shutdown.

A person suffering from D.T.s hallucinates and is unable to control his body. He shakes, sweats, vomits. He sees things–red bowels exploding over mountains, snakes and sharks and moray eels, purple eyes staring from the walls, the proverbial pink elephants of drunk jokes, except they are not funny to the person experiencing them.

One woman experienced D.T.s every afternoon in her kitchen as she waited for the clock to strike five so she could begin her cocktail hour; she thought this was normal.

In a hospital setting, the medical staff conducts the detoxification process with great care. The vital signs are monitored on a regular basis to avoid D.T.s and medication is administered properly and in the dosage required to insure a safe withdrawal.

Many people who sincerely want to stop drinking or taking drugs continue to ingest the substance to avoid the pain of withdrawal. Many try it on their own and are thrown into the throes of unmedicated, unmonitored withdrawal; they resume drinking to stave off the pain.

The assurance of a relatively comfortable, safe withdrawal is critical to one's beginning treatment and can communicate to a confused mind that somewhere, somehow, down the road there is a world where one can be safe and comfortable without alcohol or drugs.

GOALS

The goals of a successful treatment program are primarily:

1. That the person emerges with a commitment to a life of total ***abstinence*** from alcohol and other mood-altering drugs;
2. That he accepts the fact that he has a chronic, progressive, fatal ***disease*** and that he understands the nature of this disease;
3. That some of the damage his drinking has caused him and his family starts to ***heal***;
4. That he begins the long process of personal ***change*** that will insure his continued sobriety.

ABSTINENCE

Abstinence means the complete and unequivocal freedom from any and all drugs. With pride, a friend of Johnny Cash said that he was 95% free from drugs. Cash replied, "That other 5% will kill you."

There is absolutely no cure for Jellinek's disease. However, its deadly progression can be arrested by not drinking; it can be seen as going into remission, but reactivating again with that first drink.

If there is no understanding of the irreversible nature of the alcoholic's metabolism of alcohol, then the commitment to total freedom from alcohol makes no sense.

In other words, if someone with Jellinek's disease has the wild, erroneous illusion that he can drink again after an imposed period of sobriety, he will indeed drink and will end up in a worse state than he began.

Treatment programs or other cures that promise to teach the alcoholic to drink properly and with moderation, perpetrate the most cruel of hoaxes on the public. Such promises are based on a pervasive, culpable disdain for the very concept of chemical addiction and are guilty of manipulating the pain and confusion of the Jellinek's disease sufferer for monetary gain.

In addition, to promise alcoholics that they will be able to drink within a normal range is to dangle an illusion before people already out of touch with reality.

For someone with Jellinek's disease there is no recovery even remotely possible that does not have abstinence, total and continuing, as its primary goal.

During the phase of treatment following detoxification, the person is not allowed to drink or to use drugs. It is not possible to undergo treatment as long as the person's mind is clouded. For many people, this period of imposed sobriety is the first time in many months or years that they have been free of chemicals.

And although the person with Jellinek's disease is in a protected setting, unlike the home or office or factory, he is getting his first taste of living without drinking or using. He is beginning to sleep and eat and laugh without booze. He may be restless and jumpy, but finds to his relief that he has not disintegrated or gone mad without it.

With a relatively cleared head, with calmer nerves, without having to expend energy to keep a supply of alcohol or pills on hand, the individual can begin his treatment with the odds being at least even that he will learn and experience whatever he needs to begin his recovery.

ACCEPTANCE OF DISEASE CONCEPT

It is impossible to overstate how critical it is that the alcoholic come to understand and accept the fact that he has landed in a treatment center or a chemical dependency unit of a hospital because he has a disease that is killing him.

(The ***understanding*** of alcoholism as a disease and the ***acceptance*** of the fact that one has contracted this disease are of paramount importance in the recovery process. The entire next chapter deals specifically with this issue.)

In this very early stage of recovery, the person who has Jellinek's disease, because he is no longer on alcohol, gets hit with the tidal wave of reality: He's just a drunk drying out with a bunch of other drunks. He is awash in a sea of guilt and shame and profound self-repugnance, for he is also part of the human community which hates its drunks. Drunks are selfish and weak and abhorrent to all he stands for, but now, yes, he must stand and be counted with one of the most despised of the world. Life indeed has dealt him an ugly hand. He's a drunk.

In treatment parlance, this is called "cutting through the denial," as one cuts through fat, bone, and grizzle to get to the tenderloin of reality waiting inside.

Previous chapters have dealt with the impairment of the memory system through chemically induced blackouts, euphoric recall, and repression. Because, for all practical purposes, his mind has been a blank with regard to his drinking, the alcoholic has had the ***luxury of denying*** that he is in trouble with drink. And, as has been said many times, he is not lying: He ***feels*** and ***thinks*** that if there is any little problem at all, it is caused by persons, places, or circumstances around him.

When a person is left without the marvelous defense of denial, guilt and shame wash over him, drowning him in self-loathing. This cannot be avoided and serves well to knock down the last vestiges of his denial; the degree to which he is still able to disown his alcoholism is the degree to which he will not recover. All the denial must go. He does not need it anymore.

Part of the treatment program is educational. There are lectures by physicians and nurses and other staff members on the medical aspects of alcoholism. Film, books, charts, and other teaching aids introduce the Jellinek's disease sufferer to the nature and progression of his disease, much like the diabetic who must learn the workings of the pancreas and liver, the metabolism of sugar, the nature of insulin, and how to test urine, administer shots, and regulate a diet.

It is said that alcoholism is the only disease that tells you it isn't a disease. There are those who go through an entire three-or-four week program, sitting through one or two lectures a day on the nature of Jellinek's disease, who still refuse to accept the fact that they have a fatal disease, and that if they continue to drink they will die.

Because someone cannot stand naked to the guilt and shame and self-reproach for long, he must move on: He will either shore up his denial system, lying to himself again that the world is square, yet using enough of the right words and doing the right things so that he can get out and back to his drinking–this is called ***compliance***; or he will admit that he has a disease that he is powerless over and that all the unmanageability in his life has been caused by his drinking–this is called ***surrender***.

While the long-term goal of treatment is total abstinence, the immediate goal is that the person with Jellinek's disease understand and accept that his disease is why he is in treatment. He will naturally go through a period of sorrow and grief, pitying himself for this most horrible of things that has happened to him. But he is doing this in a safe place and he is told that it is all right, even healthy that he feel this way.

He has to understand, despite the fact that he may have done bad things, that he is not a bad person; he is a sick person. Unless he can begin to pay much more than lip service to the disease concept (and that is good enough at the beginning), he will wallow in self-pity and miss the meaning and benefits of treatment.

Self-esteem has to take root, shaky at first, but soon it will grow and the person will learn to hold his head high and take a good look at his illness, finally embracing it and saying, "Yes, you are all mine."

The person who has the courage and grace to move through self-pity to self-understanding and finally to self-acceptance is well on the way to a peaceful, joyful, comfortable sobriety. This is the major task of treatment.

HEALING

The person in treatment cannot remain in a state of utter shame and self-loathing for long. It serves its purpose of allowing him to feel intensely the effects of his drinking without the buffer of denial. It has allowed him to be naked, feeling every current of shame and repugnance as he begins to remember and to look at himself. It is not pretty.

In the 1954 film, ***The High and the Mighty***, a plane piloted by John Wayne begins to run out of fuel on the flight from Hawaii to California. He can't turn back, because they have passed the point of no return.

Jan Sterling plays a woman of dubious morals. When we first see her, her face is so caked with makeup that the person underneath is hidden. After John Wayne tells the passengers that they might not make it back, she takes out a jar of cold cream and a box of tissues and proceeds to take off the makeup. As she removes layer after layer, the soiled tissues pile up in her lap and her real features grow stark under the glistening cold cream. She wants to die with her real face on.

Someone undergoing treatment for Jellinek's disease finds himself without his makeup. He looks in the mirror and screams. It all seems so horrible and ugly and unforgivable. He thinks he is going to die.

The violence and infidelities and lies. The moral bankruptcy and unlovingness and duplicity. The running and dodging. The black-outs and pass-outs and degradation. He knows he is going to die.

Guided by the skill and experience of the staff and supported by others in treatment, the Jellinek's disease sufferer begins to learn about his disease and what has happened to him because of it. He starts to get real. He learns that all of the things that happened were inevitable, given his drinking.

He starts to hear that all of that is in the past; it's over. He has to forgive himself for all his shameful deeds, for the shameful person he has become. As he starts to really grasp the dimensions of his disease and trusts those responsible for his care, he will forgive himself, tenuously at first, for the havoc he has wrought.

And as he grows in the understanding of his disease and takes in the first pure breath of air that has been blessed with self-forgiveness, he finds that he is already on his way to a greater healing and to a joyful recovery.

The moment of crisis that propels the drinking person into treatment is likewise the moment of crisis for the family, and for those business associates who may have been responsible for the intervention. Everyone hurts. The mental and/or physical beatings have gone on too long; no one can take any more.

Most reputable treatment centers have a family treatment component. The sophistication of the family may vary; the important element is that the damage that has been done to the family–to the marriage, to the individual children, to the extended family–be addressed.

F. Scott Fitzgerald wrote, "When drunk, I make them pay and pay and pay and pay." Everyone has paid enough; they are bankrupt. It's time to cancel the loan.

Families may be seduced into thinking that once the family member with Jellinek's disease stops drinking, all the problems will be over and that things will return to normal. The focal point of their lives has been the drinking; just remove the drinking and all will be well. This is not the way it works.

The family Codependency has taken a long time to develop. Slowly, painfully, the fabric of family life has been picked away. There are big holes, even craters and gorges in that family. The family members are truly the walking wounded. Three or four weeks is simply not enough time to fill up the holes.

Despite the counseling and education the family receives during the time of treatment, the addicted person receives much more comprehensive, concentrated help. He may emerge with new ideas, with hope, and with enthusiasm for his recovery. He attends A.A.

meetings, calls his sponsor, goes back to the hospital for aftercare and talks with his counselor. But the wounds of the family are much slower to heal.

A.A. will most probably be mandatory for the patient and Al-Anon will be suggested for the family. There are Alateens and Alatots for the children. These programs are based on the premise that Jellinek's disease is a family disease; they have all gotten sick together and they can all get well together.

A spouse or child's joining Al-Anon has been the key to many Jellinek's disease sufferers getting into treatment. For a family to remain sick, all the members have to stay sick. If one member begins to get well, it breaks up the pathology holding them all together. Sickness no longer works. There are other options.

In addition, Children of Alcoholics (COA) chapters are springing up throughout the country. While many of these deal specifically with the problems of adult children who may no longer live at home, participation in such groups may well precipitate a long overdue healing and may call a halt to the madness and suffering that still exist in the mind of the child, regardless of her age. She has to do her work, sooner or later.

Likewise, there are counselors, social workers, pastoral ministers, mental health workers, psychologists, and therapists who are ready to help the marriage, the children, the family. It is essential that these people have some knowledge of and training in chemical addiction as a disease and understand how this effects the life of the family.

Unless the family truly understands the profound toll that Jellinek's disease has had on each and every one of them and on the family as a whole, recovery will be a hollow reward, incomplete and temporary. Unless they are willing to address their own hurts and are open to receiving help, the healing and joy that are within their grasp will run from their fingers like water.

CHANGE

The goal of treatment is long-term sobriety. The initial step is understanding and accepting the disease of alcoholism, thereby forgiving oneself and moving on toward recovery. In order to insure this commitment to sobriety, the alcoholic must change. If he does not change, he will not recover. Or, as it is said, "The same person will drink again."

In treatment with the help of counselors and a group of peers, the individual begins to look at the person he has become and to realize the underlying fear or dishonesty or arrogance that has been the overriding theme in his behavior. If fear or dishonesty or arrogance continue in the sober alcoholic's life, he will not be sober for long. Uncomfortable, he will drink again, seeking that comfort that patiently waits for him in the bottle.

He must change.

Change is a terrifying notion. If I have become what I have become, I at least know what I am. If I cease to be me, then I will die, the blip on the screen that monitors the heart smoothing out to a straight line before they pull the sheet over my face. The devil you know is better than the devil you don't know.

A recovering priest, in recalling his time in treatment when he didn't know which way to go with himself, commented that he would just look at the faces of the people in A.A. who came to the hospital and would focus on the ones who seemed the happiest and try to get near them so what they had would rub off on him.

Anatole France wrote: "All changes, even the most longed for, have their melancholy, for what we leave behind us is a part of ourselves; we must die to one life before we can enter into another."

The recovering person has to change her inner world and her outer world. Within, she must leave behind her old ways of thinking and of behaving, of seeing the world and of reacting to it.

Her outer world includes those old people, places, and things that were a part of her active alcoholism. As her old thoughts and attitudes become dangerous to her new sobriety, so do old friends, favorite taverns, the race track, the bridge club—anything that will draw her back to the life she has left or to that person she must cease to be.

Almost all treatment programs make A.A. participation mandatory at this point in order to fix the idea of long term sobriety. There is just no such thing as a quick fix. The Jellinek's disease sufferer must make a commitment to a life of sobriety; without A.A., it would be like trying to scuba dive without an oxygen tank.

A.A. says to the newcomer, "If you want what we have and are willing to go to any length to get it, we have a program of recovery for you. If you are looking for an easier, softer way, we are not what you are looking for."

Yet the paradox of A.A. is that it actually is the easier, softer way. It is a gentle, honest way of life, one that most people with Jellinek's disease have been looking for all their lives and without knowing it.

It is the people on the Program who serve as real, flesh-and-blood symbols of a commitment to lifelong sobriety and to the fact that change does not mean death or a barren life, but a second chance at living.

Chapter Ten

Surrender: The Heart of Recovery

I triumphed and I saddened with all weather,
Heaven and I wept together,
And its sweet tears were salt with mortal mine.
FRANCIS THOMPSON

The nurse hesitated at the door, glanced again at the chart, and walked over to the man in the bed. Three-day beard darkened his sunken cheeks and chin. Clear liquid dripped rhythmically from a plastic bag into the narrow tubes that ran into the blue veins in his right hand. The hand was discolored. Beneath his eyes was darkness and his left cheek and forehead were bruised. The shades were drawn. The television was silent.

She opened the patient's chart and reread the doctor's notations, as if the repetition of the words would blunt their meaning: "Father John Hurley: Alcoholism, Malnutrition, D.T.s."

She reached for his left hand, gnarled, bruised, lifeless – the very hands that changed bread and wine into the body and blood of Christ, the hands that baptized and forgave sins. The nurse refocused her thoughts, clocking the weak beats of his heart with her watch. Waves of pity, disgust, and sadness washed over her as she tried not to picture him saying Mass. He was simply a patient, a very sick man who needed care. Still, he was a priest . . .

John opened his eyes and looked around the room. He knew he had to get up and get to class. They would be waiting and he had to find his notes. His eyes closed as he tried to center himself. All he could remember was sitting in the red leather chair in his room. Cracks ran like lightning through the smooth fat leather and John felt electricity charging into his legs and back and across his face. Blood sprang from his flanks and ran onto the floor and out the door into forever.

Two figures came to the bedside. John opened his eyes and saw his doctor and his prior. He closed his eyes as he awaited their lecture. He had heard it all before: Killing himself, treatment, willingness, needing time to sort things out.

The doctor said nothing; the prior said nothing. John read only disapproval and rejection on their faces; he missed their concern.

Sadly John shook his head, for the two men had been through this with him many times before. "You know, Doc, you don't know when you're beaten, do you? This old Irishman has been sent to you to teach you a little humility. I'm hopeless and worthless and you and the rest of them with all your training and programs and big ideas to reform us drunks are only a long road with no turning. Give up, Doc, and learn your little lesson in humility, now won't you?"

The prior, a stocky man in his middle forties, walked to the other side of the bed. John looked down at the needle taped to the back of his hand. He lifted his arm to the prior "Well, Tom, at least you don't have a junkie on your hands. Just a first-class drunk. Tom, just let me be and don't be wasting your breath on dead embers."

"John," the prior spoke firmly, "John, this is it. Either you get well or you're out. The Bishop wants you off the faculty and Father Simeon is starting proceedings to dismiss you from the order. You've played your last card, John, your very last card. It's either up or out. You've got to make that decision."

"Ah, so now they're all ganging up on me, are they? And my old student, Tom Walsh, won't even defend me, will you?"

"John, you've got a decision to make. We're at the end with you and you are dragging us all down. The seminary, your classes, the order. This is the end of the road, John."

The priest lifted his worn blue eyes and faintly smiled in the face of his defeat. "You know, Tom, you speak of my drinking . . . but never of my thirst."

"Never mind your poetry, John. You'll be finished with the detoxification by the end of the week. I've made reservations for you at the Chapel Hill Rehabilitation Lodge in New Jersey next week. You go from the hospital to rehab or you leave the order, as of your discharge from the hospital."

John closed his eyes. This was truly the end of the line. He looked to the doctor and then to his superior. He nodded his head. He would go.

On Saturday the prior came to the hospital with John's suitcase and a bus ticket. He took John to the bus station, waited until the bus was ready to leave, wished him well, and put him on the bus.

The Greyhound rolled eastward across the Indiana farmlands as the wheat, corn, and oats swayed in the early summer breeze. Barns and silos shrank before the vast sea of soil and grain that stretched as far as he could see.

John thought of the little farms at home that had to feed a family of eight or ten or more. He thought of his own little cottage in Tipperary and the bog growing purple every evening when the sun stole behind the mountains and of the blue smoke from the turf fires gathering in soft clouds over the whitewashed cottages. It's a long and disgraceful road you've traveled, John Hurley, for what you're worth now.

He thought of how his parents had sacrificed to send him to the seminary and how he was chosen to study in Rome and after that in Louvain. How proud the whole village was that one of their own had become a priest. They said he was brilliant and he began to write and teach and he was called to Rome to advise the bishops and cardinals during the Vatican Council.

After that he was asked to head a new ecumenical theology department at a major university in America. He continued to write and speak and debate some of the finest minds in the church. There was standing room only in his classes and they continued to call him brilliant. He dazzled then all.

It was during this time that John discovered comfort and solace and warmth in the bottle. Naturally shy, he became congenial, even gregarious with a few drinks. His thoughts became even more lofty and he was able to conceptualize theological truths on a level that dazzled even himself. And when he drank, the burden of being brilliant Father John Hurley somehow softened and, indeed, it was a lovely thing to be himself in all his glory, bringing such service and scholarship to the order and the church.

Ever so slowly, the gentleness of the bottle turned against him. He unwittingly and unknowingly began to lose control. John changed from congenial and expansive to aggressive and mean, attacking people when they least expected it. The following day he would suffer profound embarrassment when reminded of the night before; he rarely remembered what happened after he started drinking.

He started drinking earlier and alone. He always intended just to have one or two but he would end up in oblivion; he could never stop once he began. At some point, the water started to boil and there was no lowering the flame. His will power was useless.

His work suffered. His writing became repetitious and soon people realized he had nothing to say. He was no longer asked to speak or to debate. His classes grew smaller and smaller and he was relieved of much of his responsibility at the university. John Hurley became a has-been, a bad priest.

At first there were subtle hints, then open remarks, then out-and-out confrontations. He had become an embarrassment, a liability, a drunk.

They sent him to dry out, much like his mother would hang wet sheets on a line. Then there were the psychiatrists and the therapists and the thirty-day retreat with the Trappists so he could pray. He had not prayed for years. He couldn't. His mind couldn't hold a thought and he couldn't feel anything anymore. He was as dead and numb as a wet tombstone.

He really didn't care what they were going to do with him. He felt nothing–not shame or pity or revenge. The tombstone theologian, he thought. John Hurley was truly dead. It seemed only a technicality before they put him in the ground.

John was met at the bus depot by two members of the rehab staff. It was another forty miles drive to the center. The nurse spoke kindly, trying to put John at ease. He said little, staring at the bruise on his hand. He felt like a fool. They didn't even know who he was.

The treatment center was stark in its simplicity, more like a monastery than a clinic. For days John walked in grayness. All feeling and emotion had been sucked out of his being. The graveyard growth was in him, for he was more dead than alive.

The days were filled with lectures on Jellinek's disease, films, individual and group counseling sessions, tasks to be done, and meals to be eaten. New people came and old ones finished their treatment, but John walked through the schedule, untouched and untouchable. John had his own timetable.

John stared at his counselor sitting behind the desk in his small office. His curly gray hair clung to the sides of his head, leaving the broad rounded crown bare as if nature had sculpted her own tonsure. His skin was dark and rich like buffed mahogany. His long arched nose contrasted with the full lips as if a Roman ancestor had passed on part of himself on a long African night centuries before. John continued to stare, too distanced to understand his rudeness.

Gordon Cole, his counselor, stared back at the shrunken man with sloped shoulders, faded blue eyes, and limp white hair. John looked down at his hands.

"I'm a priest."

"You're a man."

"A priest with a disgrace . . ."

"A man with a disease . . ."

"I'm a priest first . . . called from among men . . ."

"John, you're being invited back to the human race, you're called to rejoin the rest of us who get sick and laugh and love and make mistakes. It's sweet to be a man, John."

"You don't understand . . . I've betrayed everything . . . I'm a priest and I've sold out."

"To what?"

"Evil, weakness, my own corrupt nature."

"You're human. You've contracted a disease. Do you ever get a cold? Do priests get cancer? Bad hearts? Alzheimer's?"

"Alcoholism is a sin, a profoundly evil, twisted, inordinate offense against God."

Gordon leaned back from his desk, folded his arms, and looked at the ceiling. "God, John, you're getting a lot of mileage out of beating yourself, aren't you? Keep up the flagellation and you'll be too busy, too absorbed with yourself to hear the things you were meant to hear."

"May I leave?"

"I'll see you tomorrow at ten."

The following morning John appeared in Gordon's office. His mood had changed from defeat to control. The theologian, the scholar was back in charge and about to put the counselor in his place. Self-control had always been the great regulator of his life. He'd get it back. He'd show them all.

"You're looking different, John,"

"Nothing like a good night's rest. I've been working too hard. All I need is a rest and I've got this thing licked."

"What thing?"

"God, if you don't know, what the hell are you doing behind that fancy desk?"

"What thing, John?"

"'What thing, John? What thing, John?' Christ Almighty, you know as well as I do. 'What thing, John?'"

"You said that all you need is a rest and you'd have this thing licked."

"Don't you ever get tired? Are you people so strong and resilient that you never get tired?"

"How many classes do you teach?"

"None."

"Do you do parish work."

"Sometimes."

"When was your last book published? Your last article?"

John said nothing. He looked past the counselor's shoulders to the hills and valleys of New Jersey. Gordon said nothing. John drew a Camel from his pocket, lit it, and coughed.

"I'm just so goddamn tired."

"It takes a lot of energy to keep on fighting, John. And it's going to keep on controlling you. You could stop fighting, let go, release it, relax. You could, you know. You just have to be willing."

"I'll lick it yet."

"You're licked, John. You were down for the count, and they've all gone home, and you're still in there swinging. It's all over and you're still fighting. The last bell rang hours ago. The lights are out. Doors locked. You are still swinging and dancing and jabbing at the phantom, at the 'thing,' as you choose to call your disease. It's all over, John. It's exhausting to have to keep this up, isn't it? The 'thing' won, John."

"So what do I do now?"

"Enjoy your defeat."

The Camel burned itself out in the ashtray. He stared at the framed inscription on the desk: "You can't think yourself sober." What did that mean? All his life he had been rewarded for his brains. John Hurley could think himself out of this one.

John knew that Gordon and the rest of the staff were watching him. They were putting pressure on him, yet it was all so gentle. And that very gentleness made him nervous.

They didn't seem to have a timetable. Weeks were passing, fusing into one. He had already been there for two months. What did they want from him? What was he supposed to understand? When would they leave him alone?

He had time and space and in a strange way, he began to feel safe. He knew that they could see things that he could not see, but he did not know what they were. Where was he going? Who was he?

John awoke one morning. He was angry. He lathered his face, looked in the mirror, and threw the razor down. If I'm a bum, I'm going to look it. He put on a soiled shirt, broke the laces in his shoe, and left the room, slamming the door. He walked into the dining room and left quickly before he smashed the cups stacked on the table.

A blue-white rage was searing through layer upon layer of shame and guilt. He shook his fists at his God who would have allowed, even willed, that John's life should have come to such a shameless end. How his parents had sacrificed themselves so that he could become a priest and now all his learning and teaching and ministering were as dung around his feet. It was God who had played this cruel trick on them all and John was helpless in the face of such cruelty.

The anger grew and grew until John thought he'd explode. Blood bubbled in his veins as the adrenaline poured into his system. Gordon watched from afar, knowing that John's very core had been touched.

During the third month of treatment, a late afternoon storm arose. The air became heavy as dark clouds rolled off the hills into the river valley where the center was located. He sat on his bed and watched the rain pelting the window and soaking the curtains that were blowing in the wind.

Slowly, like a child waking from sleep, John felt a great sadness settle over him. It was a magnificent sadness, one that blanketed him completely with sorrow and grief. The sadness grew deeper and deeper and tears rose to his eyes and he fell on his knees and wept.

John prayed as he wept. Over and over he prayed, "Father, into Thy Hands I commend my spirit . . . Father, into Thy Hands I commend my spirit . . . Father, into Thy Hands I commend my spirit." For five days he walked in the garden and prayed the same prayer, allowing himself to touch his own desolation and grief, his shame and guilt and loss.

In the depth of his heart, John felt strangely willing. The fight had gone out of him. He had lost. There was no more struggle. Something had shifted. He had surrendered, and in the surrender came the acceptance, the embrace, the healing.

Perhaps for the first time in his life, he had been truly touched by the grace of God. Something had happened to him on a level he did not even know existed. He had been touched–deeply, profoundly–as if God himself had held John's dead heart in His hands and had breathed him back to life.

BODY/MIND

Physical disease, by definition, resides in the body's tissues, bones, organs, metabolisms. It can be seen, touched, probed, measured, counted, removed. It is in the realm of the physical, material, tangible.

But because man is not simply a material or physical entity, the diseases and illness contained within the body effect and are effected by the mind. (And by the mind, we are referring to the psyche, the soul, the spirit, the "Inner Body," or whatever we choose to call that non-bodied part of us.)

The flu makes us depressed; a headache makes us agitated; sore feet make us irritable. Likewise, major illness causes grave emotional, mental, and spiritual suffering. What goes on in the body rebounds throughout our entire being, and may cause additional problems of a psychological or psychiatric nature.

The obverse of this is that healing of the body can come through the mind, the soul, the spirit. Norman Cousins laughed himself well and went on to write of the unlimited resources within us to conquer our fears and diseases.

In one of the most significant writings of our time, Dr. Elizabeth Kubler-Ross, a psychiatrist, has outlined the emotional and spiritual struggle that must be experienced by everyone who faces his own mortality. She has detailed the five critical steps: Denial and Isolation; Anger; Bargaining; Depression; and Acceptance.

Her work is in the context of patients facing immediate death from fatal diseases, notably cancer, but her insight is just as true, just as applicable to anyone who must learn to live with any crippling, chronic disease.

Burn victims, quadriplegics, those with Hanson's disease, Parkinson's disease, Jellinek's disease, multiple sclerosis, facial or physical disfigurements–all these people experience universal stages in the acceptance of their disease. Many do not go through all of these stages and remain frozen along the way–in denial, in isolation, in anger or depression.

These various stages can be interpreted in strictly psychiatric terms. Freud laid the groundwork for much of what we now understand about regression and denial. These can also be interpreted in religious terms, as the great writers of Buddhism, Judaism, and Christianity have shown.

Norman Cousins wrote that we are on a new frontier of health and healing. At no other time in the history of the universe has man been able to draw from the learning and understanding of the human person as we do now. The universality of the human experience in facing illness and in facing wellness has been presented to us for our deeper understanding of the healing process.

It is critical to note again the universality of this experience: It is applicable to any and all diseases; it is applicable to any and all persons, regardless of level of education, faith or creed, age or race or sex. The agnostic, the child, the young uneducated mother, the priest, the old and the young are all members of the human community and they all experience human feelings, human emotions, human aspirations.

The following is an analysis of this process. The story in this chapter follows one man, who simply happens to be a priest, through the stages of acceptance. It is a form of "Death and Dying," as Kubler-Ross so beautifully shows us.

This experience is not a religious experience, per se, but rather a spiritual experience, one that is universal, one that every man, woman, or child who has faced their own mortality, their own illness or diseased state, understands.

One of the classic treatises in the field of alcoholism studies is ***"The Ego Factors in Surrender in Alcoholism"*** by Harry M. Tiebout, M.D. This work, together with his other monograph, ***"Surrender versus Compliance in Therapy,"*** foreshadowed the process of acceptance/surrender that Dr. Kubler-Ross described in her 1969 work.

Dr. Tiebout wrote in the early 50's, setting forth the critical and necessary psychological basis for the surrender process as THE condition for recovery from alcoholism. Dr. Tiebout was a psychiatrist, not a minister. He writes of a universal psychological, spiritual process, and not of a religious process.

Much of the following concepts are drawn from both the Tiebout and Kubler-Ross works.

REGRESSION

While the roots of Jellinek's disease lie buried deep within a skewed body chemistry, they spring forth and effect the emotions and personality, the mind and spirit. Normal growth and development are not only arrested, but the person regresses, the spirit slackens, becomes wizened, and the emotions grow primitive, the personality infantile. Ego reigns.

The adult so effected by Jellinek's disease is reduced to a more immature state, as if 20, 40, or 60 years of growth had vanished. The emotional clock runs backward, and the adult meets the child again. The adult world of responsibility, maturity, and conscience pales; slowly an infantile state becomes vibrant and clear and natural.

The person with Jellinek's disease assumes the omnipotence of an infant, the ego expanding and filling the psychic horizon. He becomes the all-consuming center, the heart from which everything radiates. While the self-absorption of the infant safeguards its own survival, the self-absorption of someone with Jellinek's disease is a precursor of the living hell that is to become his home.

The infant, the young child, cannot tolerate frustration and makes the world of the adult so uncomfortable that the adult reduces the child's frustration, whether it be the need for food, sleep, or stimulation. Likewise, the regressed adult suffering from Jellinek's disease must have life flow to his comfort and satisfaction; he cannot tolerate the normal static of living, much less its stresses.

In addition, the child plunges through life, unaware of its dangers, unfamiliar with reflection, circumspection, patience and prudence. The infantile adult acts precipitously, unpredictably, scornful of those who deal with life in a rational, even manner. Freud summed up the primitive ego of the very young in the term, "His Majesty the Baby."

There is pain in ***living with*** a regressed adult; there is pain in ***being*** a regressed adult. Like the stroke victim who wants to shout at his therapist, "This isn't really me . . . I don't know what happened to me . . . I haven't always been like this," the Jellinek's disease sufferer has painful flashbacks to days of sanity and equilibrium, or perhaps yearns for what never really was if alcohol became dominant before he acquired any level of maturity.

The earlier one begins treatment, the less psychic damage needs to be repaired, and the easier and swifter the recovery. Conversely, the longer treatment is avoided, the harder is the recovery. The expression "Some are sicker than others" takes on additional meaning when a prognosis for recovery is considered.

MAKING ORDER OUT OF CHAOS

It is well for others to understand the destructive path of alcohol in objective terms, for it places an order upon chaos. To look at the path of alcoholism, rather than that of a particular alcoholic, helps one understand the predictability of the disease. It takes the madness that is felt in the emotions and places it within the dimensions of the mind, imposing a naturalness about the path of madness upon which the diseased person is running.

Yet for a person suffering from Jellinek's disease to look at his illness in an objective, clinical mode is virtually impossible while he is still drinking, even if his disease may not be far advanced; he is only aware of his emotions, to the demands of "an inner unsatisfied king." Or as John said to his prior, "You speak of my drinking, but never of my thirst."

Much has been written about denial. The alcoholic simply cannot see and understand what is happening to him. The family also suffers this denial. Most frequently, the family is the first to move out of denial and needs to comprehend the nature of what has really happened. Initially, it does not matter that the alcoholic understands; once the family understands and is willing to do something, the alcoholic can then be forced to deal with reality.

SIN VS. SICKNESS

A person with Jellinek's disease cannot perceive of himself as being truly diseased. Like the rest of the world, he has been taught that alcoholism is a sin, or at least a serious social problem. It is not a real illness.

To him there is a certain nobility or eloquence in the thought of suffering from any other fatal disease. Comparing the "thing" that attacks him to the nobility of leukemia or tuberculosis, he feels doubly cheated, for he feels that society can empathize with victims of other illnesses, but the victim of alcohol is perceived to have brought it entirely upon himself, and he shares this perception.

He therefore sinks into the untouchables caste, the pariahs who provide the rest of society with a sense of their worthiness; members of society can gaze at the victim of alcohol as the deviation from the norm and feel secure and smug that they are normal, for without deviation, where is the norm? Someone with Jellinek's disease understands that he is providing others with a sense of normalcy, since he is so far from normal with his weak will, his aberrant behavior, his deviant thoughts.

Alcoholism is THE symbol of sinfulness and weakness. This is what makes it also difficult for anyone who helps and serves others through religion, (ministers and rabbis, priests and nuns), and others in the helping professions, (social workers, teachers, doctors and nurses, psychologists) to admit to being an alcoholic. Their entire lives have been dedicated to helping and healing, to goodness and rightfulness, not to sin and harm.

In an attempt to stabilize the elusive wall of normalcy, society casts off those who impinge too forcefully against its ramparts. It has been said that the Chinese would leave their infant girls by the side of the road to die and that Eskimos would place their old and infirm on ice floes to float to their deaths.

The Jellinek's disease sufferer feels himself to be in the company of society's unnecessary, undesirable, unwanted beings, to be relegated to the underbelly of urban life where others can come and point, relieved that they are normal.

NAMING THE MADNESS

In the fable, Rumpelstiltskin tips his hand and reveals his name, as if the heightened secrecy of being nameless is too much even for a demon to contain. The disease of alcohol finally reveals itself to the one it possesses, but not until it is sure of its possession, confident that the entire mortgage has been paid and the title to his soul is in its hand.

For long, the person has grabbed at straws, trying to name his affliction, to get a handle on his troubles. He has blamed everyone and everything, but on some level, he knows that isn't true. It must be stress. The job or the family are just too much. It's depression. It's immaturity. It's lack of adjustment. Mid-life crisis. Postnatal depression. The crisis of retirement. Maybe it is even a mental problem, a little neurosis. Anything . . . what the hell is it?

At first the name is heard in a muffled rumble, then in a whisper, then aloud, and finally, it resonates magnificently throughout the mind and spirit of its victim, and he can only say "Yes! Yes! You tyrant, you demons who own me! Yes! You son of a bitch, at last I know your name! Yes, I am your prisoner, but now at last I know your name!"

RAGE

As the initial relief at being able to name the "thing" subsides, the reality of the "thing" comes into focus. As one looks the source of one's insanity in the face and calls it by name, the formerly confused mind is sparked back to life, only to confront a seething rage that transports the disease person into the antechamber of a living, breathing hell.

Breyten Breytenbach writes in ***The Double Dying of an Ordinary Citizen***: "Hell doesn't exist. It comes into being, each moment it is created relentlessly, and then it is strictly personal and individual, that is, proper to each individual." The strictly personal, individual hell unique to someone initially confronting alcohol in his life is spun from the rage he feels at the gross injustice that such an ignominious, ugly thing happened to him.

And he rages at the glorious, mad injustice of it all. Life has backfired. John is a priest, one called from men to touch the face of God; alcohol has touched John's face and now he is called from among men to serve as the outsider, the pariah. John rages at the enormous cruelty of his God, who seemingly pulled such a trick on an innocent, unsuspecting servant. Give God your life and look at the joke He can make of it.

The rage that John experienced is experienced by all in their journey to surrender. With some, it is a fist-pounding rage; with others, a quiet depression so deep that one can miss that it is rage in disguise.

GRIEF

The unspeakable rage which envelopes one first looking at his illness provides the essential heat to begin the melting-down process, a necessary juncture in the process of recovery.

At some moment the rage is spent. The flailing, pounding, cursing cease. The blue-red flames of anger have done their job and they grow quiet, still.

And out of the stillness of the spent anger burst forth the tears which are the harbingers of the healing that is soon to follow. For some these are the first tears in many years; for others, the first of a lifetime.

Tears are made of water and salt. Water cleanses and cools and makes things grow. Salt flavors and preserves and is placed on the tongue of an infant at baptism. Tears cleanse and heal.

In his book ***Man's Search for Meaning***, Viktor Frankl wrote on the suffering of inmates of a concentration camp. He felt that there was ". . . no need to be ashamed of tears, for tears bore witness that a man had the greatest courage, the courage to suffer." When Frankl, a doctor, questioned an inmate on how he had gotten over a case of edema, the man confessed, "I have wept it out of my system."

While there is the emotional release that only tears provide, tears also signal deep and profound mourning over the death of one's former self, the person who at one time could cool off with a cold beer, who could toast in the New Year with champagne, who could enjoy a glass of white wine or a martini with a twist before dinner. That person is no longer; in his place stands no one.

One's life has slipped away and the person gazes at himself, cold and taut with death, lifeless, with no future, with only a past. So many, many parts of that old life were good, but now all that remains is death and one can only weep at its passing.

All who recover experience this grieving, in some way or another. With some, it comes with actual tears, as John experienced; with others, it comes in a quiet sadness, but it must come to all.

These tears are also the crying that springs from fear, for if I have ceased to exist, then who will I be? What is to become of me, since I am no longer? Nature abhors a vacuum–if the self that was known so intimately and tenderly has gone, will not a stranger of monstrous proportions come and reside in the place of the old self? In the face of such terror, one can only kneel and weep.

ACCEPTANCE

And after a time, perhaps an hour, perhaps in many days, the tears cease. The cleansing is complete and the soul stands at dawn. The reality of one's life, of one's disease manifests itself in its entirety; it cannot be changed. The reasons, the causes, the situations that have precipitated it have no weight; it simply is there in all its fullness.

At that moment, the choice is clear: Rejection or acceptance.

Robert Ostermann describes this phenomenon: "There is a moment in every man's life, crucial to the definition of his destiny, which, if fled or passed by without decision, is irrevocably lost . . . one of those rare occasions for a conclusive yes or no . . . Such moments do not occur twice . . . the gift is offered, in one or another disguise and one has the opportunity of consenting or not."

To accept or reject the gift is an act of the will. Confusion has cleared, rage is spent, tears are no longer; now the mind is free to act. The decision at this juncture determines the very course of the disease from this point on.

If the decision is to reject it, one becomes frozen in time, as the citizens of Pompeii were locked forever in the molten lava of Mount Vesuvius, their crippled bodies marbleized in anguish. The person with Jellinek's disease cannot unwalk the path he has walked: He now knows and has raged and has wept. This cannot be undone.

But he may choose to stop, to abort his healing, leaving the wounds open and festering, a fugitive from the wholeness that lies before him.

If the decision is to accept, to assent to what cannot be changed, to say "yes" to his destiny, he has taken the irrevocable step into the bright light of day where his recovery is waiting. And nothing will ever be the same again.

And so from the twilight of confusion, through the dark night of rage and tears, into the dawn of acceptance the Jellinek's disease sufferer has come, a pilgrim in a strange land on the border of recovery. The land is foreign, frightening; in the background is always the siren's call beckoning one to go back, to the illusion of the comfort and predictability of slavery, as the Chosen People looked back longingly to their days in Egypt when the journey became too demanding. Acceptance is critical, yet it is not enough; it is a truce, not a peace.

SURRENDER

The final act–of the will, of the emotions–is ***surrender***, that total and exquisite relinquishing of the illusion of all claim, ownership, control over alcohol and its presence, effect, and history in one's life. It is the abandonment of everything rational.

It is an action of simple grace that has been compared to a child standing over an open trapdoor above a cellar. The cellar is dark and the child can see nothing. The father calls from the dark and tells the child to jump. The child jumps and is caught.

To surrender is to take that magnificent leap in the dark, abandoning every human instinct of self-preservation and self-protection. To surrender is to relinquish all, to let go, to release, to abandon.

The sweet paradox is that after leaping into the depth of the darkness, one stands in the brightness of high noon, the sun streaming down and bathing one with healing and joy and release. The compulsion to drink has been lifted, drawn out from the hidden recesses of the body and mind by a force that cannot be defined, for the insane leap of surrender was the price of freedom. This is what John experienced as he received the grace to surrender. This is what all people who recover experience–regardless of faith or race or station in life.

The person with Jellinek's disease has now crossed the threshold into the Promised Land flowing with milk and honey, the fleshpots of servitude holding no allure. Healing and recovery are no longer abstractions but are as real and imminent as freedom itself.

Chapter Eleven

The Recovering Couple: The Courage To Change

Love consists in this, that two solitudes protect and touch and greet each other.

RANIER MARIA RILKE

Carl flipped on the right turn signal, pulled the white Cherokee van into the right lane, and turned off the highway onto the road that circled the lake. Tents and makeshift shacks dotted the frozen waters. Puffs of smoke hung over the tents and shacks–the only sign of life in the winter watercolor.

The sun was setting behind the snowy Minnesota hills and a blue chill covered the land as the winter fishermen sought warmth against the cold as they fished through holes in the ice. Carl turned up the heat and smiled to himself.

Carl had been an devoted ice fisherman, but that life was over now. For three years, since November of 1983, Carl had not had a drink. He had gone through periods of not drinking before, but he had never meant to live a life of sobriety, with all the changes that new life implies.

Now when friends congratulated him for being "on the wagon," he'd shake his head, because he was not on the wagon. He had tried that too many times: Wagons move fast and are not stable and people fall off them.

This time it was different. Now it was just one day at a time and if that got too hard, he only had to do it hour by hour. But this time he was open to A.A. and a new circle of men who were also recovering.

He had been through treatment four years before, but this last time he had listened and learned. He had truly been willing to go to any lengths to get sober. The first time around, he had just done it to get people off his back. And that wasn't good enough. He had had to do it for himself.

He thought of his old friends huddled over their kerosene stoves, fishing lines limp through the hole in the ice, tumblers of whiskey cradled in their raw and cracked hands. He had to be honest–he missed those times with the old gang, the booze and cards and jokes. The red-flannel, big-booted friendship of men who had grown up together, watched each other marry and have families. They saw each other through the good times and the bad, never questioning each other's loyalty.

But it was different with Carl. They all knew he drank differently than they did and they encouraged him to slow down. There was the time he lost his temper and started the fight in the tent, and the time he walked out naked into the night and they all had to get up and look for him.

He drank more and faster than any of them. But when he started to drink, he became a different person–mean or crazy or maudlin. Or he would start to cry whenever he thought of his grandfather, and he thought of his grandfather every time he drank. But by the next morning, he'd forget, like a sword slashing through time, cutting off the painful, embarrassing memories.

When he went into treatment, he learned that not remembering was a "blackout," one touchstone of Jellinek's disease. He learned about the different biochemistry that he had inherited, and how his brain had been permanently altered with its chemistry and wiring to produce the addicted state.

Now that he was truly living a life of sobriety, that he had understood his treatment, and that he was involved in A.A., peace would settle within Carl when he least expected it: Driving along, at work, at a meeting. He felt peaceful now in the late January evening as the men on the ice fastened the doors for the night. That was no longer his life.

He had to let it go, but not without mourning. It had been good while it lasted, but it was no longer a choice for him. That old existence was over and he had a new life to live.

Carl's old life had all come to an abrupt end that October of 1983 before he had gotten back into treatment: An apprentice was killed by a forklift because Carl, his supervisor, had not warned him about the emergency lever; Carl also had cramping heart pains in the chest; and his license was suspended for another DWI. There was nowhere to go. Carl had his crisis. His choice was to stay there and die or to be willing to recover.

Strange, how the doctors, the management at work, even his wife, Fern, had only asked that he be willing to recover. ***Whether he'd make it or not did not seem to matter; they only asked that he be willing***. Carl became willing–he went back into treatment. The treatment he had been through four years previously had been a joke because he remained closed, arrogant, and angry. Predictably, he drank.

It was not easy for Carl starting over again. He was stubborn, his strong neck with cords like steel. Now he had to be willing to let himself go, to abandon who he was and what he had been for fifty-four years. Control, not willingness, had been his way. That didn't work anymore.

He had to start over, despite the fact that his life was more than half finished. He had to become someone else, for the old Carl was sick and dying and destroying everything that lay in his path. And Carl was frightened, profoundly frightened as never before, for to abandon who you are is to die.

As his life lay in a heap around his ankles, Carl touched his own powerlessness. For the first time in his life he prayed to be willing, to be open, to listen and learn and maybe even not to die.

At the rehabilitation center that November, Carl grew willing to listen and learn. In his second treatment he finally accepted that he had a disease, Jellinek's disease, and that over 18 million other Americans shared this illness. As the symptoms and signs of Jellinek's disease progression were explained, Carl grew to understand the nature of his affliction and was willing to accept that he also had contracted it.

In the accepting came Carl's surrender, and in the surrender came the recovery. In abandoning his illusion of control over alcohol, or what he had imagined as his control, the indomitable compulsion to drink was lifted. The days of trying in vain to control his drinking were over.

No longer did there have to be times of forced dryness, with every cell in his body screaming for a drink. No longer need he go on the wagon, putting himself through the torments of the damned. That was all over; sobriety is not being dry, nor being "on the wagon. ***Sobriety is the exquisite freedom from the compulsion to drink***.

In court, Carl had to settle his part in the responsibility for the death of the young forklift operator. He had to get squared away with his wife, his boss, his children, his brothers and sisters, and with his minister. It all had to be done, for it was overweight luggage that could not be taken on his new journey.

Fern's life, her disease, her recovery were very different from Carl's. Despite the fact that they had been married for over thirty years and had shared so much, her drinking and using were done in private, whereas his was out in the open. It was hard for her to recognize her own disease, which seemed so mild in comparison with his violent, drunken rages.

The two of them, both from respectable but simple Swedish Lutheran stock, had been walking lies, a reproach to their people, a scandal to their neighbors, an agony to their children. Fern knew she was walking a tightrope, but there was no way off.

Just four short years ago, they were two drowning souls, clinging to each other, dragging each other down. If they had kept up their drinking, they would both be dead, and they both knew it.

They hid bottles from each other: Carl, under the seat of his pickup, in his tool chest, in the oil drum behind the garage; Fern kept her pills in her sewing box, and in dark, little spice cans–places where Carl or the children wouldn't look. And she hid her empty bottles of booze in the attic.

Fern was a nurse and she had betrayed herself and everything she believed in. She spent her time planning how to steal from the drug cart, balancing out the patients' needs, playing one off against the other, dancing from one chart to another, playing off doctors, other nurses, colluding and co-opting others to keep herself supplied. She was exhausted, having to keep one step ahead of the game: How to get it, how to keep it, how to space it so she'd have enough to function, but not too much so she couldn't work.

Her patients, her children and marriage, nothing mattered. She knew of the sordidness of her life, but she could not bear to think of it. And there was nothing she could do about it, for she was crashing down a well that had no bottom.

She woke one cold morning after a fitful, nightmarish sleep. Her mouth was parched, her hands shook, her mind vacant, unable to focus or think. She needed a drink, but the supply in the closet was gone. She became desperate. She had to have a drink! She would kill for a drink!

Dressed in only a nightgown with a torn shoulder, she ran down to the basement to the tool cabinet, but there was nothing. Behind the sofa, beneath the bed, in the linen closet, in the potato drawer, with the Christmas decorations–nothing.

In a last attempt, she ran to the garage, climbed a ladder in her bare feet, and reached her hand into the loft, hoping for a lost can of beer, sour wine, anything. The loft was empty– Carl must have found a new hiding place.

She remembered the attic. Maybe she had left some in a bottle. Maybe there was even a fresh bottle. A big, unopened bottle of clear vodka that she could open quickly and pour down her throat. She had to have it or go mad. Fern tore up the stairs to the attic and flung the door open.

The early morning sun shone through the small window, filling with light the empty bottles that sat row upon row along the rafters. The wooden eaves were suffused with a glow, an amber glow that one would find only in a church or a chapel. The eaves thrust upward as they would in a house of prayer and Fern went to her knees in the drafty, still room and asked for deliverance from her living hell.

Fern sought help, earnestly, but treatment was not easy. Carl agreed to come for the family weekend. Four years before, he had been through treatment himself, but he continued to drink. To protect himself and his right to drink, he patronized her and the staff.

Fern could tell that he was trying to sober up so the staff couldn't tell that he had a problem. But she knew he had been drinking. His hands were shaky and he wouldn't look her in the eye.

During the lectures on the nature and progression of the illness, Carl looked bored and excused himself. The truth was getting too close to him, but when Fern complained to the counselors, they told her that she was there for herself, not for Carl. She had to get better; she was as powerless over his disease as she was over her own.

It was strange. Carl had been drinking for over thirty years, and for so long it didn't seem to hurt him. Yet Fern hadn't begun drinking until she was in her forties, when the children were on their own in the world and she had gone back to work.

Within a relatively short time, less than seven years, alcohol ruled her life. Pills seemed a natural companion to the booze. They were easy to get in a hospital; they were easy to take when she was working; they didn't smell. Her system was different than his, perhaps more finely tuned. In short, it didn't take long before her addiction became the focal point in her life.

Fern finished her treatment, only to return home to a situation that was deteriorating quickly. He resented her new life: A.A. meetings, her sponsor, her new language and ways of looking at life, her daily readings and time spent quietly and alone. Carl missed his drinking partner and interpreted her new found sobriety as a reproach to his own drinking.

He saw her as a hypocrite, basking in her nondrinking and non-using. When she tried to ask for his support, he felt she was making a fool out of him. He struck out at her, sabotaging her efforts at her new-found sobriety. When she went to an A.A. meeting in the evening, she found herself locked out of the house. When friends called, he told them she was out; if they were on the program, he told them she was drinking and couldn't come to the phone.

He poured her a drink as they watched television. The refrigerator was stocked with beer. When they went out, he stopped at the tavern where they both used to drink, and when she refused to drink, he'd call her names and entice others to belittle her.

During treatment and at the meetings, she heard over and over that she should avoid "slippery persons, places, and things," lest she herself "slip" from her sobriety. She heard that there was no one or nothing so important as to place her sobriety in jeopardy, for sobriety was a gift to be treasured and guarded.

Fern heard again and again about HALT: "H" for hungry; "A" for angry; "L" for lonely and; "T" for tired. These are the things to avoid, for we drink when we are hungry, angry, lonely, or tired.

She became angry and tired of trying to defend herself from him and she felt the delicate new life she was trying to build was endangered by his aggression. While she knew it was his disease that provoked this behavior, she could do nothing about it. All she knew was that she had to stay sober, one day at a time, and that she could not do it with him in her life.

Fern moved out of the house. It was that or find herself back where she started. There was nothing that could stand between Fern and her sobriety. By this time the children, who were estranged from both of them, took Carl's side, accusing her of abandoning him when he needed her most. She knew that as long as she stayed there, she was endangering herself and enabling him to use her as an excuse not to confront his own disease.

Their individual recoveries were just the beginning. They were a couple and their marriage had taken a beating. It too needed time to recover.

Soon after Carl left treatment the second time, he and Fern began marital counseling with a counselor trained in Jellinek's disease. It was difficult trying to communicate after years and years of talking at each other, of insidious power plays, of playing "guess how you hurt me today." He said she talked too much and she said he didn't listen.

Their list of grievances was long and they had few resources to deal with them head-on. Being in the presence of a counselor who negotiated their needs, arbitrated their differences, translated their angers, frustrations, and hurts gave them a safe and protective spot to begin listening to each other with their hearts.

Slowly, they each felt a willingness to give a little, not too much all at once, but just enough to move to the next step and to do the next right thing. Their progress was marked by fits and starts, but both Carl and Fern were committed to making it work. They had come so close to losing everything. They were given a second chance and they were not about to blow it.

THE MEANING OF RECOVERY

Recovery from Jellinek's disease is a paradox. Primarily, one never completes one's recovery, unlike a case of the flu or a cold. The analogy of diabetes is more closely related to Jellinek's disease: The biochemistry has been so changed that it remains a permanent physical condition.

The harmful effects of the altered physical condition can be controlled through a program of vigilance. If a person does not do what he must to stop the progression of the disease, he welcomes it back in full force.

Thus, one never truly recovers from Jellinek's disease. The individual is in a state of recovery for the rest of his days and may say that he is a "recovering," rather than "recovered." Recovery means much more than simply ceasing to drink or to use.

Recovery means to enter into a state of well-being; every facet of one's life moves from the state of deterioration that alcohol has wrought into a state of health. Recovery means a constant and gradual leaving of what was sick and entering, slowly and painfully, into what is well.

It has been wisely said that the same person will drink again; one must change if one is to remain sober and to grow well and peaceful in sobriety.

RELAPSE PREVENTION

Relapse is a process rather than an event. We begin by returning to old behaviors which put us at risk, by thinking or saying "I'm fine", when deep inside we are falling apart. We're pulling apart from the group, perhaps not physically but emotionally. We bring the body, but the mind and spirit are in a different place.

Frequently we de-focus from our own interior lives and focus inappropriately on the lives of others. We sponsor 12 people, do a lead twice a week, are on the phone hours at a time, offering advise, a listening ear, a ride to a meeting or money. This fuels our own denial that we are in trouble, because drinking is the farthest thing from our minds. But we are well on the path of relapse, emotionally tumbling backwards with nothing to grab. The center doesn't hold.

POST ACUTE WITHDRAWAL

Terence Gorski, a pioneer in the field of understanding and treating Relapse, has focused on those sobriety-based symptoms that are a set-up for accelerating the process of relapse. The primary symptom is ***Post Acute Withdrawal*** (PAW) which can begin anytime after the acute withdrawal phase. It may appear 2 weeks into abstinence, reaches its peak at 3 - 6 months, and may last up to 2 years.

The severity of PAW depends on the severity of the neurological, biochemical damage and the emotional and social stress caused by the demands of sobriety.

Gorski lists the symptoms of PAW:

- not thinking clearly
- difficulty managing feelings and emotions
- inability remembering
- sleep disturbance
- problems with physical coordination and accidents
- difficulty managing stress

A critical dynamic in breaking up the relapse process is recognizing these symptoms and managing them so they become less often, less severe, less intense. Perhaps of all the Red Flags of Relapse, the one that is the reddest is STRESS: A high-stress job, a high-stress family, a high-stress relationship, neighborhood, hobby or sport.

HIGH STRESS = HIGH RISK FOR RELAPSE.

When we are highly stressed, we are, by definition, in some phase of relapse although we are not actively drinking or using. Like violin strings that are turned too tightly, we are ready to snap. Stress is a killer. It may also be a precursor to relapse and may serve as a stumbling block to recovery.

Change is not what systems do best. According to systems theory, a system seeks to maintain itself at any cost. When change is unavoidable, tremendous stress may be experienced.

According to the Life-Event Test which ascribes values to various life events, recovery is extremely stressful because it involves:

Personal injury or illness (alcoholism is a disease)	53
Business readjustment	39
Death of close friend (alcohol)	37
Change in number of marital arguments	35
Revision of personal habits	24
Change in recreational habits	19
Change in church activities	19
Change in social activities	18
Change in sleeping habits	16
Change in number of family gatherings	15
Change in eating habits	15

The above variables are experienced by most newly recovering persons. (There are other variables which may easily enter into the picture.)

According to the Life-Event scale, if the total is 300 or more, a person has an 80% chance of getting sick in the near future. The point is not whether a given change is good or bad, but simply that any change creates stress. The old ways are gone; there is nothing yet to take their place. More energy is needed to just keep a balance until the new ways are established.

The stress also causes a chain reaction in the brain which triggers the fight/flight response. Adrenaline roars through our veins until we are ready to jump out of our skin. This worked well when wild boars chased us over swampy marsh lands, when tigers glared down from jungle trees, when alligators snapped at our ankles, but it does not serve us well in recovery. Alcohol, being primarily a tranquilizer, would blanket the agitation of the stress.

However, an alcoholic cannot drink and is caught in a double-bind. A double bind means that there is no good alternative. You are damned if you do and damned if you don't.

THE CLASSIC DOUBLE BIND

Many years before Jellinek's ***The Disease Concept of Alcoholism*** (l960), Dr. William D. Silkworth described alcoholism with the shattering phrase "The obsession of the mind that compels us to drink and the allergy of the body that condemns us to go mad or die."

Dr. Silkworth's information reflected medical knowledge of the late 30's. While he did not have access to what we know now about how the brain works, he articulated with stunning accuracy the double bind that traps alcoholics:

- We must drink or go crazy.
- If we drink we will go crazy.

Alcoholics find themselves in a psychological dilemma as well as a biochemical one: They cannot get drunk and they cannot get sober. They hang in a twilight of pain. "Protecting your supply" is not just a cynical description of hiding drinks. It is a biological order, for without alcohol in their systems, they might literally die. And for the recovering alcoholic experiencing Post Acute Withdrawal, there is no supply to protect anymore. There is no mitigation from the pain.

THE TORMENTS OF WITHDRAWAL

This disturbance creates havoc in the entire brain. All the functions of thought, judgment, behavior and emotion are thrown off. This is why the alcoholic feels incredible pain in withdrawal and tries desperately to create a better balance by taking more alcohol into a system that cannot hold anymore. When a recovering alcoholic is in Post Acute Withdrawal, she does not drink but experiences the full force of untempered withdrawal without the consolation of more alcohol to buffet the biochemical hurricane.

Suppose there is a line to depict the difference between the system of the alcoholic and the system of the non-alcoholic. The non-alcoholic begins at the mid-point, O, and goes up to +3 with a few drinks. The alcoholic begins below the midpoint, at a -3, and simply gets up to 0 with the same number of drinks. This is why so many alcoholics report "feeling normal" with their very first drink.

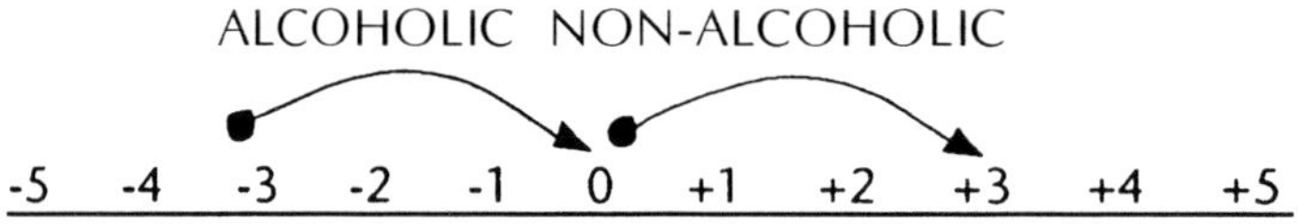

As the disease progresses and the alcoholic's system is changing with each drink, the baseline may well begin to drop to a -4 or -5. The number of drinks to come to normal is more, but the number of drinks it takes to get drunk is fewer. Tolerance goes up and the alcoholic has to drink just to stay away from the worst pain of withdrawal.

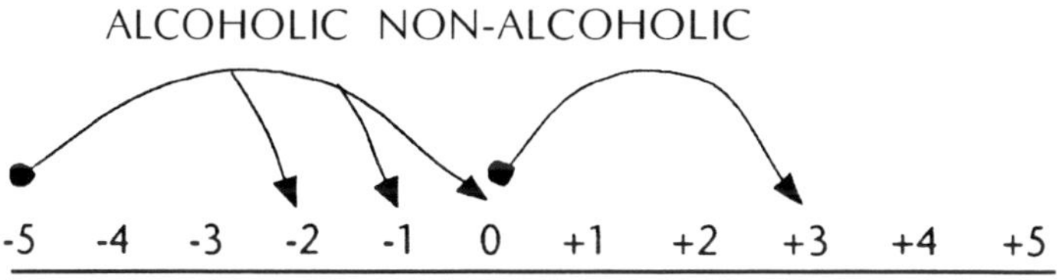

An appreciation of the alcoholic's double bind in the latter stages of the disease process is not difficult. The alcoholic cannot get drunk and cannot get sober. The recovering alcoholic is likewise in an ugly biological predicament while suffering from Post Acute Withdrawal: He needs a drink but a drink will kill him.

BIOCHEMISTRY OF THE ALCOHOLIC

There is strong speculation that the alcoholic is born with abnormally neurochemical systems that utilize the neurotransmitters dopamine and serotonin which regulate mood and "well-being". Endorphins can effect dopamine and serotonin levels.

Endorphins have 200 times the pain-killing power of morphine and attach at the same place (receptor site) in the brain where morphine attaches. It has been called the endogenous opiate.

Persons sustaining major physical trauma frequently report feeling nothing before the wound is treated. The body floods itself with its internal painkillers and allows the wounded person to seek treatment or care for a child or finish a football game. Not only is the actual pain not registered in the brain, but the stress that accompanies the injury is also reduced.

Some of the places that receive endorphins are located along the spinal cord. The highest concentration of opiate receptors, however, is in the ancient part of the brain (the limbic system), which is the source of emotional behavior. In other words, the brain receives its own natural tranquilizers right where emotions begin.

Education in the proper manipulation of endorphins is the key to a more comfortable adjustment to sobriety and to maintenance of serenity for recovering alcoholics.

Pat had been out of treatment for three months. It was hard staying sober, especially at the end of the day when she used to reward herself with a drink. Or two. Or ten. She dialed her sponsor. She felt like a fool, not knowing exactly what to say. But it was The Hour and Pat could feel herself getting into trouble. They spoke briefly. Pat hung up the phone, reached for her down jacket, whistled for the dog, and shot out the door.

"Get out of the house and walk. Fast. Keep walking. You'll feel better when you get home." Her sponsor's words carried authority, but they did not make sense. Nevertheless, she had been taught in treatment to pick a good sponsor and do what she was told. As the winds blew in from the lake, Pat quickened her gait, feeling safe in knowing that she was doing what she had been told. Pat's sponsor told her to take a fast walk. The exercise raised her blood flow, increased her endorphins, energized her body and calmed her mind.

Her sponsor also directs her to attend as many A.A. meetings as she can. So Pat goes to her A.A. meetings with newly emerging feelings. Sometimes she feels like a "cat on a hot tin roof" and is mourning the loss of her best friend, Jack Daniel. People are laughing and smiling and saying they are grateful recovering alcoholics. All she wants to do is lop off her head. Or theirs. She feels cynical and arrogant and wants to jump out of her skin. Yet, by the end of the meeting, she actually feels better. Her brain's reward circuits have been naturally stimulated by the smiles, by the handshakes, by the sharing, by the laughs, by being understood, by understanding, by enjoying her powerlessness, by not having to control, by the sweetness of surrender.

ENDORPHINS & DOPAMINE: MESSENGERS OF PARADISE

They have been called the "messengers of paradise." They are the biologically right way to come to the peace and freedom from pain that the alcoholic first sought through alcohol.

Reducing pain and elevating peace is within everyone's reach. The results are immediate:

- Recovering people are able to cope better with emotions that have been buried.
- There is less stress experienced when making the changes that recovery demands.

Dopamine is simply the brain's natural chemistry to make us feel better. Nature has put within our reach the means to feel better. Dopamine can be raised by such simple things as exercise, laughter, or pleasant experiences.

Listening to music, laughing, taking a walk or a swim, playing a game of tennis, having a massage, eating lunch with a friend, planting tulip bulbs, taking someone to a meeting, reading a meditation or a psalm, volunteering at a hospital. Of all of these activities, the most effective are the ones that demand the greatest output of energy.

The person who is going to seven meetings a week and still feels squirrelly obviously needs a more physical outlet for all the energy. Taking a long walk before a meeting or, even better, walking to a meeting and getting a ride home with a friend will provide a healthy boost in dopamine. Both the body and the mind will feel relief.

TRYING TO "FEEL NORMAL"

With the very first drink, many alcoholics report that at last they feel normal, feel like other people, feel comfortable. The system uses alcohol to compensate for what it does not have naturally. This may well be why alcoholics have a higher tolerance for alcohol at the beginning of their drinking.

BIOCHEMICAL STRESS OF RECOVERY

Since alcoholics are in such terrible pain when they drink, why don't they feel great when they stop? Why don't alcoholics bounce back after the poison is removed?

Chapter Twelve

A Life of Sobriety: The Fellowship of A.A.

I will restore to you the years the locusts have eaten.
Isaiah

The 1992 beige Dodge stopped before the small frame house on Walnut Street. Lou picked her purse up from the seat beside her, got out of the car, reached for her cane on the floor in the back, and closed the car door. She waved to her friend Mattie who was sitting on the porch, negotiated the high curb, and gingerly made her way up the sidewalk to the house.

A group of little girls on the sidewalk stopped jumping rope and shouted out in unison, "Hi, Mrs. Patterson." Lou smiled at the girls and looked up at her friend. Two teenage boys, sauntering down the street, stopped, propped themselves against a tree, folded their arms, and stared at Lou.

Mattie jumped to her feet and shouted, "You two move along! Get where you belong! You don't belong here!" The boys rolled their eyes, stuck their hands in their pockets, and slowly began to saunter away. The little girls waved at Mattie, relieved that the intruders were gone.

Mattie put an arm around Lou's waist, plumped the oversized red cushion, and motioned for her to sit in the wicker chair. Mattie sat back on the porch swing and lifted her feet onto a small pillow.

Lou looked down at her friend's feet, "Look at those ankles, Mattie!"

"Think it's the heat. The doctor said to take two of those water pills. Then I'm runnin' all night."

Mattie was a small, wiry woman with short gray curls that framed her small dark brown face. The green housedress hung loosely from her thin shoulders, the belt falling below her hips. Her stockings were rolled at the knees and her pink flip-flops sat on the floor. Lou had given her the slippers for Christmas three years before.

Mattie looked away in the distance. "Today Jessie and I would have been married sixty years."

"I thought you seemed a little melancholy."

"He's been gone nearly eighteen years. Imagine, Jessie Williams in one place for eighteen years," Mattie laughed. "I wonder what he'd be like now, over eighty."

"Jessie was a good man, Mattie. He loved you."

"Well, it wasn't always so good. He had his hands full with me, Lou. This girl had her day . . . I had my day."

"That's long over, Mattie. You made it up to him. You've been sober over thirty-five years now. You've made it up."

"Thirty-seven years, Lou. April 27, 1947 . . . that was the day. One day at a time. The bitter . . . the sweet . . . it all goes in together."

The two friends sat in silence, sipping ice tea, enjoying the bright July morning. Two blue jays flew to the sprawling buckeye tree on the front lawn. A red squirrel scampered down the tree, noted the Irish setter walking on the sidewalk, and ran back up the tree.

Lou looked over at her friend. Her pale freckled skin contrasted with Mattie's dark skin, her plump arm with Mattie's thin one.

"We've been through a lot together, Mattie. I hate to think where I'd be without you."

"Girl, you'd be just fine. I just did what anyone else in A.A. would have done. Some people just take longer."

"You stuck with me. All those years, all those wasted years."

"They weren't wasted, Lou. You came around in your own good time, but I'd have to say you weren't in any rush. You just couldn't let go."

Lou and Mattie laughed. It had taken Lou eight years to get sober and to stay sober. Mattie had stayed by her side through relapse after relapse, hospitalizations, treatments, family breakdowns. It took Lou years of fighting her disease, of trying to control it herself, of pretending that she wasn't really as bad as they were trying to tell her.

Lou had been married to Jim Patterson, an attorney in the small Ohio town where they had both grown up. They were one of the prominent young couples in town. Jim served on civic and church boards and Lou was involved with the women's clubs and church functions. Three daughters were born and Jim regretted not having a son, but he figured that the girls would marry lawyers to come into the practice when he got older.

Jim and Lou were both golfers and much of their social life centered around the club. He began spending more and more time at the club as his lunches extended into the afternoons. He began drinking, and as his drinking increased, he neglected his practice, knowing that his brothers would pick up the slack.

Soon rumors of other women reached Lou. She did not believe them. As Jim's drinking got more out of control, his affairs became more flagrant. He was seen with a younger woman, divorced, a secretary at the club. He began staying out nights, coming home in the morning to shower and change his clothes.

Lou was demoralized. Jim had always been so sure of himself and his behavior was never questioned. He had always been able to defend himself, to cross-examine Lou in such a way that any problems in their marriage had always seemed to be of Lou's making. She didn't know what to say. She begged him to stay home, pleading with him that the girls needed him. Jim moved out of their rambling colonial on Main Street and moved in with the secretary.

She couldn't face the stares of her friends, the abrupt change of conversation when she walked into a room. The girls clung to her, unable to handle the taunts of their classmates. Lou closed the doors and began drinking.

Shortly after Jim's forty-fifth birthday, he had a massive stroke and Lou took him back. Lou's drinking was not out of control, but she drank enough to mute the pain. She was glad to have him back, regardless of the terms. Lou loved him, and if she was a fool for love, then that was the way it had to be.

After his death six years later, her drinking escalated. She had always been a binge drinker, going for months without a drink and then drinking steadily for three or four days on end. The periods between binges became shorter; the times of extended drinking became longer. The girls moved out of the house, leaving Lou to ramble around alone in the empty rooms with her bottles, and her memories.

One morning her eldest daughter found her on the floor of the kitchen. She hadn't eaten for days and was bruised, dehydrated, disoriented. Lou was taken to the hospital where she was stabilized. Her doctor, spoke to Lou about her drinking and the effect it was having on her health. She agreed to get help and called A.A. from the hospital.

Within an hour, two women from A.A. were at her bedside. One was a farmer's wife from outside of town. The other was Mattie, a small black woman, a cleaning lady who worked for one of Lou's friends. From her bed, Lou listened to their stories of what it had been like for them, what happened to change their lives, and what their lives were like now.

They were simple, kind women who had been where Lou was now. They did not talk down to her, make her feel guilty, chide her for her lack of control. They told her that she had alcoholism, the same as they had, and that there was hope for her. She did not have to live a living death any longer.

When Lou was released from the hospital, they took her to her first A.A. meeting. Lou was frightened–who would she see there–who would see her? The women poured her a cup of coffee, introduced her to their friends, sat with her. They told her that she didn't have to speak if she didn't want to. She could just listen.

People were laughing, easy. As the meeting opened, she looked around the room. It was a strange cross section of the town. The banker, the librarian, the Episcopalian priest, the school cook, some farmers, a son of one of Lou's friends, other people she had never seen, others she had known.

There was a look on the faces of the men and women that Lou had never before seen. Peace and joy and freedom fused into a serenity that was absent from most gatherings. The members spoke easily about their lives, their families, their jobs, their sobriety. There were some who had been in the Program for many years; others for only a few weeks or months.

They all spoke of the present and seemed to be living in the present, for as one man said, "Yesterday is a canceled check, tomorrow is a promissory note, but today is cash."

The simplicity of the meeting hit hard. There were only first names used; it was orderly but casual; you could speak or not; contribute a dollar or not; drink coffee or not. Yesterday was over and they were all living soberly, one day at a time. A man told his story–a grim tale of illness, lost jobs and marriage, dishonor. Lou looked away from him. It wasn't her story—she drank at home where no one could see her. She looked back; he was telling Jim's story but Jim was no longer there.

Lou could feel the tears well up in her eyes as the terrible sadness of her life, of Jim's life washed over her. Mattie reached for her hand and held it tightly. Lou was alone no longer.

The following day Mattie visited Lou. Mattie had been sober for six years and told Lou that if she wanted to get sober, she'd have to go to meetings, depend on the group, get out of herself, break the isolation, and call for help before the ice hit the glass, not after.

It worked for three months. After twelve weeks, Lou felt she had been good and was entitled to reward herself with a little Jack Daniel's. What started out as a single drink ended up as a three-day bender. Mattie called and called but Lou had did not answer. She did not want to be disturbed. Finally she called Mattie and asked for help. Lou was filled with guilt and remorse and shame. She was afraid to go back to the group; she thought they'd be mad at her.

This pattern repeated itself over and over again. Lou's longest period of sobriety lasted two years and eight months. She never called Mattie or anyone else when she was troubled or was thinking of drinking. Things would go along for her and then she'd begin to dwell on her life. She felt cheated, gypped. He had made a fool of her. At this time of her life she should have money, travel, live in comfort and status. Jim Patterson was a first-class bastard. Lou couldn't get even with him, but she could drink at him.

Lou had periods of ***dryness*** when she simply would not drink. She had periods of ***sobriety*** when she would go to meetings and work her Program and be more comfortable not drinking than drinking. She even had periods of ***serenity*** when she experienced the peace that comes with surrender, but that would not last long.

The Program was there for her with all its fullness, but it eluded her grasp because Lou was not completely willing to do what she had to do. The degree that she was willing was the degree to which she felt peace.

There were repeated detoxifications and treatments. She'd come back, remorseful, stay dry for a period of time, and begin again. She just couldn't let go of her outrage, her feelings of having been wronged. It ate at her like acid eating metal, the stench and taste of resentment burning her soul, leaving no room for forgiveness or peace. She would not change her thinking and she could not get sober.

And every time, Mattie would appear–in the house, in the hospital, by her bedside–a symbol of hope through surrender. She kept saying to Lou, "You've got to let it go, you've got to release it, Lou, holding on is just poisoning your very soul. You'll never get sober as long as you need to punish him. You're only punishing yourself and you'll never understand peace."

It was before dawn one February morning in 1961. Mattie's phone rang. It was Lou, drunk, crying, "Mattie, please help me. I can't stand this any longer." Mattie and another woman went to Lou's house, dressed her, helped her into the car, and took her again to the hospital.

Lou cried. It was a grand and glorious weeping that begun in her toes and filled her whole being with its tears and its sobbing. Mattie put her arm around Lou's shoulder and softly bade her cry, knowing herself the sweetness of release that only tears can provide.

From the hospital Lou again went into treatment, but this time it was different. For the first time she began to understand the nature of the poison she was sheltering within herself and she understood that she had to get rid of it if she was ever to heal. And as she struggled to release her hold on the past, Mattie stood by, not close enough to smother, but near enough to warm.

She had heard many times at A.A. meetings about resentments. They called them "the killers." To hold on to resentments is to hold on to old hurts, thereby giving them the power to continue inflicting their pain. Lou had her private war to wage with her husband and as long as she continued to fight him, to let him hurt her, she would continue to drink. She still had him to "drink at."

During treatment, she heard lectures on grief and anger. She trusted her counselor and slowly began to share with her the hurts and anger of the past. The counselor allowed Lou to express these horrible feelings that were buried alive.

She helped Lou to understand that, yes, she had been wronged but that she had made choices, also. Lou had to own up to her choices, to take responsibility for them. She had gotten a lot out of taking him back and nursing him–she was able to feel noble and receive admiration from her friends. She was able to be a good wife, even if he hadn't been a good husband. She had been a martyr, but she had chosen that role and it was time to let it go. Her Codependency had back-fired.

Slowly, ever so slowly, Lou began to let go, to release the ghost of Jim Patterson, who haunted her day and night. She began to let go of her resentments, to release the feelings of wronged love, of humiliation, of revenge.

In their place a soft and delicate peace settled in, a peace too vulnerable to be examined, but strong enough to be felt. For the first time, Lou felt that she might have a chance at sobriety. A sobriety that did not vanish with the first crisis, with the first kicking up of the old desire to drink, with the first cloud of boredom or complacency.

Lou had always referred to her drinking as "slips," as if she were walking a narrow, icy path and, quite beyond her control, her feet went from under her. Mattie said that she was "relapsing" and that process could be interrupted at any time. Lou refused to get help before she picked up the drink.

Throughout all her days of relapse, Lou maintained some contact with A.A. The only requirement for membership in A.A. is the ***desire*** to stop drinking, not to stop drinking. Although weakly at times and firmly at other times, she held on to her desire not to drink and that was all she could do. Sometimes her participation was wholehearted and at other times she could only hide in the shadows. Mattie believed that if Lou would stay around long enough, eventually she would make it, and eventually she did.

There is no such thing as getting kicked out of A.A. Primarily, there is no authority in A.A. but a loving God, and He who had brought Lou so far was not about to abandon her.

Before her last and final drinking episode, her sobriety had been tenuous, the first thing to snap when she was under pressure. As Lou finally began to make peace with her past, the quality of her sobriety changed. Her tenuousness was replaced with commitment, her anticipated "slips" were replaced with dependency upon the Program and upon the God of her understanding. And today Lou maintains her sobriety, one day at a time.

Mattie was resting on the swing that creaked gently with her weight. A breeze from the south brought the scent of honeysuckle to the front of the house. Lou and Mattie said little, as if words would dispel the mood of warmth and harmony they so treasured.

Lou looked at her friend, nearing eighty, half dozing, half awake. She seemed to be sleeping more, as if her frail heart were giving up the struggle. A twinge of panic shot through Lou as she thought that one day, perhaps soon, Mattie would be gone. Lou and Mattie, two such unlikely peas in a pod would have never met, much less become friends, without the Program. And without the Program, they both would not likely be alive.

Their lives were so very different. And their struggles for sobriety had been so different. Lou had to fight her resentments and struggle not to drink; Mattie had to deal with other things–with her family and with herself.

As she watched Mattie's chest lift up and down with each breath, Lou thought of her own many years of slipping and sliding and of Mattie's struggles with tragedy, depression, poverty. Mattie's young daughter was killed by a hit-and-run driver, her husband Jessie developed Parkinson's disease and could not work, her grandson was shot in a gang fight in Detroit, and Mattie herself developed heart problems.

Of all the struggles, Lou knew that the hardest for Mattie had been depression. Slowly her world grew gray and flat. Mattie was incapable of spontaneity, laughter, even tears. The most perfunctory of jobs became a chore. She was chronically fatigued but couldn't sleep. Food was tasteless and people were bothersome. Life was a supreme effort as she fell deeper and deeper into depression. ***But she did not drink***.

She felt unconnected–to people, to the past, to tables and chairs, to the church, to flowers, trees, everything. An exquisite grayness enveloped her and with it came the pain that she had never experienced in all her crazy days of drinking. The pain of grayness where the flatness and emptiness kept slapping her down until the line between life and death seemed to vanish. Her shame reappeared and minimized death.

In accepting her profound and total powerlessness over alcohol, Mattie had turned her will and her life over to the care of her God. Her dependency had to be upon Him. In the midst of her depressions, she clung to the realization that she could not take that first drink, no matter how sweet would be the relief. To take that first drink, regardless of how many weeks and months and years of sobriety, would be suicide; the pain of the depression could not justify that act.

During these times of overwhelming depression, Mattie clung to A.A. like a drowning woman clings to an slippery, yellow life raft. It was her one contact with reality, with normalcy. And the people in the Program did not let her slip from their grasp.

It is the essence of depression to feel that it will last forever and that there is no way out but suicide. A.A. taught her to forget ***forever*** and to live one day at a time.

It also taught her how not to drink. Apart from avoiding a painful relapse, her not drinking was a critical factor in her recovery from depression. If Mattie had drunk, she would have stuck a pin in her life raft, jeopardizing her very life.

As previously explained, alcohol is a sedative, a central nervous system depressant. To further depress with alcohol or tranquilizers an already depressed nervous system could have killed her. In simply giving Mattie the people and the tools to help her not drink during this critical time, A.A. may well have saved her life.

Finally, Mattie went to a therapist, a woman who understood Jellinek's disease. Together, they traveled hand-in-hand through Mattie's soul, touching those sources of pain that dragged her down and crushed her. Those issues that were too painful for Mattie to discuss were left for when she grew stronger; she handled only what she could at the time she was ready.

It is said that those who will go to any length to stay sober will stay sober. A doctor prescribed a non-habit forming antidepressant that needed to be carefully monitored to correct for dosage. This was hard for her to do, because taking pills seemed to be against her Program. She had to be educated in the appropriate use of antidepressants mitigated the severity of the depression.

And when she thought she could no longer handle it, she came to admit her powerlessness, and as she ceased to struggle for control, the depression began to lift like an early dew frosting a meadow.

Ever so slowly, the sun rose again. Day by day, Mattie grew stronger and more alive. But just when she thought she was out of it, she would slip back in and grayness would again curl around her heart. But she kept on and the regressions became less pronounced and the progress more steady. And finally one day she was free of depression. Her getting and accepting this help was not easy, because Mattie had been able to do so much with her own natural strength and because she had been able to help so many others. But this was the length she had to go to continue her sobriety.

Mattie lifted her face, opened her eyes, took a sip of her ice tea, and nodded at Lou. "I know what you're thinkin' . . . but I'm not checkin' out for a long time. Who'd keep their eye on you?"

Lou laughed and stirred her tea with the straw. "Stop takin' my inventory, Mattie. Leave me to my own thoughts."

Lou and Mattie looked at each other, knowing that they were truly the Chosen People.

ALCOHOLICS ANONYMOUS

Lou and Mattie and two million other people have been able to arrest the progression of Jellinek's disease through the fellowship of Alcoholics Anonymous. A.A. is a loose-knit organization whose only requisite for membership is ***a desire to stop drinking***.

BEGINNINGS OF A.A.

A.A. was founded nearly 70 years ago in Akron, Ohio. A stockbroker from New York, Bill W., found himself in a hotel lobby. The year was 1935, June.

Bill W. had lost a fortune because of his drinking. He was trying to get on his feet financially, but was facing a law suit. And he had not had a drink in six months.

It was a dismal afternoon and he was depressed and alone. The smell of rubber from the tire factory clung to his suit, his hair, his hands. At the end of the lobby was a bar. He could hear the crowd inside and felt that if he went in, he could forget his troubles. He needed friends and felt he could now handle a few drinks.

With a shiver, he turned away and walked to the other end of the lobby to find a church directory. He knew that he needed to find another alcoholic, someone who would understand, and that a priest or minister would know of one. He ran his finger down the list of churches, selecting one at random.

A minister put Bill in touch with Dr. Bob, a man whose life was in shambles because of his drinking. Bob wanted to stop drinking, but he simply could not stop. He was trying to do it alone.

Neither Bill nor Bob could stop drinking by himself, but together they began to find their sobriety. And soon they went off to find a third person who could not stop drinking.

Bill W. was inspired to know that he had to talk with another alcoholic to stay sober himself. This inspiration laid the foundation for the fellowship of Alcoholics Anonymous which they were to establish.

It was in the mutuality of their disease that they knew each other. In this shared knowledge, they were able to connect, like two stones striking each other, and the flame of healing leaped out from their coming together.

Without this mutuality, this connection of two like spirits, each would have remained isolated, perhaps seeking understanding from professionals or family or friends who did not have it within themselves to connect with the alcoholic.

That simple, inspired meeting of a depressed, dry stockbroker and a drunken doctor gave birth to Alcoholics Anonymous. Today A.A. chapters exist in 114 countries.

HOW IT WORKS

The book ***Alcoholics Anonymous*** was first published in 1939. Chapter five explains how A.A. works:

"Rarely have we seen a person fail who has thoroughly followed our path. Those who do not recover are people who cannot or will not completely give themselves to this simple Program, usually men and women who are constitutionally incapable of being honest with themselves. There are such unfortunates. They are not at fault; they seem to have been born that way. They are naturally incapable of grasping and developing a manner of living which demands rigorous honesty. Their chances are less than average. There are those, too, who suffer from grave emotional and mental disorders, but many of them do recover if they have the capacity to be honest.

"Our stories disclose in a general way what we used to be like, what happened, and what we are like now. If you have decided you want what we have and are willing to go to any length to get it–then you are ready to take certain steps.

"At some of these we balked. We thought we could find an easier, softer way. But we could not. With all the earnestness at our command, we beg of you to be fearless and thorough from the very start. Some of us have tried to hold on to our old ideas and the result was nil until we let go absolutely.

"Remember that we deal with alcohol–cunning, baffling, powerful! Without help it is too much for us. But there is One who has all power–that One is God. May you find Him now!

"Half measures availed us nothing. We stood at the turning point. We asked His protection and care with complete abandon.

THE TWELVE STEPS

"Here are the steps we took, which are suggested as a Program of Recovery:

1. We admitted we were powerless over alcohol–that our lives had become unmanageable.
2. Came to believe that a Power greater than ourselves could restore us to sanity.
3. Made a decision to turn our will and our lives over to the care of God as we understood Him.
4. Made a searching and fearless moral inventory of ourselves.
5. Admitted to God, to ourselves, and to another human being the exact nature of our wrongs.
6. Were entirely ready to have God remove our shortcomings.
7. Humbly asked Him to remove our shortcomings.
8. Made a list of all persons we had harmed, and became willing to make amends to them all.
9. Made direct amends to such people wherever possible, except when to do so would injure them or others.
10. Continued to take personal inventory and when we were wrong promptly admitted it.
11. Sought through prayer and meditation to improve our conscious contact with God ***as we understood Him***, praying only for knowledge of His will for us and the power to carry that out.
12. Having had a spiritual awakening as the result of those steps, we tried to carry this message to alcoholics, and to practice these principles in all our affairs.

"Many of us exclaimed, `What an order! I can't go through with it." Do not be discouraged. No one among us has been able to maintain anything like perfect adherence to these principles. We are not saints. The point is, that we are willing to grow along spiritual lines. The principles we have set down are guides to progress. We claim spiritual progress rather than spiritual perfection.

"Our description of the alcoholic, the chapter to the agnostic, and our personal adventures before and after make clear three pertinent ideas:

"a) That we were alcoholic and could not manage our own lives.

"b) That probably no human power could have relieved our alcoholism.

"c) That God could and would if He were sought."

THE PEOPLE

It is a truism in A.A. that it is a Program of ***principles*** rather than of ***personalties***. The principles include the Twelve Steps, the concept of ***anonymity***, the requirement for membership being only ***a desire to stop drinking***. There are no fees or dues and there are no leaders; those who do lead the meetings are "not leaders but trusted servants–they do not govern."

In addition to the Twelve Steps of A.A., the second tradition states that there is only but one ultimate authority–a loving God as He may express Himself in our group conscience. This is a radical departure from most organizations to which we may belong. And yet, which of us could set himself up as the head, for are we not all but one drink away from where we have come?

Despite the lack of central authority and the absence of a decision maker, A.A. is not an anarchy. It is a group held together by a firm commitment to the principles of the Program and to a daily choice of sobriety.

And yet, despite the disclaimer about "principles over personalities," it is a simple Program of ***people*** who share their strengths and hopes with each other. It is simply people who are held together by a strong desire not to drink and by a commitment to change their own lives and to help others change their lives.

NOT GROUP THERAPY

Many professional people, when asked how A.A. works, state that it is simply "group therapy." It is not group therapy. Group therapy means that people come together under the auspices of a psychologist, counselor, or social worker for a specific time, for a specific price, for a specific goal. Under rather specific ground rules, people speak of their own problems and receive help from the professional person and from others in the group. It is usually conducted in conjunction with individual counseling.

Group therapy is usually a part of a good treatment program, but it is not A.A. And persons who try to use group therapy jargon ("What I hear you saying") at an A.A. meeting are quickly advised not to do so.

While meetings are conducted along a somewhat regulated format (an opening reading of "How It Works," an initial talk about the steps or another part of the Program–forgiveness, joy, "one day at a time"–and open discussion by those at the meeting), what is said and how it is said are totally unpredictable. What is heard is likewise unpredictable.

Unlike group therapy, if one chooses not to speak, there is no pressure. If one chooses to discuss something that appears unrelated to the topic, that is acceptable.

Group therapy has a set of regular people who attend every session. A.A. meetings are fluid; probably no two meetings ever have the same people.

Most importantly, while group therapy has a definite time frame, the program does not. The participant begins at a definite date, and when he and the group feel he is ready to terminate, he is free to withdraw.

Because recovery is ongoing and lasts until death or until the individual decides that he wants to drink again, participation in A.A. is never over. One does not graduate. One does not have a problem or an issue that needs resolving. An alcoholic or a chemically dependent person has a chronic, fatal, progressive illness that can be arrested, not cured, by a constant vigilance over the non-use of alcohol and other drugs.

A recovering person is attempting to live a life of sobriety, a life that is not natural to one dependent upon alcohol. He must learn to live without resentments, with forgiveness, with humor. He must learn to get through the uncertainties of everyday life without alcohol, with serenity. He must ask others to help him through the major crisis of his life. There is no time frame for these things.

THE SOUL OF A.A.

It is difficult, if not impossible, to articulate the essence of A.A. One can relate the principles and steps, describe meetings, state what it is not. One can testify what A.A. means in one's life and project what it would be like without it.

And because of snippets of an A.A. meeting on television or on film, the picture of faceless people, with styrofoam coffee cups in hand, sitting on hard chairs in a church basement and listening to a speaker say "Hello. My name is John. I'm an alcoholic," seems to define what it's all about. Something between a Rotary Club luncheon and a Bible study group.

Or the celebrity on a "Merv Griffin Show" who talks about how she stopped drinking and can say the steps by heart.

And regardless of family members or friends who go to A.A., the image somehow remains of something a little bit tacky. After all, people think alcoholics are really quite tacky and those we may actually know are the exception to the rule. They really don't belong in A.A., they've just gotten a little scrupulous about their drinking.

But because of the anonymity (Jack M., Rose T., Josie P.) and because there aren't any rules and because it can't really be spelled out, we are left with the question, What is A.A.?

A.A. calls itself a Fellowship. It isn't a church, a religion, a club. It isn't a secret society, because the membership is open. It is more of a community, a large family without the fights.

Community means a ***unity with***, a binding together, a oneness. There is a oneness, a singleness of purpose, a unity in A.A. People come together simply to stay sober by helping others to do the same. That was the model that Bill W. and Dr. Bob created in their first coming together. Then they went to find someone else, and in helping another, they found that they didn't have to drink either.

When one begins the long journey along the path of Jellinek's disease, one is embarking on a path of utter aloneness. As the disease progresses and the chemistry of the body and the brain take over, the person grows more and more solitary, wrapped up in his own compulsions and madness and illusions.

And soon, the alcoholic, the drug dependent finds himself standing in the depths of a hell created by his utter isolation from himself, from his family, from his fellows, from his God.

It is this very isolation that often drives one to contemplate suicide, for man was not created to live alone.

The essence, the soul of Alcoholics Anonymous is that the man and woman, in the throes of this disease which has cut them off from every living being, are called out of their solitary hell into communion with others.

To the man and woman suffering alone in their own private hell, A.A. says, "Come, you are not alone anymore. We know. We've all been there. It isn't nice. We know that. You can be a part of us and we'll help you get better. You don't have to be alone anymore."

And that man and woman look up and find that there is a big wonderful family waiting with its arms outstretched, overjoyed that others have connected with them, making them all richer and stronger and more fully alive.

The love and acceptance that are the soul of the Program somehow create the energy for the healing and for the courage to begin a new life of sobriety. It is not a club or group therapy. It is not an organization with specific goals and rules. It is not a refuge for bored people with nothing better to do.

Rather, it is a sort of miracle, isn't it?

THE PROMISES

Thousands upon thousands of recovering alcoholics have experienced the blessings promised by living the A.A. way of life. The Promises read:

"As God's people we stood on our feet; we don't crawl before anyone. If we are painstaking about this phase of our development, we will be amazed before we are halfway through. We are going to know a new freedom and a new happiness. We will not regret the past nor wish to shut the door on it. We will comprehend the word serenity and we will know peace. No matter how far down the scale we have gone, we will see how our experience can benefit others.

"That feeling of uselessness and self-pity will disappear. We will lose interest in selfish things and gain interest in our fellows. Self-seeking will slip away. Our whole attitude and outlook upon life will change. Fear of people and of economic insecurity will leave us. We will intuitively know how to handle situations which used to baffle us. We will suddenly realize that God is doing for us what we could not do for ourselves."

Chapter Thirteen

National Policy on Alcoholism: Denial

All great truths begin as blasphemies.
GEORGE BERNARD SHAW

There are 18 million Americans with Jellinek's disease, the total number of people who live in the Scandinavian countries of Sweden, Norway, and Denmark. Among American children from the age of 13 to 17 years, there are 4.4 million alcoholics. Yearly, 100,000 people die from Jellinek's disease. We as a nation choose to ignore these facts.

In our classrooms, one out of every 4 or 5 children have an alcoholic parent. In a school of 450 children, there are 100 who have an alcoholic parent. We prefer not to deal with this issue.

In any given year, 16,000 people die and 650,000 people are seriously injured by a drunk driver. Before he gets into his car, that driver has about 15 drinks. He has driven drunk 80 times each year for nearly 4 years without being arrested; for ever time he gets arrested, as many as 2,000 other drivers in similar condition drive unnoticed, unbothered by the law.

Before he killed or did bodily harm to people, he drank with other people, but no one stopped him. No one wants to be the bad guy. Long before he harmed another person and that person's family with his car, he destroyed his own family with his behavior, with his drinking, with his attitudes.

There is strong evidence that those people who kill and harm other people with their drinking and driving have Jellinek's disease. (Fewer social drinkers are responsible for fatal crashes.) We really do not want to look at this.

Jellinek's disease, or alcoholism, costs us $276 billion each year. This is four times the total budget for the entire state of New York.

For fiscal year 2001 the federal government budgeted billions of dollars for medical research. There are two distinct categories of medical research that receive attention: those diseases that threaten us with their random selection and power to kill, such as AIDS and cancer; and those diseases that carry prestige because of the highly sophisticated technology that has evolved around them, such as diseases of the heart, kidney, and eye.

Jellinek's disease evokes neither fear nor medical elitism. Consequently, alcoholism is the stepchild of the medical profession, of medical research.

Officially, the Number One killer is cancer, a disease that we all fear. Presently, 5 million people have cancer.

Officially, the Number Two killer is heart disease. Likewise, there are 5 million people who have had heart attacks or who suffer from angina pectoris, pain in the heart.

Alcoholism is the Number Three killer. There are 18 million people with Jellinek's disease.

However, alcoholism is the primary cause of cardiomyopathy, a leading cause of death among the alcoholically impaired, and of different cancers. Because of current medical practices, the root cause of these diseases never appears on the death certificates.

In a historical, but greatly overlooked 1985 study, Dr. R. T. Avenholt, Director of World Health Surveys, Inc. and a former member of the National Institute on Drug Abuse, stated that drug abuse is the Number One cause of death in America, a "striking fact obscured in the nation's vital records and statistics by failing to note the addictive practices underlying such deaths." Alcohol is the number one addictive drug in this country.

Because we do not consider alcoholism a primary disease, but perhaps as an adjunct to a disordered personality, we diminish its death potential, like gazing at the cobra's skin while we shut our eyes to its venom.

We consider the killing power of alcoholism far below that of other diseases and our allocation of federal research funds for 2001 bears this out.

Research Expenditure

Disease	Numbers	Total	Per Person
AIDS	1,000,000	2,111,000,000	2,111
Cancer	5,000,000	3,250,000,000	650
Heart	5,000,000	2,070,000,000	414
Alcoholism	18,000,000	389,000,000	16

Alcoholism evokes neither fear (like cancer) nor respect (like heart disease). It's the stepchild of the medical profession. We know it's there, but it's not of our own making and we don't really have to take it seriously.

Disorders of the skin, teeth, eyes and kidneys, arthritis, diabetes, strokes, allergies and many other chronic illnesses get first call on the research dollar. As a matter of fact, Child Health and Human Development received $521 million more than research on alcoholism for 2001.

The most powerful, most informed nation in the world denies the existence of Jellinek's disease. Yet our scientists and doctors have wrought cures and understanding for diseases that once put us in an early grave or sent us to bed for life.

From our laboratories have come the polio vaccine, artificial hearts, kidney dialysis artificial limbs. We are unwrapping the mysteries of Alzheimer's disease and will inevitably be able to control AIDS. We can conceive babies out of the womb and operate on fetuses before birth.

Our moral/ethical dilemmas revolve around issues of abundance, not of want. We Americans are learning to do just about everything, medically. We can keep people alive artificially who just a few short years ago would have died a natural death.

Yet we refuse to look at the chronic, fatal, progressive disease that touches into the very heart of our families. Public policy-wise, it is not important that 76 million Americans, one out of every three adults, say that Jellinek's disease has plagued their homes. We refuse to fund the very research that may help us to understand and prevent our Number Three Killer.

The United States government spent 20 million dollars on advertising alcohol abroad. According to a 1991 Marin Institute report

Gallo wine received over 5 million dollars to advertise table wine in the United Kingdom and Canada and $315,000 to promote brandy in Thailand, Canada and the Philippines. It was the same year that treatment centers throughout the country began closing because of a lack of financial support.

To insure that we keep our collective awareness away from the real problem, we have been seduced into thinking that drugs are the real problem. Each year 21,000 people die from drug abuse or drug addiction; 94,000 die from alcoholism.

True, alcohol is a drug and your nervous system does not know the difference if you drink it, pop it, snort it, shoot it, smoke it. However, collapsing alcoholism under the umbrella of drug addiction trivializes the ferocity of Jellinek's disease.

Massive public monies and energy have been directed to resolving the ***War on Drugs***, the ***Just Say No campaign***, the ***Partnership for a Drug Free America***. No such monies have been directed to resolving the issues of alcoholism, which kills 5 times as many people as drugs.

The word ***drug*** is linguistically ambivalent: Good drugs (aspirin, amoxicilin) keeps us well; bad drugs (heroin, coke) kills us. This ambivalence keeps us thinking fuzzy about the problem.

Drugs are associated with the fringes: Minorities, Hippies, kids, the homeless, women. Alcoholism is Mainstream: Middle-class, ball games, dinners, cocktail hours, power-lunches. The All-American lubricant.

So, there is a psychic reward in keeping the public eye on ***drugs,*** subtly, preying upon our collective racism and fear of Hispanics, Blacks. It keeps the public eye off the real problem which is alcoholism, but that would hit too close to home.

Why is it that most of the 18 million Americans, our mothers and fathers, our sons and daughters, our brothers, sisters, and best friends, will someday die from Jellinek's disease? Wringing our hands, we stand and watch, hoping somebody will do something. Someday.

How long must the children of the Jellinek's disease sufferer, showing the same signs of depression and shock that soldiers in prolonged combat show, sit and wait in our classrooms for a teacher or social worker to touch them?

How long will our doctors turn a blind eye to the obvious signs of prolonged drinking or to the more subtle signs of early drinking, reach for their pens and continue to write prescriptions for tranquilizers, and say not to worry, it's just a touch of stress? And the patient leaves in despair.

Does anyone really think that the Jellinek's disease sufferer likes being the way he is? Does he like being out of control? Does he like to feel that he would walk over his children for a drink? Does he like his blackouts? His headache and aching gut and D.T.'s? Does he like to watch himself hit his wife or kick the dog?

Does she like to pass out in front of her kids? Does she like to lie to her boss about being sick? Does she like to sneak pills? Does she like to try again and again to control it, only to find herself pouring another drink?

And what about those 4.4 million teenagers who have Jellinek's disease? Do they think they are cool? Or are they frightened? Do they want to kill themselves because they don't know what's really wrong? They know they couldn't be alcoholics, because that is so LOW, so GROSS. It would be better to commit suicide than to have to admit to being an alcoholic. And many of our kids do just that.

Our government pretends Jellinek's disease doesn't exist. Our teachers pretend that these children come from pretty regular homes. Our ministers and priests like to think that all the alcoholics go to another Church. Our doctors and judges and policemen don't want to deal with it. Our companies look at it only when they can't do anything else.

Because we are so ashamed, we must bear the burden of unchecked Jellinek's disease. We have put the head of a monster on the body of a simple man and have allowed him to embarrass us. So we turn our heads. Yet, we pay dearly, every single day, for the risks of not looking. It is still there even if we close our eyes, put our fingers in our ears, and whistle in the dark. It's here to stay--killing, destroying, devastating.

We pay lip service to prevention or education. But if it doesn't exist, there is no real need to prevent it or to educate our children. What if those 4.4 million alcoholic teenagers had been told what they were getting into? Did they not have a need to know? A right to know?

We as a nation no longer have the luxury of denial.

Some of the engineers responsible for the ***Challenger*** launch shirked their duty. Afterward, they pointed fingers at each other, claiming innocence for themselves. And yet 7 people lost their lives one bright, cold Florida morning. Someone was responsible. They could not pretend it didn't happen. We all saw it.

It is now our time, all of us, to open our eyes to the disaster of alcoholism strewn before us. The time is long past for us to take off its monster head and see it as an illness. We have long since done that for our 5 million cancer victims, for our parents with Alzheimer's disease.

Won't we do it for our 18 million alcoholics? For their 15 million children? For the 141 million of us whose lives have been scared by Jellinek's disease?

We must all take part of the blame for our collective denial. We deny because we are ignorant of the nature of alcoholism. Or once we have been shown, we refuse to believe, because our old ideas die hard.

A simply syllogism illustrates this point:

1. Alcoholism is BAD
2. My mother is GOOD
3. Therefore, my mother cannot have alcoholism

If we proceed from a more enlightened premise, the syllogism would read:

1. Alcoholism is a disease (Jellinek's disease).
2. My mother has alcoholism.
3. My mother is sick.

We have all been ignorant, and in our ignorance, we laugh at "drunk jokes"; we speak of the "alcoholic personality," rather than "alcoholic body chemistry"; we allow the media to divert our limited attention to the sensationalism of crack or cocaine; as we sip our scotch, we feel superior to the alcoholic in the long coat with a wine bottle in his pocket; we patronize our family members and friends who go to A.A., telling them how proud we are that they have "overcome" their problems.

All of us--teachers and tailors, our mothers and ministers, rabbis and priests, our social workers and salespeople, our employers and community leaders, our actors and writers and poets, our doctors and nurses, our students, our media writers and producers, our lawyers and law enforcers, our plumbers and electricians and carpenters--must stop pretending that this does not exist.

On a bright Wednesday morning in January of 1993, a young President whose father was alcoholically impaired, spoke to us from the joyful mountain, celebrating his Inauguration and inviting us to hear the call to service in the valley. To celebrate the mystery of American renewal. To force the spring. To bring forth the courage and vision to reinvent America.

What better way to begin on the path of transformation for our spirits, for our economy, for our homes and communities that by declaring a National Year of Sobriety, a year of raising our individual and collective consciousness, a year of educating, of healing, of renewing our spirits and forcing the spring.

Our National Year of Sobriety could be the clarion call for all segments of our society, both public and private, to pool our collective energies, to retrieve the very soul of America that is daily trampled by the disease of alcoholism.

Together, we must harness the energies of truth about Jellinek's disease, about alcoholism, and for the second time, man will have discovered fire.

Appendix

SELF-TESTING

The following seven tests are to be administered by yourself, as needed. These include two tests of chemical dependency, one for Jellinek's disease (#1) and for cocaine addiction (#6) and four tests for affected family members (#2, 3, 4, and 5). There is also a Recovery Indication Scale (#7).

How to score yourself and where to go for help is included at the end of each test.

These tests are not meant to be used as a final diagnostic tool and do not take the place of consultation with those professions trained in Jellinek's disease and chemical dependency and any testing they may wish to administer.

They are simply personal checklists that may assist you in determining to what degree you are or have been affected by your own chemical dependency or by the chemical dependency of another. In addition, these tests may help you to determine whether or not you are in need of support from the various groups suggested at the end of each test.

SELF-TEST 1: DO YOU HAVE JELLINEK'S DISEASE?

1. Do you loose time from work due to drinking?
2. Is drinking making your home life unhappy?
3. Do you drink because you are shy with other people?
4. Is drinking affecting your reputation?
5. Have you ever felt remorse after drinking?
6. Have you gotten into financial difficulties because of your drinking?
7. Do you turn to lower companions and an inferior environment when drinking?
8. Does your drinking make you careless of your family's welfare?
9. Has your ambition decreased since drinking?
10. Do you crave a drink at a definite time daily?
11. Do you want a drink the next morning?
12. Does drinking cause you to have difficulty in sleeping?
13. Has your efficiency decreased since drinking?
14. Is drinking jeopardizing your job or business?
15. Do you drink to escape from worries or trouble?
16. Do you drink alone?
17. Have you ever had a complete loss of memory as a result of drinking?
18. Has your physician ever treated you for drinking?
19. Do you drink to build up your self-confidence?
20. Have you ever been to a hospital or institution on account of your drinking?

If you have answered yes to any *one* question, you may have Jellinek's disease.

If you have answered yes to any *two,* the chance is that you do have Jellinek's disease.

If you have answered yes to *three or more* questions, you definitely have Jellinek's disease.

IS THERE ANY OTHER WAY TO TELL IF I AM BECOMING OR HAVE BECOME PHYSICALLY ADDICTED TO ALCOHOL?

1. Do not go "on the wagon". (That simply means to stop drinking. Anyone can do that, unless you are in the latter stages of Jellinek's disease and withdrawal occurs when you do not have enough alcohol in your system.)
2. You drink only two drinks per day for three months. Two drinks means:
   a. two 12 oz. cans of beer; or
   b. two 5 oz. glasses of table wine; or
   c. two 1 and 1/2 oz. of hard liquor.
3. This is a test of control.

SELF-TEST 2: IS AL-ANON FOR YOU?

1. Do you worry about how much someone else drinks?
2. Do you have money problems because of someone else's drinking?
3. Do you tell lies to cover up for someone else's drinking?
4. Do you feel that drinking is more important to your loved one than you are?
5. Do you think the drinker's behavior is caused by his or her companions?
6. Are meal times frequently delayed because of the drinker?
7. Do you make threats, such as, "If you don't stop drinking, I'll leave you"?
8. When you kiss the drinker hello, do you secretly try to smell his or her breath?
9. Are you afraid to upset someone for fear it will set off a drinking bout?
10. Have you been hurt or embarrassed by a drinker's behavior?
11. Does it seem that every holiday is spoiled because of drinking?
12. Have you considered calling the police because of drinking behavior?
13. Do you find yourself searching for hidden liquor?
14. Do you feel that if the drinker loved you, he or she would stop drinking to please you?
15. Have you refused social invitations out of fear or anxiety?
16. Do you sometimes feel guilty when you think of the lengths you have gone to control the drinker?
17. Do you think that if the drinker stopped drinking, your other problems would be solved?
18. Do you ever threaten to hurt yourself to scare the drinker into saying "I'm sorry" or "I love you"?
19. Do you ever threat people (children, employees, parents, co-workers, etc.) unjustly because you are angry at someone else for drinking too much?
20. Do you feel there is no one who understands your problem?

If you have answered yes to three or more, Al-Anon or Alateen may help.

SELF TEST- 3: IS ALATEEN FOR YOU?

1. Do you have a parent, close friend or relative whose drinking upsets you?
2. Do you cover up your real feelings by pretending you don't care?
3. Does it seem that every holiday is spoiled because of drinking?
4. Do you tell lies to cover up for someone else's drinking or what's happening in your home?
5. Do you stay out of the house as much as possible because you hate it there?
6. Are you afraid to upset someone for fear it will set off a drinking bout?
7. Do you feel that nobody really loves or cares what happens to you?
8. Are you afraid or embarrassed to bring your friends home?
9. Do you think the drinker's behavior is caused by you, other members of your family, friends, or rotten breaks in life?
10. Do you make threats, such as "If you don't stop drinking, fighting, etc., I'll run away"?
11. Do you make promises about behavior such as, "I'll get better school marks, go to church or keep my room clean" in ex change for a promise that the drinking and fighting stop?
12. Do you feel that if your Mom or Dad loved you, she or he would stop drinking?
13. Do you ever threaten or actually hurt yourself to scare your parents into saying, "I'm sorry" or "I love you"?
14. Do you believe that no one could possibly understand how you feel?
15. Do you have money problems because of someone else's drinking?
16. Are meal times frequently delayed because of the drinker?
17. Have you considered calling the police because of drinking behavior?
18. Have you refused dates out of fear or anxiety?
19. Do you think that if the drinker stopped drinking, your other problems would be over?
20. Do you ever treat people (teachers, schoolmates, team mates, etc.) unjustly because you are angry at someone else for drinking too much?

If you have answered yes to some of these questions, Alateen may help you.

SELF-TEST 4: DO YOU NEED FAMILIES ANONYMOUS?

1. Do you ever lie awake worrying about your child?
2. Do you ever feel frustrated in your attempts to control your child?
3. Do you disapprove of your child's life-style?
4. Do you argue with your child about his or her friends?
5. Do you find it increasingly difficult to communicate with your child?
6. Does your child's behavior have you "climbing the walls"?
7. Do you often ask, "Where have I failed"?
8. Do you feel it necessary to protect your child because he is unusually sensitive?
9. Are you trying to compensate for some family misfortune—divorce, death, illness, etc.?
10. Are you afraid to discuss your situation with your friends or relatives?
11. Do you find yourself lying or covering up for your child?
12. Do you feel resentful or hostile toward your child?
13. Do you find it increasingly difficult to trust your child?
14. Do you worry about your child's behavior affecting other members of your family?
15. Do you blame your spouse for your child's problems?
16. Do you blame yourself?
17. Are your child's problems starting to undermine your marriage?
18. Do you find yourself playing detective, fearful of what you'll find?
19. Do you go from place to place, seeking help for your child?
20. Is concern for your child giving you headaches, stomach aches, or heartaches?

If you have answered yes to any three of these questions, this is an early-warning sign.

If you have answered yes to four, chances are that you could use some help.

If you answered yes to five or more, you are definitely in need of help.

SELF-TEST 5: DID YOU GROW UP WITH ALCOHOLISM?

1. Do you constantly seek approval and affirmation?
2. Do you fail to recognize your accomplishments?
3. Do you fear criticism?
4. Do you over-extend yourself?
5. Have you had problems with your own compulsive behavior?
6. Do you have a need for perfection?
7. Are you uneasy when your life is going smoothly, continually anticipating problems?
8. Do you feel more alive in the midst of a crisis?
9. Do you still feel responsible for others, as you did for the problem drinker in your life?
10. Do you care for others easily, yet find it difficult to care for yourself?
11. Do you isolate yourself from other people?
12. Do you respond with anxiety to authority figures and angry people?
13. Do you feel that individuals and society in general are taking advantage of you?
14. Do you have trouble with intimate relationships?
15. Do you confuse pity with love, as you did with the problem drinker?
16. Do you attract and seek people who tend to be compulsive?
17. Do you cling to relationships because you are afraid of being alone?
18. Do you often mistrust your own feelings and the feelings expressed by others?
19. Do you find it difficult to express your emotions?
20. Do you think parental drinking may have affected you?

If you have responded positively to most of these questions, you have been affected by alcoholism and are still carrying around the wounds. Help is available through counselling, Adult Children of Alcoholics, Al-Anon.

SELF-TEST 6: IS COCAINE AFFECTING YOUR LIFE?

1. Has spending money on cocaine kept you from buying necessities, such as food or clothing, or from paying the rent or mortgage?
2. Do you worry about how you'll pay for the coke you use?
3. Have you ever borrowed money to buy cocaine?
4. Have you ever missed a day's work because of using cocaine?
5. Have you used cocaine for "fun" or to "help you get through the day" while at work?
6. Do your co-workers use cocaine and try to get you to join them?
7. Have you been worried lately about losing your job because of your use of cocaine?
8. Have you ever driven a car while under the influence of cocaine and/or drugs and/or alcohol?
9. Have you ever had an accident or been given a ticket while you were using cocaine and/or other drugs?
10. Have you lost a friend or friends because of your use of cocaine?
11. Do you lie about your cocaine use? Even to your close friends?
12. Do you sometimes argue with people about the way you use cocaine?
13. Do you take cocaine to improve your performance on the job, among friends, in bed?
14. Do you use cocaine to feel good, self-confident, the center of the universe?
15. Do you take cocaine to help you forget your problems?
16. Do you sometimes take cocaine before breakfast, perhaps to get the day off to a "good" start?
17. When you don't use cocaine for a day, do you feel depressed?
18. Do you feel "left out" when not using cocaine?
19. Do you sometimes feel sick - a headache, upset stomach, etc.- when you stop taking cocaine for a day or longer?
20. Have you lost interest in sex - even a little - since you've been using cocaine?

21. Have you ever stopped doing cocaine even temporarily, because of an unpleasant physical or mental feeling?
22. Have you ever felt sick while taking cocaine but kept on taking it anyway?
23. Have you tried to cut down your cocaine use?
24. Do you sometimes worry that your cocaine use is out of control?
25. Have you ever wondered whether you are addicted to cocaine?
26. Do you ever feel guilty about taking cocaine?
27. Do you have trouble waking up or feel as if you have a hangover the morning after you use cocaine?
28. Do you suspect that your use of cocaine has increased over the past few months?
29. Do you think about cocaine at least once a day? More often than that?
30. Have you sometimes thought of suicide since you've been using cocaine?
31. Do you sometimes accept cocaine without even wondering about its purity when a friend offers it to you?
32. Are you able to remember what happened after you've used cocaine?
33. Do you have trouble concentrating when you've used cocaine?

The cocaine hot-line is 1-800-COCAINE.

RECOVERY INDICATION SCALE

	Almost Always	Frequently	Sometimes	Infrequently	Very Rarely
1. I have let go of trying to control people and events in my family that I could never control anyway.	5	4	3	2	1
2. I get a good night's sleep and feel rested when I get up.	5	4	3	2	1
3. I can pray and meditate without feeling that I'm wasting time.	5	4	3	2	1
4. I am really in my body, in my self, connected and whole.	5	4	3	2	1
5. I eat, sleep, drink, watch TV, shop, work and exercise appropriately.	5	4	3	2	1
6. I can say no when I feel that it is not good or right for me to do something.	5	4	3	2	1
7. I am free from headaches, back-aches, upset stomachs, allergies and nervousness.	5	4	3	2	1
8. I can recall traumatic events that happened in the past without reliving the intensity of the feelings.	5	4	3	2	1
9. I don't fear the future – I know I'll have the strength and wisdom to do whatever I have to do.	5	4	3	2	1
10. I have friends that I see and have fun with – they each connect with a different part of me.	5	4	3	2	1

RECOVERY INDICATION SCALE

	Almost Always	Frequently	Sometimes	Infrequently	Very Rarely
11. While there are things that I might have done differently, for the most part I am at peace with my past.	5	4	3	2	1
12. My work is right for me. I am able to use my talents and am rewarded both financially and emotionally for what I do.	5	4	3	2	1
13. When I find myself slipping back into old patterns of thinking or feeling or acting, I know what to do to avoid relapse.	5	4	3	2	1
14. Resentments no longer burn through my heart; I have let go of them.	5	4	3	2	1
15. I like myself. I like my own company and my own thoughts.	5	4	3	2	1
16. I care for and honor myself. I protect myself from abuse.	5	4	3	2	1
17. I can now look at old photos of myself and embrace who I was at that time.	5	4	3	2	1
18. I no longer fear peace. I no longer confuse it with death. I seek peace in all of my life.	5	4	3	2	1

Please total your score on each of the questions. If you scored:

90 - 72: Congratulations! Your recovery program is working.

71 - 54: Your hard work is paying off. Things are moving along well for you.

53 - 36: You're off to a good start. Don't be discouraged.

35 - 18: Recovery isn't easy but please take that first step.

Glossary

A.A.: Alcoholics Anonymous, an organization open to anyone who has a desire to stop drinking, founded in 1935.

Abstinence: Complete freedom from and non-use of alcohol and other drugs.

Acceptance: Belief in something; agreement; assent.

Acethylcholine: A neurotransmitter that can bind to two kinds of receptors, the nicotinic receptor (nerve-skeletal muscle junctions) and the muscarinic receptor (located in cardiac muscle cells). Both types are present in brain.

Acetaldehyde: The principal metabolite of alcohol, occurring in higher levels of those with Jellinek's disease.

Addiction: A chronic, relapsing disease, characterized by compulsive drug seeking and use and by neurochemical and molecular changes in the brain.

Al-Anon: Organization offering support and recovery to those directly affected by the alcoholism of a family member, friend.

Alateen: Al-Anon's component for teenagers.

Alatots: Al-Anon's component for children.

Alcohol: A colorless, volatile, flammable liquid, C2H5OH, obtained by fermentation of sugars and starches, and widely used as a solvent in drugs, cleaning solutions, explosives, and intoxicating beverages.

Alcoholism: A chronic, fatal, progressive disease characterized by an inability to control drinking; Jellinek's disease.

Amphetamine: A colorless, volatile liquid, C9H13N, used primarily as a central nervous system stimulant; speed; diet pills.

Analgesic: Painkiller.

Anesthesia: Entire or partial loss of sensation or feeling; a state of paralysis of sensory apparatus caused by disease, hypnosis, or drugs.

Axon: Nerve-cell process which conducts electrical impulses and at its end (terminal) releases neurotransmitters that can bind to receptors in the target cell.

B.A.L.: Blood Alcohol Level; a measure of alcohol in the blood system, .08 signifying legal intoxication.

Barbiturate: A central nervous system depressant often prescribed to promote sleep.

Benzodiazepine: Family of sedatives that include the tranquillizers Valium, Librium; family of drugs that are cross-tolerant with alcohol.

Binge drinker: One who drinks to excess on a sporadic pattern but is sober between drinking episodes.

Biochemical: Pertaining to the chemistry of the body.

Blackouts: The state of temporary amnesia and/or loss of consciousness that occurs with alcoholism; the alcoholic behaves normally but has no memory of what has happened.

Central Nervous System (CNS): the brain and spinal chord.

Central Nervous System depressants: A class of drugs that slow CNS function, some of which are used to treat anxiety and sleeping disorders; includes barbiturates and benzodiazepines.

Cirrhosis: The most severe and, presumably irreversible form of alcohol-induced liver disease; Excessive scarring of the liver with hardening caused by excessive formation of connective tis sue followed by contraction; simply, a plugged-up liver; major cause of death in alcoholics.

Cocaine: A colorless or white crystalline alkaloid, C17H21NO4, extracted from coca leaves and used as a surface anesthetic; stimulant, known as "snow" or "white gold".

Codeine: An alkaloid narcotic, C18H21NO3, derived from opium or morphine, used for relieving coughing; as a painkiller and as a hypnotic.

Counselor: One, professionally trained, who listens, advises, supports.

Crack: A mixture of cocaine, baking soda and water which "cracks" as it cooks; like free-basing, it is smoked, creating an instant high.

Crash: Pertaining to cocaine; the depression that sets in when a cocaine user withdraws from the drug.

Dendrite: Any of the branching, tapering processes of a nerve cell which receive nerve impulses from the axon of another cell.

Denial: In Jellinek's disease, the process of refusal to acknowledge that one has the disease.

Dependence: The state of being determined, influenced, or controlled by a drug; addiction.

Dependent: One controlled by a drug, such as alcohol; one with Jellinek's disease.

Depressant: A depressant drug: opposite of stimulant; serving to lower the rate of vital activities.

Detoxification: The process of safely ridding the body of drugs, usually done in a hospital; also known as "detox".

Dopamine: A neurotransmitter in the catecholamine family. Dopamine is produced in two principal cell groups in the brain - The substantia nigia (motor region, involved in Parkinson's Disease) and the vertical tegmental area which projects to the nucleus accumbens forming the "reward circuitry" of the brain; regulates movement, emotion, motivation and feelings of pleasure.

Dual-addiction: Being addicted to or dependent upon two drugs at the same time, e.g., cocaine and alcohol.

D.U.I.: Driving Under the Influence (of alcohol).

D.W.I.: Driving While Intoxicated.

E.A.P.: Employee Assistance Program, a program in a business or industrial organization, whereby help and support is given to a chemically dependent employee.

Enabler: One who inadvertently helps the Dependent to continue drinking or using.

Endorphin: A neurotransmitter derived from a larger molecule that also give rise to several hormones. Beta-endorphin is used in the pathways that perceive pain sensations.

Esophageal Hemorrhage: Excessive bleeding of the esophagus, frequently the cause of death in an alcoholic.

Euphoria: A feeling of great happiness or well-being; bliss.

F.A.: Families Anonymous; support group based upon principles of A.A. for families of chemically dependent children.

F.A.S.: Fetal Alcohol Syndrome, irreversible physical and mental damage inflicted by a chemically dependent pregnant mother upon the baby she carries.

Flashbacks: Hallucinations that occur after the hallucinogenic drugs are no longer in the body.

Free-basing: The extraction of cocaine base, freed from adulterants, for smoking.

GABA: Gamma amino butyric acid; this is a main and abundant inhibitory neurotransmitter in the brain.

Glutamate: The main excitatory neurotransmitter in the brain. This small molecule neurotransmitter interacts with AMPA and NMDA receptors.

Halfway House: A temporary residence for those having completed treatment but not well or stable enough to return home.

Heroin: A white, odorless, bitter crystalline compound, C17H17NO(C2H2O2)2, derived from morphine; a highly addictive narcotic.

Hypnotic: An agent that produces sleep; an opiate; a narcotic.

Intoxification: The state of being drunk, wherein the toxins (poisons) in the body exceed what the liver can usually metabolize; legally defined as having a B.A.L over .08.

Intervention: The process whereby a chemically dependent person is presented with objective statements regarding his behavior and is given an choice between continuation of addiction with concomitant loss of marriage, job, etc., or rehabilitation; as opposed to letting the Jellinek's diseased "hit bottom".

Jellinek's disease: A fatal, progressive, chronic disease characterized by an inability to control one's drinking, named after Dr. E. M. Jellinek (1890-1963) who first described and charted it's progression; alcoholism.

Junkie: Slang word meaning heroin addict.

Kindling Effect: Increasing toxic reactions, including seizures at lower doses, experienced by cocaine and other amphetamine addicts upon relapse.

Marijuana: The dried flower clusters and leaves of the hemp plant, which are used to induce euphoria. Slang terms include pot, weed, grass, dope, and joint. Estimated 20 million marijuana addicts.

Membrane: Thin, soft, pliable layer of lipids and proteins that makes up the cell "wall".

Metabolite: Any product of metabolism.

Metabolize: To change chemically in living cells, a process by which energy is provided for the vital processes and activities, and new material is assimilated to repair and replace the waste.

Methadone: An organic compound, C21H27NO HCL, used as a pain killer and in treating heroin addiction. However, there are now methadone addicts among persons who have never used heroin.

Morphine: An organic compound, C17H19NO3, extracted from opium, used as a painkiller and light anesthetic or as a sedative. Repeated dosage causes addiction.

N.A.: Narcotics Anonymous; an organization for those whose primary addiction is to drugs other than alcohol, based upon the principles of A.A.

Narcotic: A drug, such as opium, which, in moderate doses allays sensibility, relieves pain, and produces sleep; in excess, may cause stupor, coma, or convulsions.

Neuron: Brain cell.

Neurotransmitter: Chemical message carrier between brain cells, released from the axon of one neuron to the dendrite of the second neuron.

Nucleus accumbens (NAC): Cluster of neurons located deep in the brain; the reward center activated by the release of dopamine.

On the Wagon: Term for one who has temporarily stopped drinking but has not admitted disease or started true recovery.

Opioids: Controlled drugs or narcotics most often prescribed for the management of pain; natural or synthetic chemicals based on opium's active component - morphine - that work by mimicking the actions of pain-relieving chemicals produced by the body.

Opium: A bitter yellowish-brown drug prepared from the dried juice of unripe pods of the opium poppy, containing alkaloids such as morphine and codeine, used as an anesthetic; habitual use induces strong addiction; excessive use is fatal.

Physical dependence: An adaptive physiological state that can occur with regular drug use and results in withdrawal when drug use is discontinued.

Polyaddiction: Dependency upon many drugs at the same time.

Post Acute Withdrawal (PAW): A secondary stage of withdrawal beginning at 14 days abstinence and extending to 2 years. PAW is characterized by emotional, neurological and social stress.

Primary addiction: The drug most frequently used and abused by an addicted person.

Program: Term used to signify way of life as suggested by Alcoholics Anonymous; members of A.A. may identify themselves as "being in the Program".

Psychedelics: Hallucinogens; drugs capable of producing hallucinations.

Rebound: To bounce back to a level of anxiety which was avoided by the use of alcohol; rate of rebound increases as abuse continues.

Recovery: The arrest of the progression of Jellinek's disease by total abstinence from drugs and alcohol; a "recovering" person.

Rehabilitation: The beginning process of recovery, conducted within a hospital or treatment center; commonly called "rehab".

Relapse: When a recovering person breaks abstinence by taking a drink or drug. A process that can be interrupted at any point.

Ritalin: Amphetamine-like drug administered to children for hyperactivity, minimal-brain-damage, attention-deficit syndrome; its principle action is within the cortex of the brain; exact action unknown.

Rush: Feeling of immediate relief experienced by the Jellinek's disease upon ingestion of alcohol.

Serotonin: A neurotransmitter in the "indolamine" family. It is produced mainly in the raphe nuclei region of the brain and is involved in maintaining mood and emotion.

Sedativism: Addiction to all drugs in the sedative-hypnotic category, including alcohol.

Serenity: State of being at peace; used specifically to denote quality of sobriety, abstinence.

Sobriety: State of being nonintoxicated, free from alcohol.

Sponsor: A member of A.A. who acts as guide, friend, and sometimes counselor to a newer member.

Stimulant: A drug that arouses or accelerates physiological or organic activity; includes cocaine and amphetamines.

Straight: State of being nondrugged, freed from chemicals; used as a distinction from "sober" which pertains to alcohol.

Surrender: To give over or totally resign oneself to something; abandonment; a necessary and critical condition of recovery.

Synergism: The combination of two or more drugs which produces an effect unobtainable by one alone; the principle that the whole is greater than the sum of its parts.

Tolerance: The capacity to absorb a drug continuously and in increasingly larger doses without adverse effect.

Toxic: Causing temporary or permanent effects that are detrimental to the functioning of a body organ or group of organs.

Tranquillizers: Drugs prescribed to promote sleep or reduce anxiety, including benzodiazepines, barbiturates and other types of CNS depressants.

Ventral tegmental area (VTA): Major neural input circuit of the midbrain; delivers and releases adequate amounts of dopamine.

Withdrawal: The pain and craving experienced by a chemically dependent person when detoxification occurs; characterized by tremors, anxiety, and even hallucination; a sign of addiction.

Bibliography

Advances in Alcohol and Substance Abuse. Vol. 1. Binghamton, N.Y.; Haworth Press, 1981

Alcohol and Health: Eighth Special Report to Congress: U.S. Department of Health and Human Services. September, 1993.

Alcohol and Health: Ninth Special Report to Congress: U.S. Department of Health and Human Services. June, 1997.

Alcohol and Health: Tenth Special Report to Congress: U.S. Department of Health and Human Services. June, 2000.

Al-Anon Family Groups. Adult Children of Alcoholics (1979); Al-Anon Faces Alcoholism (1975); Alcoholism: The Family Disease (1972); The Dilemma of the Alcoholic Marriage (1967); How Can I help My Children? (1973); Living with Sobriety: Another Beginning (1979). Cornwall, N.Y.: Cornwall Press.

Alcohol World: Health and Research. Summer 1984: Vol. 8, No.4; Winter 1984/85; Vol. 9, No. 2, Summer 1985: Vol. 10, No. 1; Winter 1985-86: Vol.10, No. 2. National Institute on Alcohol Abuse and Alcoholism.

Barnett, P.G. and Swindle, R.W. "Cost-effectiveness of Inpatient Substance Abuse Treatment", Health Services Research 32(5):615-629, 1997.

Baurac, Deborah Rissing. "Cocaine Babies: With Therapy, Normal Childhood's Possible", Chicago Tribune, Section 6, P. 1, March 7, 1993.

Berke, Joshua D. and Steven E. Hyman. "Addiction, Dopamine, and the Molecular Mechanisms of Memory", Neuron, Vol. 25, 515-532, March 2000.

Black, Claudia. It Will Never Happen to Me. Denver, Co.: M.A.C., 1982.

Blum, Kenneth. "Alcohol and Central Nervous System Peptides", Substance and Alcohol Actions/Misuse, Vol. 4, pp.73-87 (1983).

________, Ernest P. Noble. "Allelic Association of Human Dopamine D2 Receptor Gene in Alcoholism", Journal of The American Medical Association, April 18, 1990, Vol. 263, No. 15, pp. 2055-2060.

________, Kenneth, John G. Cull, Eric R. Braverman and David E. Comings. "Reward Deficiency Syndrome", American Scientist, March-April 1996.Blume, S.B., "Early Intervention: A Clinicians Guide to Secondary Prevention of Alcoholism." Postgraduate Medicine, Vol. 74 No.1, 1983

Burrows, Loretta Cameron. The Burden Booze Begets. Chicago Sun-Times, Feb. 9, 1986

Caldoret, R.S. et al. "Adoption Study Demonstrating Two Genetic Pathways to Drug Abuse", Archives of General Psychiatry 52(1):42-52, 1995

Changeux, Jean-Pierre. Neuronal Man. New York: Pantheon Books,1985.

Christner, Anne E., Ph.D., ed. Reference Guide To Addiction Counseling. Providence, RI: Manisses Communications Group, 1991.

Cohen, G. and M. Collins. "Alkaloids from Catecholamines in Adrenal Tissue: Possible Role in Alcoholism, Science, Vol. 167, pp. 1749-51 (1970)

Davis, Joel. Endorphins. Garden City, N.Y. The Dial Press,

Davis, Virginia E. and Michael J. Walsh. "Alcohol, Amines, and Alkaloids: A Possible Biochemical Basis for Alcohol Addiction", Science, Vol. 167, pp. 1005-1006, Feb. l3, 1970.

Davis, V.E., Cashaw, J.L. and McMurtrey, K.D. Catecholamine-derivative Alkaloids in Dependence", Addiction and Brain Damage. Baltimore: University Park Press, 1980.

Dawson, D.A. and Grant, B.F. "Family History of Alcoholism and Gender: Their Combined Effects on DSM-IV Alcohol Dependence and Major Depression", Journal of Studies for Alcoholism 59(1):97-106, 1998.

Duggan, Anne K. and Hoover Adger, Jr. "Detection of Alcoholism in Hospitalized Children and Their Families", American Journal of Diseases of Children, 145:613-617, 1991.

Duncan, David, and Robert Gold. Drugs and the Whole Person. John Wilet and Sons, 1982

Eckardt, Michael J. et. al. "Health Hazards Associated with Alcohol Consumption", Journal of the American Medical Association, Vol. 246, No. 6, pp. 648-666, Aug. 7, 1981.

Falkowski, Carol. Dangerous Drugs: An Easy-to-Use Reference for Parents and Professionals. Center City, MN: Hazelden, 2000.

Finn, P.R., et al. "Heterogeneity in the Families of Sons of Alcoholics: The Impact of Familial Vulnerability Type on Off-spring Characteristics", Journal of Abnormal Psychology 106(1):26-36, 1997.

Finney, J.W. and Monaghan, S.C. "The Cost Effectiveness of Treatment for Alcoholism: A Second Approximation", Journal of Studies for Alcoholism 57(3):229-243, 1996.

French, M.T. and McGeary, K.A. "Estimating the Economic Cost of Substance Abuse Treatment", Health Economics 6(5):539-544, 1997.

Garrett, R.C., U.G. Waldmeyer and Vivienne Sernaque. The Coke Book: The Complete Reference to the Uses and Abuses of Cocaine. New York: Berkley Books, 1984.

Gilling, Dick, and Robin Brightwell. The Human Brain. New York: Facts on File, 1983.

Goodwin, D.W., F. Schulsinger, L. Hermansen, S.B. Guze, and G. Winokur. "Alcohol Problems in Adoptees Raised Apart from Biological Parents", Archives of General Psychiatry, Vol. 28, pp. 238-43 (1973).

________, ________N. Moller, et al. "Drinking Problems in Adopted and Non-Adopted Sons of Alcoholics", Archives of General Psychiatry, Vol. 31, pp. 164-69 (1974).

Gorski, Terence and Merlene Miller. Staying Sober: A Guide for Relapse Prevention. Herald House, Independency Press. 1986

Grant, B.F. "Estimates of U.S. Children Exposed to Alcohol Abuse and Dependence in the Family", American Journal of Public Health 90(1):112-115, 2000.

Griffin, Emilie. Turning: Reflections in the Experience of Conversion. New York: Doubleday and Company, Inc., 1980.

Hamilton, Murray C., Blum, Kenneth, and Hirst, Maurice. "Identification of an Isoquinoline Alkaloid after Chronic Exposure to Alcohol", Alcoholism: Clinical and Experimental Research Vol.2, pp. 133-44, 1978.

Harlow, Enid. Crashing. New York: Bantam Books, 1981.

Harrison, Prof. M. Trice. Alcoholism in Industry. Mill Neck: N.Y.: The Christopher D. Smithers Foundation, 1979.

Hawkins, C.A. "Disruption of Family Rituals as a Mediator of the Relationship between Parental Drinking and Adult Adjustment in Offspring", Addiction Behavior 22(2):219-231, 1997.

Himwich, H.E. "Views on the Etiology of Alcoholism. The Organic View". In Alcoholism as a Medical Problem. New York: Hoeber- Harper, 1956.

Humphreys, K. and Moos, R.H. "Reduced Substance-abuse-related Health Care Costs Among Voluntary Participants in Alcoholics Anonymous", Psychiatric Service 47(7):709-713, 1996.

Hyman, Steven E. "Addiction to Cocaine and Amphetamine", Neuron, Vol. 16, 901-904, May, 1996.

_______, Steven E. and Robert C. Malenka. "Addiction and the Brain: The Neurobiology of Compulsion and its Persistence", Neuroscience, Vol 2, 695-703, October, 2001.

Jackson, Joan K. The Adjustment of the Family to the Crisis of Alcoholism" Quarterly Journal of Studies on Alcohol. Vol. 15, No. 4, P.P. 562-86, Dec. 1984

Jellinek, E.M. The Disease Concept of Alcoholism. New Haven: Conn. Yale College and University Press, 1960.

Johnson, G. Timothy, M.D.. "Biology Linked to Alcoholism", Chicago Tribune, Dec. 4, 1985

Johnson, Vernon E. I'll Quit Tomorrow. San Francisco: Harper & Row, 1980

Julien, Robert M.. A Primer of Drug Action. San Francisco: W.H. Freeman and Company, 1978.

Keller, Mark. "The Disease Concept of Alcoholism Revisited", Journal of Studies on Alcohol, Vol. 37, No. 11, pp. 1694-1717. (1976)

_________."Perspectives on Medicine and Alcoholism", Alcoholism: Clinical and Experimental Research, Vol. 6, No. 3, pp. 327-32. (1982)

Kellerman, Joseph L.. "Alcoholism: A Merry-Go-Round Called Denial". Center City: Hazelden Educational Service, 1980.

_________."Guide for the Family of the Alcoholic." Long Grove, Ill.: Kemper Insurance Company

Kessel, Neil and Henry Walton. Alcoholism. New York: Penguin Books, 1977.

Kinney, Jean, and Gwen Leaton. Loosening The Grip: A Handbook of Alcohol Information. St. Louis: The C.V. Mosby Company, 1983.

Konner, Melvin. The Tangled Wing. New York : Harper Colophon Books, 1983.

Koob, George F. and Michel Le Moal. "Drug Abuse: Hedonic Homeostatic Dysregulation", Science, Vol. 278, 52-70, October 3, 1997.

Kreek, Mary Jeanne, M.D., and Barry Stimmel, M.D. Dual Addiction: Pharmacological Issues of Concomitant Alcoholism and Drug Abuse. Binghamton, N.Y.: Haworth Press, 1984.

Kubler-Ross, Elizabeth. On Death and Dying. New York: MacMillan 1969.

Kurtz Ernest. Not God: A History of Alcoholics Anonymous, 1st ed. Center City, Minn.: Hazelden Educational Materials, 1979.

Lesher, Alan I. "Addiction is a Brain Disease, and It Matters", Science, Vol. 278, 45-47, October 3, 1997.

Lieber, Charles S., ed. Recent Advances in the Biology of Alcoholism. Binghamton, New York: Haworth Press, 1982.

Little, S.C. and M. McAvoy. "Electroencephalographic Studies in Alcoholism" Quarterly Journal of Studies on Alcohol Vol.6, pp. 139-140, (1945).

Luks, Allan. Having Been There. New York: Charles Scribner's Sons, 1979.

Long, James W., M.D. The Essential Guide to Prescription Drugs: 1992. New Your: HarperCollins Publishers, 1992.

Marsh, Rev. Jack. You Can Help the Alcoholic: A Christian Plan for Intervention. Notre Dame, Ind.: Ave Maria Press, 1983.

MacLeod, L.D. "Biochemistry and Alcoholism." British Journal of Addiction. Vol. 47, pp. 21-39, (1950).

McGrath, C.E., et al. "Academic Achievement in Adolescent Children of Alcoholics", Journal of Studies for Alcoholism 60(1):18-26, 1999.

Milam, Dr. James R. and Katherine Ketcham. Under the Influence. New York: Bantam Books, 1983.

Morris, Lisa B., Robert Garrett, Waldmeyer, Ursula and Lawrence D. Chilnick. The Little Black Pill Book. New York: Bantam Books, 1983.

National Council on Alcoholism and Drug Dependence, Inc., "Substance Abuse: The Nation's Number One Health Problem," Institute for Health Policy, Brandeis University, 2001.

Nestler, Eric J. "Total Recall - the Memory of Addiction", Science, Vol. 292, 2266-2267, June 22, 2001.

Niven, Robert G., M.D.. "Child Abuse Demonstration Projects," ADAMHA News, Vol. 10, No. 1 (1984)

Olds, David L., M.D. "Disease Concept of Alcoholism:; "Sedativism/ The Prescription Trap"; "Pot". Belleville, Ill: Gary Whiteaker Co. Publications.

Pattison, E. Mansell, M.D. and Edward Kaufman, M.D..Encyclopedic Handbook of Alcoholism. New York: Gardner Press, 1983

Reddy, Betty and Orville McElfresh. Detachment and Recovery

from Alcoholism: A Dilemma. Park Ridge, Il.: Lutheran General Hospital, 1978

Restak, Richard. The Brain. New York: Bantam Books, 1984

Rogers, Ronald R. and Chandler Scott McMillan. Relapse Traps: How to Avoid the 12 Most Common Pitfalls in Recovery. New York: Bantam Books, 1992.

Rouse, Kenneth. Alcoholism in Industry Series. Long Grove, Ill.: Kemper Insurance Company

Russell, Marcia, Cynthia Henderson, and Sheila B. Blume, M.D.. Children of Alcoholics: A Review of the Literature. New York: Children of Alcoholics Foundation, 1984

Schuckit, Marc A. "Genetics and the Role for Alcoholism", Journal of the American Medical Association, Vol. 245, No. 18, pp. 2614-17, Nov. 8, 1985.

______, M.A. and Smith, T.L. "An 8-year Follow-up of 450 Sons of Alcoholics and Controlled Subjects", Archives of General Psychiatry 53:202-210, 1996.

______, M.A. "Penny-wise, Ton-foolish? The Recent Movement to Abolish In-Patient Alcohol and Drug Treatment (Editorial)", Journal of Studies for Alcoholism 59(1):5-7, 1998.

Seixas, Judith S.. Living with a Parent Who Drinks Too Much. New York: Greenwillow Books, 1979.

Seixas, Judith S. and Geraldine Youcha. Children of Alcoholism: A Survivors Manual. New York: Crown Publishers, 1985.

Shah, Diane K.. "Kids of Alcoholics", Newsweek, May 28, 1979

Sher,K.J. et al. "The Role of Childhood Stressors in the Intergenerational Transmission of Alcohol Use Disorders", Journal of Studies for Alcoholism 58(4):414-427, 1997.

Smith, David E., M.D. and Donald R. Wesson, M.D.. Treating the Cocaine Abuser. Center City, Minn.: Hazelden Foundation, 1985.

Smith, Anthony. The Mind. New York: The Viking Press, 1984.

Stimmel, Barry, M.D., Opiate Receptors, Neurotransmitters and Drug Dependence. Binghamton, N.Y.: Haworth Press, 1981.

Stone, Nannette, Marlene Fromme and Daniel Kagan. Cocaine: Seduction and Solution. New York: Pinnacle Books, 1985.

Swift, Harold A. and Terence Williams, Recovery for the Whole Family. Center City, Minn.: Hazelden Foundation, 1975.

Thanos, P.K., et al. "Overexpression of Dopamine D2 Receptors Reduces Alcohol Self-Administration", Journal of Neurochemistry 78: 1094, September 11, 2001.

Triebout, Harry M., M.D. "Surrender Versus Compliance in Therapy," Quarterly Journal of Studies on Alcohol, Vol. 14, pp. 58-68, March 1953.

_________,"The Ego Factors in Surrender in Alcoholism," Quarterly Journal of Studies on Alcohol, Vol. 15, pp. 610-21, Dec. 1954.

Trice, Harrison M.. Alcoholism in Industry. New York: The Christopher D. Smithers Foundation, 1979.

Uhl, George, M.D., Ph.D. "Scientists Clone Cocaine Sensitive Brain Protein," Science, Oct. 25, 1991.

Vaillant, George. The Natural History of Alcoholism: Causes, Patterns, and Paths to Recovery. Cambridge, Mass.: Harvard University Press, 1983.

Vaughn, Clark. Addictive Drinking: The Road to Recovery for Problem Drinkers and Those who Love Them. New York: Penguin Books, 1985

W., Bill. Three Talks to Medical Societies by Bill W., Co-Founder of Alcoholics Anonymous. New York A.A. World Services, Inc., New York, 1985

Wegscheider, Sharon. Another Chance: Hope and Health for the Alcoholic Family. Palo Alto, Ca.: Science and Behavior Books, 1981.

Wickelgren, Ingrid. "Getting the Brain's Attention", Science, Vol. 278, 35-37, October 3, 1997.

Wilbur, Robert, "Kicking Cocaine", The Chicago Tribune, Feb. 23, 1986

Wise, Roy A. "Addiction Becomes a Brain Disease", Neuron, Vol 26, 27-33, April 2000.

Wittenberg, Erica. "Drug Abuse: A Handbook for Parents." Phoenix: Do It Now Foundation, 1983

Woodside, Migs. "Children of Alcoholics in the Medical System: Hidden Problems, Hidden Costs". New York: Children of Alcoholics Foundation, 1990.

Wrich, James T. The Employee Assistance Program. Center City, Minn.: Hazelden Foundation, 1980.

Zucker, R.A. et al. "The Development of Alcoholic Subtypes: Risk Variation among Alcoholic Families during the Childhood Years", Alcohol Health Research World 20(1):46-54, 1996.

Index

About the Author

Kathleen Whalen FitzGerald, Ph.D., is the President of The Institute for Recovery in Lake Forest, Illinois.

She has been published by Doubleday, Contemporary Books, Whales' Tale Press, *The Chicago Tribune, Newsweek, Christian Century, New Age, Alcoholism & Addiction* and *Professional Counselor magazines*. Her titles include *Brass: Jane Byrne & the Pursuit of Power* (1983), *The Good Sisters* (1983), and *Whatever Happened to the Good Sisters* (1992).

Dr. FitzGerald is a trained interventionist, writer, therapist, public speaker and retreat facilitator. She has appeared on national television and radio and has addressed university, political, professional, church and social groups. She received her doctorate from Northwestern University in Education and Social Policy.

Institute for Recovery

500 N. Western
Lake Forest, IL 60045
(847) 735-1827

The Institute for Recovery was founded in 1988 to provide compassionate, professional care to suffering alcoholics, their families, and others suffering from addictive illness, Codependency and Adult Child issues.

Issues

Issues that our clients bring to therapy:

Addictions	Low self-esteem	Depression
Codependency	Loss and grief	Disenchantment
Relationships	Family Problems	Incest
Anxiety	Communication	Anger
Spirituality	Crisis intervention	Adoption

Out-Patient Services

The Institute is likewise an out-patient facility specializing in:

1) After-care programs
2) Relapse Prevention Services (Individuals & Groups)
3) Intervention
4) Assessment

Community Education

Programs vary in scope, depth and immediacy and are structured to most effectively meet the practical needs of clients:

Seminars	Workshops
Consultations	Retreats
Group Discussion	Courses of Study

Staff

The staff of The Institute for Recovery are experienced professionals including licensed psychologists and master-level therapists. We are trained in addictions counseling, social work, spirituality, education, pastoral ministry, family systems and relapse prevention.

Also Available from Whales' Tale Press

Women In AA

By Kathleen W. FitzGerald, Ph.D.

In June, 1996, the National Center on Addiction and Substance Abuse at Columbia University published the landmark study, "Substance Abuse and the American Women," stating that women were as vulnerable to, and participated in alcoholism to the same degree as men. Alcoholism could no longer be accused of gender bias.

Every Friday morning for years I have attended a wonderful Big Book AA meeting for women in recovery. Every Friday morning we read stories from Alcoholics Anonymous, affectionately called the "Big Book" by AA members. Many of the stories are written by women. We seem to read and discuss these stories with more knowing, with deeper humor and with greater identification.

And so it was one cold winter night, as I sat on our front porch and watched the stars, the idea for Women in AA dropped into my lap. For years I had intuitively known that women were equally represented in the manifestation of the disease of alcoholism. I saw with my own eyes that half the folks in AA were women, and it was time for their stories of trial and triumph to be shared.

The Irish say, "When you pray for potatoes, pick up a hoe". So I sent a "Call for Manuscripts" to 900 newspapers through the US and Canada, assuring potential contributors of our adherence to Tradition 12, wherein each women's anonymity would be protected.

Eighty women from 26 states and throughout Canada trustingly sent us their stories, each in her own way articulating the issues that we, as recovering women, must integrate into our recovery if we want a peaceful, joyful recovery.

These stories and reflections invite you to use them to examine some of your own thoughts and feelings and possibly to discover the special meanings that these stories may hold for you. Take from them what you want and leave the rest.

So in giving to you this little book, we are giving back in some way what we have received from AA. Namely, our lives.

ISBN: 1-882195-03-5

$18.95 USA
$20.95 Canada

Whales' Tale Press
P.O. Box 27
Lake Forest, Illinois 60045

Also Available from Whales' Tale Press

The Good Sisters

By Kathleen W. FitzGerald, Ph.D.

It is time to tell the simple story. Hundred of thousands of adult Catholics were educated by religious women. For every horror story told about nuns there are ten memories of warm, caring women who taught us to read, to write and yes, even to love God and our fellow men & women.

The Good Sisters is a butterfly caught in amber, stopped in time and space forever. You can hold the lovely butterfly up to the light and see the startled look on her face as she was caught in the sticky flow. You can toss her in your bottom drawer with your old college yearbooks and pressed prom roses, embarrassed at such innocence. You can wear her around your neck, tied through with a black velvet ribbon, to mourn the passing of her beautiful days and grace-filled ways. You can try to release her, but the amber and the butterfly have become one.

The second coming of ***The Good Sisters*** is synchronous with the dearth of the female, of the yin in the church. It harkens us back to butterfly times in the church, when every playground and classroom in America was filled with dedicated women in brown, white, blue, gray and black habits, chalk dust on our veils and long wooden rosaries swinging from our belts. We thought it would last forever. When "The Good Sisters" kept the men in balance, the likes of Msgr. Desmond Ryan, Father Jack O'Mahoney and Father Danny Doyle didn't even think of abusing a child.

As you read ***The Good Sisters***, you will be coaxed back to a time when the church was clear and predictable, a Ferris wheel circling through the liturgical year at the same speed and rhythm as the year before and the year after. People changed but the roles remained.

If you were fortunate enough to know The Good Sisters, one may well hold your young face or your young name in her old heart. She remembers you fondly, perhaps with regret for her harshness or exhaustion. I know that good sister sends to you blessings across the years, for how could she not? Now hold that beautiful butterfly caught in amber up to the light of day and understand what it was all about.

ISBN: 1-882195-04-3

$19.95 USA
$24.95 Canada

Whales' Tale Press
P.O. Box 27
Lake Forest, Illinois 60045

Also from Whales's Tales Press . . .

Whatever Happened to the Good Sisters?

Too much has been written about nuns. Far too many tasteless jokes have peppered conversations at Catholic gatherings about "Sister Mary Holy Water" or, worse, "Sister Mary Pew". Enough you may say. Enough already.

It is time to tell the simple story. Hundred of thousands of adult Catholics were educated by religious women. For every horror story told about nuns there are ten memories of warm, caring women who taught us to read, to write and yes, even to love God and our fellow men and women.

Who were these women? What were their emotions, masked as were their bodies in those mysterious black and white robes. Which of the stories we were told were the truth? Will we allow John Powers' book *Do Patent Leather Shoes Reflect Up* serve as our collective memory or is there another story to be told?

Let's take a walk together. The path is personal; the story as complex as the church we served. The journey is meant to satisfy the curiosity of those who have questions yet to be answered. For those other readers who were characters in the plot it will be, hopefully, a nostalgic trip into the not so distant past.

Joanne Rooney

ISBN: 1-882195-00-0

$19.95 USA
$24.95 Canada

Whales' Tale Press
P.O. Box 27
Lake Forest, Illinois 60045

Now Available from Whales' Tale Press

Codependency... PowerLoss SoulLoss

By Dorothy May, Ph.D.

"When we cry all our tears, laugh at ourselves, and playfully thumb our noses at the world, then we know we are living life as it was meant to be lived."

Dorothy May, Ph.D. received a Doctorate in Psychology from Northwestern University in Evanston and a Master of Arts degree from Northeastern Illinois University in Chicago.

As a Clinical Psychologist, her professional expertise includes work in her private practice for the past 15 years with Codependents, Adult Children of Alcoholics and Adult Children from Dysfunctional families. She has served as community advisor and supervising teacher/psychologist and has taught at local colleges and universities.

Years ago, she began her personal quest for meaning to her life experience. When Codependency was identified, she knew that the ideas generated by the discovery applied to her own life as well as to the thousands of clients she was seeing. What she had thought was an idiosyncratic problem was in truth a societal/cultural problem.

The research for this book came out of her classes, lectures, workshops and practice, but the heart of this book lies in her own personal quest.

ISBN: 1-882195-02-7

$12.95 USA
$14.95 Canada

Whales' Tale Press
P.O. Box 27
Lake Forest, Illinois 60045

CODEPE
PROGRESSION

Institute for Recovery
(847) 735-1827

IDENCY
& RECOVERY

These progression and recovery symptoms are based on the common experience of those suffering from Jellinek's disease. Every symptom does not occur in every sufferer or in the same sequence. The entire process may take years or it may occur in a very short time.